MOUNTAIN DRIFTER

Mountain Drifter

*Hunting Camp Adventures
From Wyoming's Thorofare*

ZACH BOWMAN

Mountain Drifter LLC

CONTENTS

Dedication vii
Introduction ix
Acknowledgments xi

1 Fledgling Woodsman 1

2 Empty Pockets 7

3 Cuttin' Teeth Part 1- The Trail 32

4 Cuttin' Teeth Part 2- Bear Bait 62

5 Ambushed by Bullwinkle 87

6 Twistin' Off 103

7 The Bubba Mule Part 1- Outlaw Horses 119

8 The Bubba Mule Part 2- Bob Got Screwed 141

9	The Bubba Mule Part 3- Just John Wayne Em!	156
10	Surrounded on Hat Pass	175
11	Swayback Horses	186
12	Green Eyes in the Darkness	216
13	Redemption	236
14	Sore Feet	263

Closing Thoughts   293
About the Author   297

DEDICATION

This project is dedicated to several important people. First and foremost, to my wife who has been the ultimate encourager, steadfast believer and the best helper to get me to complete this project!

To my kids who will hopefully enjoy the outdoors as much as their parents do! When I'm done with the world, they'll have something to pass along to their kids.

I'd also like to thank my parents, Dave and Nancy Bowman for raising us kids to enjoy and respect the mountains and for introducing me to hunting and woodsmanship.

There are countless others who have played rolls in helping me become a better person, mountain hand and horseman. Too many to list in fact! However, Troy Wilcox and the entire family, as they are the best mountain hands and horseman I know. Outfitters like, B-Joe Coy, who gave me a good base to start learning the trade. Terry Dolland and Colby Gines, whom I worked several seasons for. And Colby, who can be directly complimented for saving my life on one particularly bad encounter. I owe him a lot!

Also, Bill Butler, a mentor of sorts as far as writing a book goes and being a cowboy and a good person. Rob Stothart, my old college English teacher who had to endure several phone calls and questions as this project progressed. And everyone else who helped with the cover and editing process!

None of this would have come to fruition without each and every one mentioned above! Along with several others who I did not mention! I hope this is something everyone can read and remember what fun it all was!

I would be remiss to not mention a good friend who just had his life cut too short. One of the best guys to have in camp, a good hand, a gritty kid and the best camp cook! Cameron Overfield. May he rest in peace.

Spooky, on top of the Trident Plateau. You can see Baldy, the Thorofare Buttes and several others in the background.

INTRODUCTION

You're in for a treat reading this book by Zach Bowman. Whether you're an armchair adventurer or a dedicated hunter and outdoorsman you'll read some pretty amazing stuff. You'll hear the voice of 15 years of guiding in the bear infested Wyoming wilderness and the danger, humor, drama and mostly hard work of these guides and outfitters. You'll never take for granted the grit these people show while doing something they swear they'll never do again but later cant wait to get back to it. You'll learn a lot about the personalities of the outfitting camp workers and the challenges offered by the unusual personalities of the hunters they guide.

These guides are tough and they get it done because they have to.

I've known Zach Bowman most of his life as a friend of his family. His evolution as a rodeo cowboy, hunting guide, author, commercial airline pilot and dedicated husband and father has been amazing. Not to mention multiple other jobs and occupations including being a local politician. His discussions of the Federal and State policies regarding bear, wildlife and hunting management show the opinion of someone on the ground rather than remote policy managers. He also happens to be a very smart guy with a wry sense of humor.

Buck Sitz

The author with a 27-inch Steelhead he caught on the John Day River in Oregon.

ACKNOWLEDGMENTS

First and foremost, I sure appreciate your interest in my book! Let me lead off by saying a few things to provide some perspectives- I consider myself an average guide. There are legends who have worked this country far longer, and better than me. Their stories are better, they're better horseman, better cowboys and better hunters. And it's a shame they aren't writing their own books! I sure wish they would because the country is magical, and their stories shouldn't be forgotten!

If you are after a book about guys killing animals and tooting their own horn, this isn't it. However, if you're looking for something that tells the tales of the adventures of everyday life in a wilderness hunting camp, the recklessness and caution, bucking horses, wild bears, Medevac helicopters, lost mules, both bad and good cooks, terrible weather, treacherous mountain passes and fun-loving guides, you've come to the right place! I hope you find this entertaining! Some "writer's liberties" were taken, which you have to expect in creative nonfiction. Remember, most of these stories were from a decade ago. I can't remember every detail or what was said yesterday! As such, I tried to keep this as accurate as I can remember, but it should not be taken as an exact account of events. They are just memories that happened to me and my fellow mountain hands while working in and around the Thorofare Area in Northwestern Wyoming.

XII - ACKNOWLEDGMENTS

Working for nearly fifteen seasons left me with a lot of stories. A lot of memories too dear to me to let slide into forgotten time. The livestock are the true workers in these camps, and I believe they deserve their due. As such, a lot is centered on the animals as they are the true characters that fill these camps. I hope you enjoy!

The author getting ready to peak into Big Buck drainage

| 1 |

Fledgling Woodsman

As a kid growing up in a middle-class family in eastern Oregon the hunting and outdoor tradition was normal. My brother and I were raised roaming and exploring the CRP fields around the house. Building forts along the creek and spending countless hours wading in the creek catching crawdads. Mushroom hunting, cutting firewood, fishing, or just for picnics, we spent a fair amount of time outdoors.

As kids, we were in boy scouts and were blessed to have a dad who took us backpacking in the wilderness, took us on Canadian fishing trips, and spent time pheasant hunting with us. Occasionally, we even were allowed to tag along on the summer trail clearing outings up at elk camp!

My dad, perhaps unconsciously, brought us up in steps with regard to being in the outdoors. I recall how big of a deal it was when he allowed me to carry a pocketknife in the mountains. With strict instructions to never have it out unless I found a morel, or another edible mushroom. After a year or so I was granted the blessing of carrying a pocketknife whenever. But that was after first proving I wasn't going to chop a finger off.

It was basically a rinse, repeat with guns. First a BB gun. And once proven he moved us to a 22. And so on. Seemed he never missed a step and we learned from the get-go that any carelessness or other safety violations were met with consequences. Maybe it's just "a kid's memory" but when we screwed up, the consequences seemed severe. In reality, we probably just had our pocketknife taken away for the rest of the day? Who knows exactly but the end result was a couple of kids who could safely roam the mountains.

We learned to appreciate nature from the beginning. Clear memories remain with me today of my dad saying, "Leave it better than you found it." That has always stuck with me and something I've tried to instill in my children. Picking up some extra trash that was there when you arrived seems to be something I still do to this day. And my young children have taken that to a whole new level it seems? I don't recall sifting through ashes in a fire ring for micro trash when I was seven years old, but I've watched my kids do it!

I remember when my older brother reached the age where he got to go on his first elk hunt. This was before I was old enough to go through the "Hunters Safety" program. I have very clear memories of the excitement in the months leading up to hunting season. The necessary purchase of a rifle large enough to bring down big game. It was a very big deal that I remember vividly. My brother was sitting on his bedroom floor counting one, five, twenty and an occasional fifty-dollar bills. I also recall him cracking open his piggy bank full of coins. It was a large porcelain clown figure with the classic slot on the top big enough to drop coins in.

I looked on from the bunk bed while he carefully counted out $150.00 of hard-earned chore money. As kids, most of the money we earned was from mowing lawns and doing little menial chores around the house for mom. That was the first time I had ever seen $150. It seemed like a fortune to me! I also have vivid memories of watching my dad and my brother sitting at the kitchen table looking through the classified section of the local newspaper. It seemed like an exciting time in the household where my brother was taking a major step toward manhood! All while I looked on, very aware that it wasn't my turn yet.

Thinking back on those days, aside from my dad's old 270, I hadn't seen many "high powered rifles." But behold, I remember when my brother brought home his newly acquired rifle. Purchased with every kind of money available, pennies, nickels, dimes and quarters! Ones, fives, tens and twenty-dollar bills. All told, he bought a very used .308 with a 4X Weaver Scope for $150. It was something most people would turn their noses up at nowadays. But back then, it was gorgeous!

My brother and I "helping" load firewood.

I'd watch as Dad taught him how to clean and care for the gun. Soon enough, it was elk season and Dad and my brother set out for the cabin while I had to stay behind with my mom and sister. The worst part was that my brother got out of school to go on the hunt. It was about the most painful thing imaginable for a young kid to endure.

The hunting season in Oregon always opened on Wednesday and closed on Sunday. I remember my dad pulling in the driveway on Friday night. He hadn't shaved and looked dirty and tired. Whenever Dad came home from a successful hunting or fishing trip, he would open the door between the garage and the kitchen and would just smile and hold his arm up flexing his bicep, indicating his success. Us kids would all jump and run to him for a hug and he'd take us out and show us his prize.

It took years to realize this, but my brother and I had the best dad we could have ever asked for. As dad stood in the doorway flexing his bicep and smiling, we knew he'd got one! "Where is he?" I screamed as I raced across the kitchen with my mom yelling at me to slow down. But this time he couldn't show me his trophy, Dad explained that he had come back to pick me up and take me to elk camp! No doubt because I threw a fit about being left behind! Although I don't recall that part. (Sarcasm emphasized). Dad prevailed against Mom's protests and the plan was set!

Dad helped me get outfitted with proper clothing and boots, mostly hand-me-downs we found in the garage and pilfered from my brother's closet. We loaded in the truck after dinner and headed for the cabin. The "Cabin" back in those days was a single-wide mobile home which belonged to one of dad's friends. He always invited us up for every elk season I attended in Oregon. Situated on roughly three acres in the Ukiah Unit in eastern Oregon, it was an absolute paradise for us kids to cut our teeth at being hunters and woodsman.

As it turned out, Dad had shot an elk on Friday morning and decided to bend the rules of the house a little and come get me. I was going to tag along the following morning and help recover the elk. In the morning after some breakfast and getting my brother sent off for the morning hunt Dad and I drove back some old forest service roads to a place I would later on get to know quite well. We called it, "the south point."

After parking and making sure I was situated we hiked down the steep embankment to the downed bull. I don't recall much about the process of getting the elk out, or even the events following. However, I do remember how important that trip was to me. I got to go to huntin' camp with all the men and "help" dad get that elk out.

In just a few years it was my turn to cash in all the coins I had saved up and I bought my first rifle as well. I don't remember how much it was, or even what brand it was, but it was a .308. By then I had shot my brother's rifle a few times and I wanted either the .308 or a 270. I think the deciding factor was what was available in the classified section of the local newspaper?

As the years passed, elk hunting was the trip we never missed. Even as I entered my teens and started to figure out girls and beer, elk hunting was the priority. And it remained so until I discovered rodeo... and beer... and girls. Then hunting seemed to drift on the list of priorities.

High School rodeo turned into Amateur rodeo and shortly afterwards onto Pro Rodeo. I hadn't hunted in many years. Being that my priorities in those days were to party, chase women and ride bulls and bucking horses (in that order), it wasn't long before I had received several thousand dollars in fines from the professional rodeo organization, I was a member of. Which also meant, until I paid them, I was ineligible to compete at pro events.

Like any young cowboy, my objective was to be a cowboy, not an everyday, average working man, so when I learned of a small town in Wyoming that had a rodeo seven days a week through June, July and August, I loaded my 1985 Chrysler Fifth Avenue and headed... East!

I lived all summer in a tent at the rodeo grounds in Cody, Wyoming. Riding every day I could and bumming around. I had various jobs from the Western Wear store, (because they had air conditioning) to finishing concrete. As chance would have it, as the summer was drawing to a close one of the Pickup Men at the rodeo asked if I knew how to hunt? Soon after I had a job as a "camp jack" in his wilderness hunting camp.

Up to that point, I had barely ridden any horses who weren't intended to buck. I knew nothing of packing, riding or even how to hunt the big country of Wyoming. But this job offer sounded like a good adventure and a way to delay my arrival back in Oregon. So, I headed in, totally unprepared and completely wet behind the ears.

The Valley Fork. Thorofare, Wyoming. My daughter's namesake.

| 2 |

Empty Pockets

As a young cowboy in my early twenties surviving ninety performances in Cody, Wyoming as a bull rider and a bareback rider you inevitably end up banged up. This particular year I had been fighting tendinitis in my riding hand. It wasn't a super huge deal; I just ran my bull rope between my ring and little finger after taking my wrap. A lot of people call it a "Suicide wrap" but I didn't see it like that as I had always taken it that way. The difference now verses regularly being that rather than set the slack of the rope on the bull's neck, I would place it under my knuckles so that when I slid up on my rope to nod, I would pinch the rope between the bull's back and the back of my fingers. Effectively tying my hand to the bull.

When you're twenty you don't consider how anything like this could be a bad idea. At the time I wasn't physically able to close my hand into a fist. But the most important thing was keeping my hand connected to my rope. Why not tie myself on? You can't win if you don't enter, right?

The bum arm had limited the number of bucking horses I was willing to ride late in the summer so I ended up mostly just competing in the bull riding. That year as the middle of August approached, I found myself in a very tight race for the year end bull riding title at the Cody Night Rodeo.

The view from camp. Looking southeast.

As the weeks went by my arm had managed to hang in there, and my riding was improving every night. In hindsight, my riding probably improved because it had to being that I was tied on? Who knows? When the final night arrived and all the money was counted, I ended up winning a disappointing second place.

After the rodeo a few contestants and myself were hanging out in the parking lot exchanging good byes and "where you headed to next" type of talk over some cold beverages. Not being twenty-one meant that we had limited options as to where we could kick back and unwind. As the conversation progressed soon the stadium lights were being shut off when we noticed one of the Pick-Up Men headed our way.

This guy was also was an outfitter in the fall. Throughout the season I had gotten to know him a little. He was a short but stalky guy, classic rodeo build. He wore glasses and was never seen without a felt cowboy hat or a denim long sleeve wrangler shirt with the white snaps. We took particular note of his approach as it was obvious that we were indulging in a few frosty beverages and we all knew he didn't touch the stuff.

He was a respected enough cowboy that my conscience caught up with me when I was around him. I felt like I was screwing something up to drink in front of him. Even though, to his credit he never said anything or seemed to pass judgement. We exchanged pleasantries and he asked,

"You're from Oregon aintcha", you ever do any huntin' out there?"

"You bet! We did quite a bit! Haven't been for a few years because I've been rodeoing, why's that?"

He said that he was in need of an extra hand in his wilderness hunting camp and explained that I'd be a camp jack, if I was interested? At the time, I knew less than nothing about the job but it sounded like a good adventure so I agreed to the job for fifty dollars a day under the condition that I not start until next week. I had one more rodeo in Pendleton, Oregon to attend and I assured him I'd be back.

The Pendleton Round-up is one of the top three wildest places I've ever been. And being in my twenties, I was in my prime. Twenty thousand rodeo fans packed into one place in September? If that doesn't sound like paradise to a twenty-year-old bull rider, I don't know what would? Saturday was the short round in Pendleton but I wasn't up and functional until Monday given the festivities and my general lack of knowledge on all things with moderation. I rolled from the camper on the back of my '88 Ford pickup and into the cab with one eye half open.

An unfortunate encounter with a deer on a Montana highway one dark and stormy night had finally forced me into a new-to-me vehicle purchase the previous winter. Having been a steadfast fan of "boat" cars, anything under fifteen feet I deemed too small, this was the first pickup I'd had in a while and the camper sure came in handy!

I rolled out of contestant parking, banged a left onto I-84 eastbound and lit out on my return trip to Wyoming. As I tapped the cruise control off at 70mph, still questioning my blood alcohol content, I was excited for the adventure that lay ahead and the chance to dry out a bit.

Fourteen hours, two fuel stops and one time zone change later I rolled the old ford into the outfitters place just east of Cody. We spent the following day packing panniers and situating gear, heading to town to meet the hunters, then back to feed horses. We filled out a Guide License application for me because, "You just never know" according to the boss.

The following morning, we loaded all the horses into trailers and headed to town to pick up the hunters. Once that mission was complete, we stopped off for breakfast at Granny's restaurant in Cody. I had bacon, eggs over easy, toast, pancakes and black coffee to wash it all down. Then we all headed for the trailhead about forty miles outside of town.

Having been on a hunting hiatus for several years, I was rusty to say the least. But when you also consider that literally all of my hunting experience was gained foot hunting in the Blue Mountains of Oregon, to now be packing mules into the Absoroka Range in Wyoming's vast wilderness, I was completely ill prepared. That was okay though, I thought, I'm just going to be a camp jack. Little did I know at that young age and experience level, the brush hunts of eastern Oregon aren't the way to hunt the big country states, as I soon came to find out!

We were riding horses, so naturally I showed up in cowboy boots and a cowboy hat. I had been given vague instructions on what to bring with me for personal gear. That amounted to an old cowboy who's spent his life in the mountains glossing over a few things and not even mentioning the "common sense stuff" such as a better hat? Anyhow, I was smart enough to bring hunting boots but they were tucked away in my duffel. As a young Oregonian I hadn't even considered that we might walk our horses downhill? Needless to say, that first ride into the mountains in Wyoming was a learning experience.

The camp I had been hired on as the camp jack was set 9,995 feet above sea level. It was primarily a bighorn sheep camp but also could support a few elk hunters. Being at that elevation, the camp would be pulled in late October and the outfitter would do a lot of what we call "Town hunts" or "Hotel hunts" which simply means that they would put the clients in a hotel rather than in a camp and hunt by driving to a chosen trailhead every morning and returning in the evening. At the time the owner was the Foundation for North American Wild Sheep's Outfitter of the year so I was in good hands.

I was unaware of all those details at the time, all I knew was that we were riding horses up mountains I never imagined a horse being able to climb. From the trailhead we climbed and climbed. Periodically, we stopped to let the horses catch their breath. Until finally, we were at a point to where we appeared to be trapped by cliffs. As we rode along the base of the cliffs we eventually came to a makeshift gate at a small notch in the cliff.

We rode through the gate, guarded on each side by roughly fifty-foot cliffs, wide enough for a car to drive between. We made a final short climb and popped out in an open meadow on the very top of the mountain. There was a small grove of evergreens where camp sat and a spring flowed not ten steps from the dining tent. The livestock were turned loose to roam in the meadow as they were trapped up there with cliffs over one-hundred feet tall on three sides of us. Assuming the gate was closed, the horses had nowhere to go except up a few miles.

The camp itself is still one of the most beautiful places I've been. A small camp by comparison to other Wyoming camps, this one had two hunter tents, one guide tent and a cook and dining tent. The cook and dining tents shared a ridge pole and the whole camp was nestled in a stand of evergreens, with a few beetle killed old growth trees.

The corrals were nestled in a small group of trees about fifty yards away, towards the nearby cliffs. All this was surrounded by a picturesque meadow with gently sloping terrain on the wind swept, grass covered meadow. In the distance was breathtaking views of what seemed like the entire state to the east, and 12,000-foot jagged peaks to the west.

A small spring next to the cook tent trickled water out of a small piece of PVC pipe the outfitter placed there. The sweetest water I'd ever tasted flowed at a rate to fill a five-gallon bucket in about ten minutes. At the time it was the most beautiful place I'd laid eyes on.

We brought with us two hunters and a hired-on guide. Several pack horses and mules carried gear and groceries. The week flew by and being such a small camp, I was able to tag along on a few hunts. We tagged out the hunters, I even cooked a few nights and we had a great time! We even found two different bighorn sheep skulls! These mountains sure are easy, I thought!

Once the hunt was complete, we saddled our stock and headed back to town. The four hour ride out was quick and painless, mostly because we had to walk the horses down off the steep sections and only rode about two or three miles out. Once we were out, before even getting back to the outfitters house to unload our horses and equipment and wash eight solid days' worth of sheep blood, elk guts, dirt and body odor off, the boss wheeled his big dually pickup and loaded stock trailer into the best-known steak house in Cody for a meal in which he paid for everything.

I came to have mixed feelings on the dinner ritual that followed every hunt. On one hand it was good food! Free food! But on the other, having just spent eight days with a group of guys, a shower was higher on my priority list than a dinner, but oh well?

Amazingly, at dinner all the hunters started handing out tips. I hadn't even considered this as a custom and my kneejerk reaction was to decline. Thankfully, I saw the boss pocket a tip just as the first hunter approached me.

The six hundred dollars I received in tips was mighty welcome too! I made two months' worth of pick-up payments, which came to a grand total of $300 and pocketed the rest as I was unsure what the schedule was or how long I'd be in camp this season? Better to be ahead of the game I thought! That $300 I pocketed allowed me to get a lot better gear too! A warm hat, gloves and I traded my cowboy boots for a second pair of hunting boots.

The following hunt we welcomed two brothers who were there to archery elk hunt and one other hunter who was there to chase bighorn sheep. One of the brothers was using a crossbow because a traditional bow would have twanged his morbidly oversized belly! I'm not saying the guy was fat just that he was about three feet too short for his weight!

Not to be disparaging but his belly size is relevant because we only had one mule who was big enough to carry this three-hundred plus, sized individual! The problem was that the mule was a pack mule, not a riding mule which set us on a path for an interesting week.

The mule tasked with this endeavor was a gigantic grey mule. She had a name, but I only knew it for a few days prior to this hunt. We branded her as the Psycho Donkey on this hunt and the name stuck! She stood a solid 15 hands, big ears and a gentle personality. She wasn't what the name suggests, rather, she was too smart for her own good and was just inexperienced as a riding mule. Usually, she was assigned the real heavy loads to pack. A whole elk? No problem for this mule!

Winter kill ram skull in the head of a high basin.

The second bobble in the plan appeared when one of the hired guides was a no-show. I remember thinking at the time how unprofessional that was. Not only for the guide, but also the outfitter. Who hires guys like that? As time went on, I figured out exactly why the guide didn't show up. It correlated perfectly with the reasoning behind me having a temporary guide license fresh and handy for that season too!

As you might imagine, the boss told me I was now a guide. And I was tasked with taking the guy shaped more like a bowling ball than a human on his hunt. Who doesn't like challenges?

"Don't worry though, I'll knock a ram down tomorrow morning and be able to help you out!" the Boss said as he walked away to pack another horse.

We made our usual trip to Granny's restaurant, then headed for the trailhead. Other than a couple minor incidences at the trailhead, we got our bowling ball shaped hunter in the saddle by using the fender of the horse trailer, everything seemed to be going smooth. The poor guy was so short legged and not quite as limber and flexible as he was in his younger years. He couldn't lift a leg high enough to get into the stirrup. The horse trailer fender solved the problem however.

As we rode up the trail, every so often the sound of the hooves walking up the trail would be drowned out by the hunter screaming "Whoa!!!" We'd look back only to see the big grey mule fart and kind of scatter off at the pace of a fast walk. Obviously, the mule couldn't do much more with that kind of weight on his back. We all tried to hide our chuckles as we watched the big fella' screaming, "WH!..WHOA!!...WHOA!!!" in a terrified voice.

As soon as it started, it seemed to stop as the Psycho Donkey would only make it fifteen or so yards before stopping and licking her lips as she returned to her place in line on the trail. Our plump little hunter would be stark white and wide eyed.

Soon we were in camp no worse for the wear, except for the grey mule who by now had been officially dubbed the Psycho Donkey. Not that the mule was doing anything wrong, she was just a big pack mule and unaccustomed to a rider. Especially, this particular guy.

By the time we climbed the 3000-3500 vertical feet into camp the poor Psycho Donkey was pretty well played out. We decided to give her a rest the following day. We opted to walk our hunters up to a nearby meadow the following morning. This all was decided by the Boss of course.

The following morning, we struck out on foot at an agonizingly slow pace to a meadow above camp. The morning breakfast of bacon and eggs were not at all helping our agility. But we wondered up the trail anyway. Stopping every fifty or so yards so our hunter could catch his breath.

As a side note, the boss was doing the cooking, and let me tell you that guy would cook a piece of bacon until it had the consistency of granite and sand. The hardest, driest, and saltiest bacon I've ever tasted in my life. You couldn't eat it without going through a whole canteen of water between bites! It only took two mornings of bacon before I just quit taking any. When the Boss finally noticed, being polite I told him I wasn't a huge fan of bacon. Which was a half truth, I actually love bacon, just not burnt to a crisp bacon. The remainder of the season I was made fun of for not liking bacon, but I never clarified my position.

When we finally reached the meadow there were some elk bugling. So, we tried to close the distance. Sliding as quietly as we could down the hill on our butts through the tall meadow grass ended up being fruitless however. The elk busted us about twenty minutes in and that was that.

At some point in the stalk my wallet slipped out of my pocket never to be seen or heard from again. I looked for that wallet for the rest of the year and never found it, or the few hundred in tip money that was inside of it. I imagine some porcupine made lunch out of that leather. My social security card was probably a side salad for it?

The following morning, we decided to go to roughly the same spot but with the help of the Psycho Donkey. We tried to load the hunter on that poor mule which by this time was well aware of our tricks. The hunter's legs being too short to reach the stirrups, and his overall lack of flexibility and athleticism forced us to use a down tree for the boarding process.

Using a tree stump or a down log for a boost is still my preferred method of getting into the saddle in the mountains, however that poor mule was aware of the drill and protested as much as she could. We would lead her up to the log, the hunter would do a slight shuffle to get his pants organized, and then he would try to get a foot in the stirrup, which one of us had to hold for him. As soon as he'd get close, the Psycho Donkey would nonchalantly step away from the log, and we'd have to lead her around in a circle to get her positioned again and repeat the process again. And again, and again. To be honest, short of cussing at her no other disciplinary action was taken as we all felt sorry for her.

The hunter eventually got a foot in the stirrup but stalled out when he had to lift his other leg over her back. After waiting a lot longer than the hunter deserved the mule had enough and let out a big fart as she began another half scatter half walk away from the log.

It only took the Psycho Donkey a few steps to rid herself of the guy. As he was half in, half out of the saddle, With one foot in the stirrup and the other about in the center of the mule's rump. The saddle was slipping as he just stood there like a fool. As the Donkey took off, with me holding onto the lead rope for dear life, the hunter hit the ground with a thud, flat on his back.

He laid there making wheezing noises and whimpering as the fall knocked all the wind out of him. After that he refused to ride the Psycho Donkey until we left camp. Soon the boss's hunter killed a ram and "Slim" the Crossbow hunter was his problem.

I still helped when time permitted though, but to no avail. At the end of the hunt the guy had the nerve to complain about not seeing enough game. You can't please everyone!

A few hunts later, I had been tasked with heading to the road on a solo mission to get more horse feed which was stashed in the trailer at the trailhead. At the time I still could just barely pack so I was nervous as could be. But you can't back down from a job when you're in the mountains. So, I happily agreed to go.

Glassing for sheep at 12,000.

Looking back, it was the perfect trip to send a greenhorn on. It was short. There is no need to weigh the feed as they come in fifty-pound bags. And the feed sacks rode so low in the soft panniers they could have made it in with a hitch or not. I would make it out and back in a day.

For some reason when you aren't leading, or at least up front on the trail, things look different. There's no need to second guess when to turn or where, when you're following other people. Although I was nervous and saw some things, I'd not paid attention to before, I made it without a hitch.

I was able to call my girlfriend on the cell phone from the cliff face a few hundred yards out of camp. She came to the trailhead with some snacks, clean clothes and a few other items I had forgotten. I put on a fresh pair of clothes and put my old ones in the trunk of her car and headed back in. She still talks about how bad my clothes stunk up her car from the trunk! A week's worth of sheep blood and body odor is no match for a plastic Walmart bag, I guess?

A couple days after the feed run, we had a big storm blow into the area. Winds kicked up to gale force velocities on the ridges which slowed our sheep hunt down. That night after dinner while we were all asleep a loud cracking noise, followed by a loud thump woke every one up! Well, almost everyone! I somehow slept through the whole thing! The following morning, we awoke to a tree down in camp. It was an old growth, beetle killed tree and by the grace of God, it fell right between the cook and dining tents. They shared a ridge pole so both tents were collapsed!

Breakfast was put on hold as we fired up the chainsaw to lop the tree into rounds fit for firewood. By noon it was all cleaned up and the only evidence was the stump and millions of small sticks that exploded off the tree when it struck the ground!

A few days later, over a pancake breakfast our hired-on guide was complaining about our fire in the guide tent the previous night. I was new and didn't know any better, and still had my little mummy bag that backpackers use. We had always had a fire because this camp stood just outside of the wilderness. Thus, we could use a chainsaw to cut our wood! I was too green to even consider that cutting wood with a cross cut saw was enough work that people really limit their fires. Either way, it seemed it got too hot for him.

His usual camp was a Thorofare camp where the guide tents didn't have woodstoves. As a result, he had a gigantic bedroll. In the years that followed I ended up working in that camp and it became one of my all-time favorites. But you'd have a miserable trip if your bedroll was inadequate in any way. As I continued to guide, I eventually bought an oversized -20-degree bag, covered it with a canvas bedroll tarp, with a wool blanket, pillow and even an inch and a half foamy. I never got along with being cold at night!

Let's just say tact wasn't this guide's strong suit. Rather than politely saying something, he turned it into a half hour rant. Which left us with no other option than to retaliate! A plan was hatched for later that night. After a supper of salad, pork chops, potatoes and corn our hired guide headed off to his bedroll for the night. We waited until he was fast asleep before sneaking into the tent. We built a fire, and packed the woodstove so full of logs we had to beat the last few in so the door would close.

About an hour had passed, we were all laying on top of our bedrolls as the temperature had risen to around eighty degrees inside the 12x14 canvas tent. A two-foot flame roared from the top of the chimney casting a glow on the surrounding campsite and the metal on the wood stove glowed red from the heat.

Suddenly, without so much as a twitch or a grown, the guide shot out of bed in one movement and was standing over me staring down with his fists clinched as hard as his teeth were! I kept my eyes shut and pretended to be asleep. Cursing and muttering he went to the next cot where one of the other hands was putting on the same act as me.

After a few moments the guide opened the door to the stove, "What the!..."

The morning after the wind storm. The cook tent had been temporarily put back up but the dining tent is still collapsed from the fallen tree.

His complaint trailed off as he turned and ripped open the tent flaps and tied them off, then jumped back in his bedroll and drifted back to sleep. The next morning, we were going to let him know it had all been a joke but he was so mad we decided to let it lay. We forgot to tell him later in the hunt too.

Perhaps fourteen years later, over a glass of whiskey deep in the Thorofare in a different camp all the hunters and guides were sitting around the fire telling stories. This same guide was across the fire from me and jogged my memory with a comment about the fat hunter and the Psycho Donkey. I retold the story to all the hunters and at the conclusion the guide just smirked.

"That was a pretty good prank! Wish you wouldn't have waited this long to tell me that was a joke!"

At this point in the hunt, I already decided I didn't like the guy. I thought he was arrogant and snobby. As I mentioned, years later this same guide and I ended up working a few other camps together and eventually figured each other out. Nowadays, I'd call him a hell of a mountain hand and one of maybe three people I would go anywhere with on the mountain. A good guy and a damn good hand!

Later on, in the season after we had pulled the camp, during the town hunts, one other guide and I were hunting a pair of buddies from southern California. To say they were high-end clients would have been the understatement of the year. My hunter was an attorney for the porn industry and the other was an owner of an Indy car race team. They bought either Governor or Commissioner's tags every year for elk and deer and used the regular draw system for antelope and bighorn sheep. One of them had bought a Governor's Sheep tag at the auction in Reno a few years prior however.

They had been coming for a few years and were happy with the hunting, but found other aspects of the outfit unpalatable. Namely, that we wouldn't allow them to ride our horses down the hills. Being the problem solvers that they were they both purchased a couple of bald, skinny, short legged and small hooved, southern California horses.

Since race season was on hold in late October, early November they had the guy who drove the race team semi-truck, drive their horses to town. They traveled in via private jet, of course. Once the horses arrived the driver would clean out the horse trailer, head to the taxidermist and pick up all the mounts from the previous year. Most were full body mounts but a few were shoulder mounts as well. The driver then would return to California with the mounts, unload them, and then come back empty, ready to pick the horses up at the conclusion of the hunt. Roughly ten days later as it were.

This process played out for years actually. Right up until they both died of heart attacks in the same year, as chance would have it.

The first day of the hunt we headed out to the sagebrush east of Cody in search of an antelope. I pulled up to the spot I had chosen to hunt when my hunter waved his nonfiltered Camel cigarette at the outside thermometer on the dash of the pickup.

"It's minus ten out there, if you think I'm getting out to kill an antelope you're crazy!"

I smiled as I put the pickup in reverse and began to leave. We soon found ourselves driving down a two track on open BLM land when a few speed goats appeared in the distance. My hunter got out, and shot the antelope with his 30-378, and got back in. Simple as that. (Of course, he moved the requisite distance off the two track and didn't break any laws, or blast any paint off the hood of the pickup with that overgrown muzzle brake!) In short order I had the antelope butchered, loaded in the truck, and by 8:30 we were sitting down for breakfast at a restaurant in Cody! And he paid for breakfast! That's my kind of antelope hunt!

A few days later, we were headed up towards the mountains, shifting our focus to deer and elk. My hunter had been having trouble finding a hotel befitting of his greatness and had moved hotels three times in as many days. On the fourth day he had found one he could bear. Which I found to be handy as the hotels would no longer be a topic of morning conversation as we made the hour and a half drive to our chosen spot.

One particular morning we pulled into a ranch that we were allowed to hunt back in those days. Now-a-days the owners don't let people on their place, supposedly because of a few bad eggs who cut fences, left gates open and tried to drive too close to their downed animals. Inconsiderate, lazy hunters brought an end to a fantastic hunting spot. Of course, none of that had happened yet. On this day we were riding out of the parking area at ranch headquarters right as it was breaking daylight. Oh yeah, these hunters also didn't like riding in the dark. So, we had late mornings and early evenings the whole hunt. Which makes things even more difficult than they already were!

As we rode our horses up the ranch road, I soon spotted four bulls above us in a basin. They all looked good but one looked quite a bit bigger than the others. We decided to close the distance and continued up the mountain. That poor little Californian horse was huffing and puffing a lot so I stopped quite a bit to let him blow. We weren't in too big of a hurry as we were the only pickup at the trailhead that morning.

Soon we rounded a canyon abeam the elk's position and tied up about twenty yards below the skyline. After tying up I hustled up the hill and peered down into the next canyon. The elk were still there, feeding in the open. Completely unaware of our presence. They were all nice 6x6's except one who was a monster 7x8. He was absolutely huge, a once in a lifetime bull to even see, let alone shoot!

I looked back to check my hunter's progress. He was still at the horses, so I retreated back down to him. He had taken about ten steps and was gasping for air, leaning with an elbow on his uphill knee. I grabbed his pack and hustled back up to our shooting position. In the meantime, the hunter made it another ten steps. I checked on the elk through my binoculars again, they were fine, so I hustled back down. The hunter was sweating like Mike Tyson at a spelling bee, still gasping for air. So, I took his rifle and headed back up. He had a bipod so I got him all set up, bipod unfolded, cleared a place for him to lay down and soon had everything ready! I even chambered a round for him so all he had to do was get there, lay down, aim and shoot. The elk were three-hundred yards down the hill.

After a long while the hunter showed up, panting, gasping and wheezing. I pointed at the elk and told him to lay down and shoot. But before the hunter could even lay down, in the distance a shot rang out. Panicked, I looked through the binoculars to find the elk before they all scattered! The shot was close, but we were the only ones here, or so I thought?

As I looked, all but one of the elk were running for the timber. The big one was lying dead, right where I'd last seen him! Before long two hunters appeared and were heading toward the elk. Having nothing else to do, and curious exactly how big the bull was, we gathered the stock and I walked, while my hunter rode down the canyon to meet the hunters and see the elk.

By the time we got to the kill sight the other hunters were there taking pictures. The bull turned out to be green scored on the spot at 405 and some change. The hunters had walked in from the other side of the ranch and camped nearby. Dejected, demoralized and frustrated my hunter and I headed back to the pick-up to find some new hunting grounds.

It was getting late in the year and all the trailheads had a good dusting of snow. The crisp smell of cold evergreens filled the air as daylight broke over the eastern mountains. We drove slowly the last several miles towards the parking area at the end of the road when we spotted some deer about four-hundred yards off the road, on the forest. This was important because we were mostly surrounded by ranches and catching game off the private property this late in the year was a tall task.

I had to park the truck and force my hunter to get off the road the required distance before shooting. But we got it done and had a nice four-point buck down right at first light. Still intending to elk hunt that day, I butchered the deer, threw him in the pickup and off we went to the trailhead.

Before long we were riding up the trail, headed to a perfect "fat hunter" spot. You just go up there and watch, build a fire, make coffee and hang out. The spot looks down on a migration trail that descends a small side canyon. The main drainage bends around the side canyon creating a large gravel bar area at the base. When the migration is on, you can watch elk pour out of that canyon. You have about forty-five minutes to see them, get them judged for size, and then get your hunter set up before the elk walks out onto the gravel bar at the bottom. A three-hundred-yard, downhill shot as you lounge high above on a cliff face. Like I said, a perfect fat hunter spot!

My hunter had been drinking Cognac from a flask 24 hours a day since he arrived. He said his doctor told him it would help some medical condition he had? Whatever. When he didn't have his flask in his hand you could count on there being a nonfiltered Camel in it instead. We looked like a steam engine wherever we went with all that smoke billowing from the trail! Sounded like one too! That flask was clanking around every few minutes. The hunter was constantly coughing or his zippo lighter was clanking. But I digress.

This was day thirteen of this hunter's ten-day hunt. We had been on several elk but could never close the deal. Finally, admitting that my hunter couldn't move, I was resigned to the migration trail. At least I was getting some good naps in!

The first migration had certainly already passed. It was a blustery twenty degrees, with parts of the main river completely frozen over. Some parts were only half frozen which had posed a few problems for the horses. We were sitting on that rock hoping for a straggler.

Finally, on the thirteenth day we noticed some elk way up on the rims above. But they were hung up on something. A few of the old, wise cows kept looking down the mountain. Finally, we spotted seven wolves side hilling across the mountain. This was back in the late 1900's so that was a really rare sight to see! But after several hours, the elk decided to come down anyway.

We had picked out a bull in the herd and were set and ready when they finally stepped out on the gravel bar. The hunter made a "perfect shot," right through the hips, hitting both femoral arteries. Dropping the elk dead in seconds just a few hours before dark. I was too tired to be mad about the bloodshot meat. I was just happy that we were about done!

The Southfork River Valley.

Some other local hunters had shown up earlier in the day and had watched the whole thing happen. Obviously, my hunter was not up to the task of helping pack the bull. We had to ride about a mile back down the trail, then take a switchback that led back up river towards the base of our shooting position. From there you crossed the river, which had ice one third of the way from each bank with open, swift running water that was about three feet deep in the center. It was dangerous going with horses and experienced mountain hands, but an absurd proposition for a fat Californian with a questionable blood alcohol content who was riding an inexperienced horse. Plus, it was going to be dark soon and my hunter was hell bent for leather to get out of the woods.

The locals were good guys and the main group volunteered to ride my hunter back to the trailhead where he would wait for me to come out with the meat. One local would stay and help me get packed. So off we went, and as we stepped out on the ice it became even more apparent how dangerous this was going to be. Not fifty yards downstream the river was completely froze over. Falling off your horse into the swift current was almost certainly a death sentence.

We had to walk our horses out on the ice, not knowing when they would break through. When they did, you had a two-to-three-foot drop until they hit the comparatively solid footing in the river bed. A good tight rein helped them keep their head up when they broke through. Then on the other side, once we reached the ice the horses had to jump that same two or three feet up onto thin ice. Which they would then break through, then repeat the process until the ice was thick enough to support the animals. Crossing back wasn't as bad because you could follow your same tracks, or broken ice path, if you will.

Anyhow, after several tense minutes of negotiating the crossing, "Firecracker" a red roan colt that I had been riding did well. The Psycho Donkey was our pack mule that day and she took some coaxing, but eventually she made it and the local hunter also made it across. Soon we were butchered and almost ready to pack the Psycho Donkey when we decided to be neighborly and drag the carcass as far to one side of the gravel bar as possible so the smell and sight wouldn't be too bad on the next bunch of elk for these local hunter's morning hunt. We hooked ropes on the carcass and dallied onto our riding horses and we pulled as hard as we could. After three or four tries we had successfully moved the carcass out of sight and stashed it in some willows a hundred yards downstream.

As daylight got short, we were packed and kicking for the trailhead. It was a good four-hour ride however and eventually we made it out safe after a few hours of riding in the dark.

When we arrived at the trailhead, not at all surprisingly my hunter was gone. His horse was tied to the trailer and he had bummed a ride to his hotel with the locals who had duded him out. That about did it for me, the guy hadn't even loosened his cinches on his horse or taken the bridle off. I was pissed and planned on giving him an earful on our next meeting.

Me, Firecracker and the Psycho Donkey packing a bull out.

When I got to town my hunter was sitting in the bar already three sheets to the wind. When I walked in, veins bulging in my forehead and ready to give this guy the "what-for" he saw me coming and smiled. He motioned for me to sit down and as I approached, I saw a huge stack of $100 dollar bills on the table, which threw me off my game. He ordered me a whiskey and told me about several other things he had for me besides the money. Which was a $1,200 tip alone. He also bought me an oil cloth outback slicker, which I still have on my saddle to this day, several pairs of elk skin gloves, a knife and meat saw and several other trinkets. Needless to say, I never gave him that stern talking to!

Twenty years later I walked into a taxidermist shop in Cody with a successful sheep hunter to drop off his ram. We were looking at all the mounts when I noticed an old dusty mount in the back that looked familiar for some reason? As we talked to the shop owner, we realized that the bull we were looking at was this same bull I had guided long ago. The hunter had paid for it but never picked it up! (And passed away soon after) The taxidermist offered him to me but at the time I had no room for him in my house but that would have been a neat one! The bull ended up being a 5x6 that gross scored 357 so he was very unique!

By the time my first season ended the snow was deep and the days were short. We had been hunting late season elk hunters and finishing up a few Governor's and Commissioner's tags out of a Lodge on the Yellowstone line. Overall, I ended up guiding several clients successfully, including guiding my first bighorn sheep hunter.

I had been surviving the season financially on my tip money. And never had gotten suspicious about getting paid, I just figured maybe payment at the completion of the season was customary? That's the way some farming jobs I'd had in the past were. We never even talked about it and I'd never thought about it.

My boss wasn't by any means a bad guy. What I didn't know at the time was some of the family's spending habits and financial issues. This eventually caught up to him and he is no longer in business as a result, I'll have more to say on that in a moment.

Needless to say, there wasn't any money when we were done hunting. And it turns out, was the reason the other guide no-called, no-showed us several hunts prior. Eventually, to his credit I did get paid most of what was owed. It took until February but never-theless, I got it. But not before several heated conversations.

Today, I consider that boss a friend. In fact, he showed up at my daughter's second birthday party! And I use him as a farrier for my horses. He's a good guy and an even better hand, but not everyone's road is smooth.

He was certainly a hunting mentor and you can say whatever you like, but the guy was the best sheep outfitter in the state for years. He taught me more than anyone else has on the subject. Taught me a lot about horses and gave me a good base to learn to be a pretty decent packer. For that I'm thankful.

Years later the Forest Service abolished his camp. The story I heard was it was due to nonpayment of fees? The Forest Service charges what amounts to a franchise fee, a percentage of the gross for the hunts conducted on that land. Every outfitter has to pay them.

I don't doubt the nonpayment, however it never sat well with me that the Forest Manager's took the guy's camp and abolished the permit entirely. Meaning no one can own it ever again. Especially, when the stated reason was nonpayment of dues.

If it was really about money the Forest could have kept the camp and sold it. Or force the guy to sell and recover their money that way? I just never thought they did it right, I guess? I certainly don't know all the details, but it sure set the precedent of what the Forest Service would do if an outfitter wasn't playing by their rules.

| 3 |

Cuttin' Teeth Part 1- The Trail

By mid-August in Cody, Wyoming the construction trade was in full swing. The entire US economy was booming and there were more jobs in the building industry than a guy could shake a stick at. Our modest town of 5000 people was no exception. We had houses, town homes, duplexes, tri-plexes, and four-plexes all popping up at an alarming rate. It seemed that a new one was up every day.

This was no small feat during that time period as Cody's primary industry was tourism. With three million tourists passing through every summer to visit Yellowstone, the town's bars, restaurants, camp grounds, hotels, and grocery stores boom from the end of May till the kids go back to school in late August. After that, it's essentially a ghost town. The economic boom of the early 2000's resulted in our small town growing by 3000 people in just a few short years. In that short time Cody was looking like a real town, complete with a brand-new Walmart Super Center and one of those Quick Lube places.

I had been sticking with my usual routine of working for one concrete company for six months, quitting because I would get bored, or because the boss had been thrown in jail...again, which looking back on, happened at an alarming rate.

A view from atop Deer Creek Pass. The first glimpse into the Thorofare.

Not to downplay how bad domestic violence is, I had one boss who was always in and out of the "Can" on domestics. The problem was, his wife was bigger and tougher than him. Both were alcoholics and thus, when the booze flowed, often there was a fight. I recall him showing up to work more often than not looking like he got the worse end of the deal.

One time in particular his wife "tuned him up" pretty well with the business end of a shovel! After a brief stay at the hospital, off to the "Pokey" he went. Despite all that, our crew would usually show up and do our work anyways. And to their credit, they paid on time and the checks never bounced!

The boss's wife would show up on Monday morning (In the Boss's pickup) to pay us, a tactic they used to keep us from drinking our entire paychecks on the weekend. She'd make a half-hearted effort to ask us how things were going while an extra-long Virginia Slim dangled from her lips. Soon she'd leave us to continue our work.

It worked well considering. Mostly because we had a good crew but it was an obvious public relations nightmare for interfacing with the customers. And it only lasted as long as we had jobs to do. Once out of work, we had to wait until the boss got out of jail. Usually, his wife would bail him out but not until the work was running out and there were new jobs to bid!

Amazingly, that process continued for a period of years. In fact, I'm sure it would still be going on like that had not both of them ended up in jail. The boss got picked up on another Domestic and his wife was in for her third DUI. At that point in my life, you could call me anything but a loyalist so I headed back to framing as soon as the gal who was supposed to be writing the checks was locked up. Most of the crew stayed on and finished out the work but once they got out that time, the damage had been done. The City jobs mostly dried up and soon the Boss and his wife split town and I haven't seen them since. Don't get me wrong! These were some of the nicest and most incredible people I've met. I'd love to see them again. I'm just saying, when they got on the bottle things went south in a hurry!

Anyway, be it that the boss went to jail or I got bored, I'd pick up my trusty hammer and blow the dust off the tool belt and go back to work for a framing crew that I had just quit six short months earlier (and so on). The bosses would just roll their eyes and cut me a check when I broke the news that I was done. To their credit they always hired me back on right away. I operated like that for about seven years straight.

Cody was a small enough town that most of the construction type employees knew each other and it seemed you hadn't cut your teeth until you had worked for at least two of the contractors more than once. And by that theory I had already exchanged my semi-pro jersey for a starting quarter back jersey in the Super Bowl. I took job hopping to a new level.

It was late summer. All the signs were upon us. The colors of the trees were starting to change and I had already awoken to frost on the windshield of my pick-up. The first signs of the tourism season drawing to a close had already came and went. Mostly defined by there only being around forty people in the bar on the last few Monday nights.

I was back working as a carpenter for a local construction company four days a week as I had just traded in my concrete job a few weeks prior. It was good to be back framing. To this day the smell of fresh cut OSB brings me back to those days. Our crew worked four ten hour shifts per week. The day I decided to head back to framing, that boss happened to be in need of some guys, so a deal was struck for the same wages as I received six months prior. I was delighted to be back.

I was quite pleased with my new situation. I was making $15.00 an hour, and had more days off than before. To most people this was a great step up in quality of life and I was no different. Actually, I enjoyed my new and improved quality of life so much that the local bar tenders ended up with enough extra cash to put their kids through college. So, as you can imagine, my pay raise and new found free time ended up leaving me with less disposable income than before.

Usually, my nights and weekends were consumed by competing in the bull riding and bareback riding events at various rodeos throughout the Rocky Mountain region. This year had been different however; the first week of August I had torn a groin muscle which sidelined me from the rodeo. Not for lack of effort on my part I did try to ride one more bull. It was the day after the injury but found out on the first jump that the doctor had probably been right.

The bruising that ran from my knee caps to the bottom of my rib cage seemed to confirm what the Doc said too. To this day there is no pain that I have experienced more intense than a torn groin muscle. But I digress. So once again, due to injury, I was a normal, everyday, average "Joe" trying to scratch out a living pounding nails. There had to be a better way.

On August 20th I was driving to the local lumber store for more job supplies when the phone rang. On the other end was the owner of a newly acquired hunting camp that happened to lay thirty miles from the nearest road. It was in the Thorofare country Southwest of Cody nestled a stone's throw from the most remote place in the lower 48 states. After a brief discussion I agreed to take a job as a guide.

Back in those days most of the town's business was conducted at one of three main local watering holes. If an outfitter needed a guide, a contractor needed a framer, or a rancher needed a cowboy, said entrepreneur would head to the bar and announce his intentions to everyone.

Even if the person inquiring had no luck, there were always twenty, half-liquored, good-hearted folks who would gather their minds and brainstorm up a volunteer and a phone number. This was the chain of events that led to me becoming known to this outfitter. Seemed I had a few buddies who knew I wanted to see the Thorofare Country and told him a few tall tales about my guiding abilities in order to secure me my next job.

I had been around town for four or five years by then and I was known to all that frequented any of the three aforementioned watering holes. I was aware of the camp and its reputation as producing large bulls' year in and out. I had also heard that the former owner, had sold out. So why not give it a try?

To this day there's a valid argument to say this camp was one of the best elk camps in Wyoming. I had wanted to go in there for a long time but the problem was… well, let's just say that I had heard the former owner decided to go to law school to keep his attorney expenses down? I'll leave it at that. I don't know if it's true, but there certainly were a few court filings and newspaper articles floating around that made the claim plausible. Add to it that I was a tad gun shy about going back to work guiding after having a rough go of collecting wages in the previous camp.

Pack strings on the initial climb out of the Deer Creek Trailhead.

This had not been the first time I acquired a job from our local "Job Service." Once I landed a two-year gig over a game of pool. A friend and I were enjoying a friendly game with a guy from L.A. Obviously, not a local, his parents had sent him out to Cody to build them a vacation home while he decided what to do with his life.

The catch in the whole plan was that the home would be built using straw bales as walls and insulation. The only problem with the whole plan was that none of us, including him, had ever done more than stack straw into a large pile.

Intrigued by the idea, the pool game eventually headed for the napkin holder located on the large cherry wood bar. Soon after, we had designed an entire home using nothing more than a few napkins, under the influence of spirits. Not without telling every "Big Bad Wolf" joke we could think of in the process.

The following morning, myself and a few friends met our new boss in front of the Silver Dollar Bar at 8:00am and followed him to our new job site. Two years later, we had the first straw bale house in Park County and to my knowledge, it is still standing. Being over a foot out of square notwithstanding. That's not a joke either, we designed and built the place off of napkins. He had the basic dimensions, but that was it!

Anyway, after agreeing to take the new guiding job, all that was left to do was quit the current one. Not without some heart burn though. Both my concrete and my framing employers always hired me back and I always stayed six months. Anyway, I had a good thing going and sure didn't want to burn the bridge. So, I broke the news to the boss at the end of the day and apologized for the lack of notice. He took it in stride, as it wasn't the first time I'd quit. And as it turned out, wouldn't be the last.

We parted company by shaking hands and he bid me good luck on my next adventure. With a fist full of dollars, I headed for the sporting goods store to stock up on essential items. Hand warmers, two rolls of Copenhagen, a carton of cigarettes, a box of cigars and a bottle of Crown Royal. I also called my girlfriend at the time, who is now my wife to see if I could find a pistol to borrow from her dad or brother. I was in luck and soon had a borrowed Colt Python, 357 for a bear protection. Back in those days, some guides didn't even wear a pistol. It was a treat to see a bear and we didn't think much of it. However, this was one of the big camps in Wyoming and I would be a long way from help. So, I figured I needed some protection. It couldn't hurt!

A day later I was laying down for the night in the camper on my pick-up in the outfitter's driveway. It had been a long day building loads, organizing and weighing panniers, and checking and fixing the pack saddles. I was tired but couldn't sleep. My mind raced as I thought of what lay ahead. I had only heard stories about the Thorofare Region of Wyoming. Tomorrow, not only was I going to see it, I was going to live in it for the next two months.

I was worried too. The logistics of running an outfitting business thirty miles in the backcountry are daunting to say the least. We had thirty head of pack mules, fifteen horses, and fifteen more leased horses on the way. Each animal had their own saddle as indicated by the name written in black marker on a piece of duct tape which was then stuck to the saddle. I wasn't much of a horseman and I wasn't sure how I was going to remember all these mules and horses?

A tickle of fear struck me earlier in the day when I saw that we had sixty loads for this pack trip. When I asked how many guys were going in with us, I was surprised to be told there was only five of us. I had packed some the year before for another outfitter but I never had to lead more than two pack animals at a time.

Camp one year ago was only seven miles in, about four or four and a half hours of riding. Tomorrow, I was going to have to lead at least ten pack animals for thirty miles, over what sounded like a treacherous trail that is known as Deer Creek.

As I laid there unable to sleep, I remembered something from time studying my map. According to my crude calculations it was only seven miles to the top of Deer Creek Pass. This gave me some comfort because I had heard that once you got over the pass it was smooth sailing all the way into camp.

From the pass I knew we would walk down Butte Creek until it dumped into the Thorofare River, from there we would follow the main trail to the tributary of the river camp was on. From that point it looked like an easy three to five miles into where I figured camp must be. Just a few short miles from the most remote place in the lower 48 states according the USGS, Bridger Lake.

Camp was barely a mile from the southeast corner of Yellowstone National Park. The old timers say that the Thorofare region got its name back in the old days for being the main thoroughfare between "Jackson's Hole" and modern-day Cody, while the younger generation insist it earned the name due to the elk migration. I was not there in the old days when guys like Jim Bridger were around but I'm inclined to believe whatever they say. You can make up your own mind? By the way, this book shouldn't be used as a historical reference of any facts!

A lot of the southern Yellowstone elk migrate to a reserve near Jackson in the winter. Where, for a small fee, you can go for a horse drawn sleigh ride in the winter and get a very up close and personal view of the elk. Few outsiders realize that there are less publicized (at the time) migrations.

A few hundred elk actually migrate north to the Sunlight Basin Areas and a few thousand others prefer to winter up on the Greybull River near present day Meeteetse, Wyoming.

As soon as the snows start hitting Yellowstone, Mr. and Mrs. Elk pack their bags and start a long walk all the way up the Thorofare River. When they get close to the head of the river, they head up a side canyon and drop off the other side into another side drainage that flows into the South Fork of the Shoshone. That's where I sat and watched a guy smoke camels and drink cognac for thirteen or so days in the previous chapter. Anyway, from there they make a short hike up the South Fork until they find, and follow another side canyon, up and over that and down through the next basin and out the other side which descends all the way to their preferred wintering grounds. Which is usually some farmer's field.

This is a long and arduous journey for the elk as that route is rougher and far steeper than the comparative stroll down to the Jackson Elk Refuge. It also has more hunters and outfitters hiding in the bushes waiting to ambush them at any moment. Not to mention the hordes of wolves and droves of grizzly bears that either do or don't exist depending on which side of the political debate you are on. But I digress.

This is wilderness like nowhere else in the lower 48 states. Nearly untouched by man to this day except for the few remains of old trapper cabins left over from the Anson Eddy's, Max Wilde's and the famous Siggins Mountain men of yesteryears. If you know where to look you can still find teepee rings in a few places as well!

It was still dark when I was awakened by a pounding on my camper door. I hustled into my clothes and out the door. Leapt from the tailgate and headed for the garage where the outfitter's mom was waiting with a cup of coffee and a cheery "Good Morning!" I was still knocking the cob webs out of my sleepy eyes, it was 3:00am. I downed the coffee, lit a smoke and headed for the corrals to help load mules into the trailer. Shortly, we were making the forty-five-minute drive to the trail head in the pre-dawn darkness.

While we were loading the last of the animals our camp cook, showed up as well as our wrangler, a bareback rider friend of mine from the rodeo. He was over from Australia for the summer and had a broken foot, so instead of sitting in the bar waiting for his visa to expire, he decided he wanted an adventure, American style, broken foot be damned! He didn't let the doctors put a cast on him and swore me to secrecy about the bum wheel, so he signed on, "under the table" of course, and did his best not to limp enough to cause concern from the boss-man.

Climbing, "Fire Box" on the way up Deer Creek.

We all sat pretty quiet on the ride up to the trailhead. None of us really knew each other very well so conversation was small talk at best. The boss and the cook were chain smoking cigarettes from the front seats while the wrangler and I sipped coffee and enjoyed our Copenhagen from the back.

You could feel the excitement and anticipation in the cab of the four door Dodge pick-up as the 5.9L Cummins Diesel powered us towards the trailhead. Seeing as how it was the outfitters first trip as an outfitter, the cook and myself were on our first Thorofare adventure, and our Aussie wrangler hadn't been anywhere resembling a mountain before, the uncertainty, excitement, and nervousness feelings were so thick you could cut them with a knife.

We arrived at the trailhead to find an older guy leaning against the tailgate of his truck. He stood quiet, and motionless except when he raised his half-smoked cigarette to his lips. I didn't recognize him, but I knew who he was. He looked to me, as a twenty something year old kid, like he was an old man. This other guide was known around Cody as one of the modern era legends of the Thorofare. I'd heard it said that he was the best reed caller that there was around this country, and I was looking forward to learning from a good hand! Although I couldn't see him in the predawn darkness, every time he took a pull on his smoke the cherry lit his face just enough to make out a week-old beard and glasses, rough looking fellow beneath a well weathered, short brimmed, silver belly cowboy hat.

I wasn't completely surprised that he didn't say a word to any of us. He just hung his smoke from his lips and turned around to find something in the bed of his truck. He didn't acknowledge any of us. He just fell in and started working.

I remembered thinking that we had a good group of guys as everyone started working. This was a crew of guys that don't need to talk about every minor detail. We all just stuck our heads down and went to work on the task at hand. No one needed to give orders, we all just jumped in and got started.

The wrangler started catching mules and horses that had been trucked up the day before, while the boss started unloading animals from the trailer. The cook and I stayed busy unloading all the pack loads and organizing our top packs.

Soon, the boss and other guide were saddling as they knew the animals and what saddle belonged to who. It was fun to watch a group of guys that for the most part didn't know exactly what to do find a task and get it done quickly and efficiently.

Turns out that the boss was pretty particular about the way we tied the lash rope. I knew the diamond and double diamond hitch and a half hitch but the boss wanted us to tie a Sierra box hitch.

As I gained experience and got better as a packer, I still chuckle at how adamant the east coast outfitter was about tying everything with that particular hitch. Don't get me wrong, it serves its purpose when used properly. When used improperly it serves as a fantastic way to sore a lot of livestock's elbows because once pulled tight, the cinch under the mule's belly goes slack. And sways back and forth for thirty-some miles hitting the livestock in the elbows. Anyway, to the wrangler's and my dismay he offered no lessons. So, we watched him tie one or two before teaming up and starting packing ourselves. Somehow, we managed and I'll admit that we were the weak links in the group when it came to packing with this new (to us) method.

By 10:30 am we were packed, had the strings of mules put together and were climbing on our horses. The boss took the lead. The guide and cook went second and third in line respectively. Our Aussie followed me, and I fell in line behind the cook.

Leaving the corrals, we rode down the gravel road and over a bridge that crossed Deer Creek. Shortly, we were beginning our ascent on the pass. The first part of the trail climbs an open, sage brush covered hillside. It twists and turns up a series of switch backs until after maybe eight-hundred vertical feet, it dives around the corner and into Deer Creek canyon. The reason for the climb on the open hillside is because Deer Creek itself has five-hundred to one-thousand-foot cliffs on either side with numerous waterfalls and cascades in the bottom thereby making it impassable to everything except ice climbers when it's frozen.

Once in the canyon, after another set of switchbacks, we were riding across a piece of solid rock that made up an unnamed (officially) side stream. The locals call it "Hangover Springs" due to a convenient spring that trickles down the rocks which makes a great place to fill up a canteen. The stream is fed from high above where there were still many snow and ice fields.

A bit farther and the trail becomes particularly unnerving due to the fifteen or so foot cliff on the uphill side and the one-hundred foot nearly vertical drop off on the downhill side. The only thing flat was the trail which is only a few feet wide.

Pack Strings climbing out of the "Wash Tub" on the way towards town.

"Well, here we go mules, pay attention" I thought to myself, as my ridding horse stepped out on the ledge with all my pack animals in tow. The trail descends a ways down through the cliffs and crosses a small stream we called "The Washtub." Eons of water has polished the rocks into a bowl that is one smooth piece of rock. The place made me nervous my entire career, even after the Forest Service used dynamite to widen the trail years later. It looked very slippery. The trail crossed the ten-foot-wide creek a few short steps from the top of the bowl of the Washtub. As the water left the tub it immediately fell into a fifty or so foot water fall.

A few sets of switchbacks and cliff faces later the trail had ascended out of the high desert style basalt rock and long needled pine trees and into the forest. Soon we were at the first creek crossing and I led the string up river far enough that the mules in the back of the line could get a good drink of water.

After the animals were satisfied, we continued up the trail which was now on the south side of the canyon. We worked our way up through another set of switchbacks through a boulder slide. Before returning back down to the creek we crested a boulder filled plateau called "Firebox." The second crossing was just a few miles upstream from the first, and the trail was proving to be far less treacherous.

Once we were across the second creek crossing, we entered the timber and ran head on into another pack string headed for town. Luckily, we had the larger string thus, according to trail etiquette we had the right of way.

The boys from a competing camp pulled their string into the timber and let us by. I was feeling a little less nervous by this time. I was starting to trust my horse, but not enough to have a drink of water or a snack the entire trip so far. I was getting a tad parched and I just needed to work up the nerve to do something other than pay an extreme amount of attention to the string of flopping ears that I was leading. In retrospect, I was probably overly concerned about my string. But every few minutes I would turn and look back to see how the loads were riding. Then look to check saddle pads, and so on.

While in the timber I could see far enough that the trail ahead was pretty good. No big rocks, mud holes, down timber, or switch backs. I took the opportunity to sneak a few gulps from my canteen and reload my lip with Copenhagen. I still wasn't comfortable enough to eat the sandwich the boss's mom had prepared.

We rounded another bend and found the trail to be fairly rough. This time however, I concluded that I could probably have a wreck here and live. The trail was bending to the right with steep timber on the same side. Below and to the left there was a large wash-out where the spring runoff managed to slice a chunk of mountainside away that was about fifteen feet deep.

Pack Strings hitting the sub alpine below Deer Creek Pass.

With my new found confidence I started digging in my saddle bag for a candy bar when I heard a loud, "CRACK" ahead of me. Just then I looked up in time to see the cook's last two mules in line slip and fall off the fifteen-foot embankment.

The mules were maybe half way through their ordeal when my horse decided that the situation was dire and he was going home. I didn't have time to pull my hand from the saddle bag and we parted company with mother earth, made a one-hundred and eighty degree turn and headed down the trail. The horse was giving it his best at leaving me and the pack string in the dust too. He was crow hopping and squealing in his effort to get around the string of mules on the uphill side.

My horse, bless his heart, tries hard to be a bronc sometimes, but he just doesn't have the talent. Not to make light of the situation since getting hurt, even this far in requires a helicopter to get you out. Not to mention that it is a long walk in either direction to get anywhere. So, the priority was to first of all, stay on his back. Secondly, get him shut down. Thirdly, you don't want to drop your mule string because there's no telling where you'll find them (assuming you actually could find them). So even if he bucks like grandma's rocking chair I wasn't inclined to relax.

Soon we are enveloped in a cloud of dust and flying hair and I'm grabbing for leather, determined to stay aboard. At the same time, I have to try to keep my pack animals in order or we'll have a huge wreck. The terrain was such that the "Pucker factor" I was feeling resulted in me performing like a world champion bronc rider.

Thankfully, the horse gathered up his marbles before it got too out of hand. When the dust cleared, I was now behind the Aussie and had him surrounded by pack mules that seemed to just follow the lead horse only having far less enthusiasm. In fact, so little enthusiasm that they just walked behind us as we had our fit right there next to the cliff. Good mules!

Still gathering my wits, I looked up to see the cook's two mules. The one in the lead pinned her ears back and bit the follower on the neck, clearly showing her disapproval of the situation. She then took a bite of some grass and walked back up to the trail and got in line, leading the other mule the whole time.

The cook was off his horse and negotiating the narrow trail back to see what happened about then. A half-smoked cigarette between his lips. He was squeezing between mules on the uphill side of the trail, cussing and carrying on the whole way. We had to tell him that the last two were no longer tied on because the mules in question had by this time regained their positions in line.

I remember being impressed with the mules' performance as they slid down the embankment. Neither one panicked, they fought the entire time to keep their footing and protect themselves. Impressive.

When I say tied on, what we did was tied a rope to the back of one pack saddle in a loop. On the loop we connected bailing twine on the rope so that, when you tie a lead rope from the following mule to the saddle of the leading mule, there is a weak spot or breaking point in the line. That way, when you have a wreck of some sort, one mule won't drag all the others off a cliff.

The plan worked for the most part. This day the last mule in line stumbled and fell, but her line didn't break. So, she and the next mule went for the ride while the third saddle twine broke. Better to only lose one or two, than to lose the entire string.

In no time we had the wreck sorted out and were back on our way. Having not seen our little wreck, the boss and other guide continued up the trail while we got resituated. Just a few more miles and the trail exited the timber and made a sharp switch back to the right. On the left there was a perfect little camping spot. There was a small flat spot, maybe twenty feet by twenty feet and there was a small fire ring made up of soft ball to pumpkin sized rocks.

The grass was green and the surrounding mountain side meadows were full of wild flowers with brilliant bluebells, Red Indian paintbrush and other bright yellow and white flowers as we ascended into the sub-alpine. It was a beautiful contrast between the reds, purples, yellows and greens of the foliage while the wind beaten boulders, some the size of houses, were shades of grey seemingly laid out into rows created by eons of erosion, rock slides and avalanches.

There was not a cloud to be seen and the brilliant blue sky created a mesmerizing back-drop against the snow fields, rocks, and wild flower meadows. Truly one of the prettiest places I've had the privilege of seeing.

Descending the avalanche chutes on Deer Creek Pass.

The beauty was quickly forgotten as the trail quickly steepened, narrowed and became far rougher and rockier. The Aussie and the cook were getting pretty far ahead of me as well. As we made our way up the endless maze of switchbacks, crests, cuts and washouts I watched as the top of the pass came into view. I wanted to breathe a sigh of relief but couldn't. The trail to the top was full of countless obstacles. I knew it was close, but I wasn't sure what lay between me and the top. Hundreds of horse accidents have occurred right at the top of this notorious pass and I wasn't ready to let my guard down.

As we continued our assault on the pass, my horse found a rhythm and was making good headway. All the mules and horses were impressive as they continued stepping out without a complaint. Soon I noticed a snow shovel laying off to the side of the trail. I knew from reading and listening to stories that these shovels stayed on the pass year around so that outfitters, hikers and hunters can dig through the snow on the trail.

I took note that it seemed quite a ways down from the pass. I figured maybe people set them that far down to ensure the shovel doesn't disappear in the wind-swept snow drifts? A few weeks later I would find out that this was not the case.

As we gained altitude and ground on the pass the trail soon turned into larger rocks. The horses were stepping up through the obstacles when we finally turned the last switch-back. We were still a few hundred yards from the pass but the trail had flattened out as the horses' side hilled around a gradual corner until I could see the trail disappear down the back side of the pass. We made it!

A mere four and a half hours earlier in the day we stood at the Deer Creek trailhead some 6 or 7,000 feet above sea level. Now it was 3:00 in the afternoon and I was standing on Deer Creek Pass, about 10,000 feet above sea level. So far, we had ridden four and a half hours covering about seven miles and gaining about 4,000 feet in elevation. I was glad to have a sure-footed, good (for the most part) horse carrying me.

To this day I can remember my first look into the Thorofare with absolute clarity. One of the first things I saw was the weather beaten, wooden sign signaling us that we were leaving the Washakie Wilderness and entering the Bridger Teton Wilderness. The grass was short on top of the pass and it danced in the wind as the sun shined down on the snow fields and meadows below.

The pass itself was a low place surrounded by what appeared to be rolling hills. They obviously are not hills, but 10,500-foot mountain peaks. The grass and gravel on the ground reminded me more of a wind beaten tundra that you would find in the Brooks Range of Alaska than Wyoming.

Far below the grass thickened and was taller and looked like a pristine pasture. It lay in a bowl-shaped canyon whose snow fields fed Butte Creek. To the right stood the Thorofare Buttes, 10,840-foot snowcapped peaks that stood by themselves on the northern rim of the canyon. They appeared to be keeping watch on the entire area.

To the left there was a small bowl of knee-high grass and wild flowers such as Indian paint brush and lupine. Below you could see the canyon where the Thorofare River flowed in from almost due south before making a sharp elbow and continuing west northwest. The Thorofare Plateau was clearly visible some twelve miles away. With everything to the distant west being Yellowstone National Park.

It was truly breathtaking, and I realized the view probably hadn't changed much in several hundred years. It was interesting to see the checkerboard pattern that the infamous Yellowstone fires of 1988 left on this land. I felt like riding over the pass was like riding back in time. Pure, pristine, untouched, wild wilderness.

It is an interesting feeling to leave civilization for months on end. Most people cannot comprehend what life is like without lattes, cell phones, electricity, and hot showers. In my experience, few people understand what it is like to not be on top of the food chain. Just like modern day dogs, we have been fed for so long via a grocery store that most people couldn't survive if they were forced to live of the land for a week. As evidenced by many reality TV shows nowadays.

This country is the last of the truly wild country in the lower 48 states. A place where the humans are no longer on top of the food chain, grizzly bears and wolves are. The amazing thing about backcountry living is when you realize that your instincts are screaming at you to find, food, water and shelter. Not fancy coffees, and the best way to avoid traffic on your way to the office. A far cry from life in metropolitan America.

From atop the pass, I followed the lead of the others, now far below me and dismounted. The Aussie and cook were already a few hundred yards in front of me, leading their horses and mules down the open mountainside. I figured that if I was going to make it into camp, I'd better eat something, at this point, Copenhagen wouldn't even hold the hunger pains at bay.

The Thorofare Buttes and July's crop of wildflowers.

At the time, I felt safer eating my sandwich while walking and leading my horse and pack mules than riding and doing so. I know now how silly that was but it accentuates what a greenhorn I was. I kept tripping and stumbling over the rocks and uneven terrain as we made our way down the back side of the pass while munching on that sandwich. The open meadow we were in was still quite steep but the view was spectacular enough that I wasn't paying enough attention.

After about a half an hour a-foot we mounted our horses and continued on, eventually ending up in the timber as we descended below the tree line. I was grateful that the trail was wide and for the most part flat. As we descended onto Butte Creek the mules were doing their best to steal nibbles of grass every few steps or so. With the exhilaration of having the worst trail behind us and some food in my belly, I reloaded my lip with a dip and relaxed as we rode down the valley. Taking in the view of pristine wilderness as we rode deeper into the tall and uncut wilderness.

Not many miles passed when we rode by another outfitter's camp, owned and operated by a certain Mrs. Outfitter (ahem). The camp is situated not one-hundred yards off the north side of the main trail so I had a pretty good view of the first Thorofare hunting camp I'd ever seen.

I don't know exactly what the circumstances were that led to her taking over her husband's camp but the word around the campfire was that she took the camp over after her husband was allegedly caught doing some illegal things and subsequently fined, given a short jail sentence, and banished from the Forest for a year or so. It's an amazing testament to the efficiencies of the bureaucracies far below that a simple title transfer from husband to spouse satisfies their criteria.

A few more miles down the trail and we came to what is known as the "Airplane Meadows." I rode into the upper end of the meadow to find the other guide busy repacking one of the mules. A pack had started to slip due to uneven weight distribution. I stopped alongside and offered to lend a hand which was rebuffed with a grunt. The meadow was on an incline and was roughly two-hundred yards across and about half a mile long with a ten-foot embankment almost smack dab in the center of the meadow.

The Airplane Meadows earned its name from one of the legendary stories of the Thorofare. A guest on a summer trip got hurt or sick or something? So, one employee high tailed it to town to rustle up some help. A local pilot ended up flying in to extract the guest and they all lived happily ever after.

Or was it the one where an outfitter had some fisherman on a summer trip when one became gravely ill? It was suspected that the client in question had an appendicitis. As a result, one of the outfitters employees "high tailed it" to the road and called for an emergency evacuation of the sick client.

This of course, was long before the advent of high-altitude helicopters. Due to the small nature of the area, word traveled fast and the town of Cody and Jackson were soon filled with rumors of the ongoing crisis. So, one of the pilots in Jackson received word of the situation and flew his airplane into and landed in, the meadows. Hence, Airplane Meadows.

The meadow proved to be too steep for the plane to taxi to the top of the hill so they managed to rig up a contraption so that the horses and mules could pull the plane up to the top. After hours of work the plane was finally on top of the hill and the pilot had his sick passenger on board.

He fired up the bird and made the short flight to Jackson. The pilot landed to a hero's welcome, complete with a waiting ambulance and a cheering crowd. Well, it turned out that once they landed the sick passenger miraculously made a full recovery. It was said that he jumped from the plane and headed for town saying, "If you think I was going to ride a horse out of there you're nuts!" The pictures of whichever event this was still hang in the terminal at the Cody Airport.

Anyhow, after the mule was repacked, we started kicking for the mouth of our drainage. We were not too far from the turn off when we passed a creek, which flows into the Thorofare River from the south with a camp that bares its name. It has a long history and at one time, was one of the premier hunting camps of the Thorofare Region.

Pack strings descending into the Thorofare.

Back when this seven mile-long, (read: very small drainage) was producing quality trophy animals year in and out, the outfitter at the time was only taking twenty or so hunters a year. Truly, the outfitter was a steward of the land and a respected "herd manager." Then, he sold to a newbie and became a politician. A pretty decent politician if there ever was such a thing, too!

The new owner subsequently started booking sixty to one-hundred hunters a year and absolutely decimated the resident herd that called the drainage home. Nowadays when you pass those guys on the trail, they usually are sporting spikes and rag horns on top of their packs and most of the time, hunters without a smile.

It is very sad to see an outfitter place the short-term dollar value generated by hunters ahead of the long-term herd management. But then again, can you blame them? When you never know how many tags are going to be available from year to year, or what other business crushing ideas the suit and ties in Cheyenne will scheme up, why not get paid?

That exact scenario has resulted in a movement to lower the number of hunting tags issued to this area. What else would we expect the Red Shirts do? They flew around during the summer, counted less elk, and thus came to the conclusion that we need less hunters. Which sounds plausible until you realize they are turning a blind eye to the rampant bear populations or the wolves running rough shod wherever they please. Rather than focus on ninety percent of the problem, they zeroed in on five percent of the problem. Yes, I'm aware that ninety plus five doesn't equal one-hundred. There are other factors that I'm not going to go into, such as winter kills and all that!

The wolves and bears are certainly doing their part on the elk population, the Forest Service, Game and Fish, and outfitters all need to realize that the short-term gains of whatever crusade they happen to be on at the moment will be at the cost of an entire industry being shut down or ruined. They need to realize the revenue being generated for the state and local economies is real. But most importantly, they need to understand that there's an ecosystem that has been thrown out of balance by special interest groups and none of them are helping fix it.

An awful lot of non-hunting type town folks rely on the aforementioned revenue brought in by the hunters. And the squabbling is most likely going to be the demise of the industry by way of grizzly and wolf populations going unchecked. The Fuzz knows what's happening. And they gripe to their bosses a little. But don't kid yourself, none of the Fish and Feather guys that I've spoken to care more about the ecosystem or the habitat than they do their government pensions. And thus, we've come full circle back to where we started! Which squeaky wheel gets the grease this time around? It certainly won't be the elk! Oh, whoops! This book isn't intended to be political! Now back to our regularly scheduled programing!

At length, we finally rounded the bend and made the right-hand turn into our drainage. I figured we were getting close to camp? The trail exited the timber into a large meadow where we saw a sow grizzly with two cubs grazing about a hundred yards away. The outfitter's Border collie took off like she was shot out of a cannon. Her barks didn't do much to scare the bears because the grass was taller than the dog. All we could see was the grass parting and swaying back and forth as the dog ran toward the bears. The dog was fearless and went head on with the sow, sailing by and biting her on the rump as she ran past. This made the sow sit down like a dog and whip around trying to swipe at the dog. She was too fast though and soon the bear was spinning in circles trying to get the dog. Finally giving up, the bear and her two cubs beat a hasty retreat up the mountainside. That's a good dog.

Finally, after ten hours of riding we crossed the creek to the western shore and rode up a small embankment and into camp. That was an awesome sight. We pulled up to the hitching rails, I bailed off my horse and tied him and my lead mule to the rail. Quickly I unsaddled, threw my saddle on the ground and started working on my mules. All of us were tired and just wanted to be done messing with the stock. I was about three mules into the job of unpacking and saddling when a clean-cut older guy walked up introduced himself. He wore a Tim McGraw type cowboy hat, flat shaped with the front dipped down low over the eyes. He had come into camp a few days before us and had a few tents set up. Which proved to be a welcome sight after being on the trail all day. He helped me finish up unloading, unsaddling, and hanging cow bells around the mule's necks before turning them loose in the meadow.

The mules were rolling and stirring up a lot of dust, obviously happy to finally be in camp and not wearing a saddle. They eventually dispersed into the meadow to graze. Some were just lying in the belly high grass resting while others went to the creek for a drink of water, still a few others just grazed on the fresh grass. A lot of mules travel in pairs, kind of like best friends, and most all of them have very unique personalities. It was fun to see them all in the meadow winding down after the thirty-mile journey to camp.

Sally the mule taking a break after the long walk into camp.

Still to this day one of the most calming sites is a horse pasture in the mountains. The calm in the air as an occasional bell dings quietly as mules graze in the distance. Pairs and other assorted groups, some laying down, others grazing, still others cooling their feet as they get a drink from the crystal-clear water in the creeks. The horse pasture is a neat place to just take in your environment!

The outfitter and wrangler headed out to the meadow to picket some of the horses for the night while the rest of us explored our new surroundings. We'd call this place home for the next few months. It was spectacular to say the least, nestled on the side of a meadow with 10-12,000-foot mountains looming over the 8,000-foot valley floor. A creek on one side and timber on the other.

A picket is just a soft cotton rope roughly twenty feet in length. One end has a hobble attached to it and the other a metal stake. This allows a horse to graze freely while still being tied up. The mules usually just get turned loose with bells on their necks so we can hear them when they are out of sight, i.e. hiding from us. Most mules stay right around the horses anyway so there is no need to tie them up or picket them.

The Trident Plateau stood at 12,000 feet to the northwest. Its seemingly gradual foothills covered with timber. In places bearing the scars of the 1988 fires as it climbed, getting gradually steeper until they became seemingly impassable towering rock faces and precipices. To the southeast, another peak, Baldy, dramatic in its own way nearing 12,000 at its sharp summit. The head of the valley was seemingly guarded by the equally formidable Rampart Pass.

Far below in the valley floor was intermittent green timber, burn, and blow down, and meadows with belly high grass. Perfect for the horses and mules that toiled under their saddles to get here. The creek ran on the southeastern end of the meadow and tucked in the green timber on the south end of the meadow was camp.

The cook soon had salad, spaghetti and meat balls with garlic bread cooking while the wrangler and I headed for the spring to fill the two five-gallon containers full of water. One of the containers is used for water while the other is reserved for Kool-Aid. The spring in this camp had been the brunt of many jokes. Now, it had an electric fence around it to keep the mules out. But a few years back a hunter allegedly took pictures of a mule urinating in the spring and took the old owner to court over it. It was good to see the new outfitter avoiding that fight!

The dining tent was mostly completed when we arrived. The 20x40 canvas tent was complete with two wood stoves in opposite corners, a kitchen on one end, tables, and benches on the other. Soon everyone was gathered in the tent telling stories about the trip in.

The guide who was already in camp also reported that he had been having some trouble with a bear coming into camp in the middle of the night. We all agreed that tonight would most likely be calm as all the mules and horses, people and dogs were now occupying the area.

After some of the most satisfying spaghetti, garlic bread, and Kool-Aid we lounged in our camp chairs making some small talk as to the plan for the next few days. The cook handed me a blend of Black Velvet and Kool-Aid to sip on without a word. I figured he didn't want everyone else to know he had any alcohol? Either way, I liked him even more now and was glad we had him as our cook. I figured I'd have to return the favor tomorrow night using my Crown Royal. Soon we all made our way to the sleeping tents and drifted off to sleep to the sounds of the breeze blowing softly through the trees.

The next few days we toiled with the camp set, cutting firewood and taking care of the livestock. After another trip or two in and out we were ready for hunters!

| 4 |

Cuttin' Teeth Part 2- Bear Bait

The first hunt was an archery hunt, and we only had a few hunters. The wrangler and I were tasked with heading up country and setting the north camp which we would use later for the rifle hunts. It was during the camp set that I saw my first wolf in the wild. A big black wolf stood watching us one afternoon. At the time, it was a real treat to see one!

In the coming days the wrangler and I set the camp quickly and developed a great system for the never-ending firewood battle. No "mechanical equipment" is allowed in the wilderness so we are left to cut wood with hand tools and crosscut saws. Just like the pioneers.

Once we had a good stash of wood split and stacked, we decided we would cut down one tree a day and cross cut them into three manageable logs to carry. We would carry them into camp and set them near the saw bucks. The saw bucks made the task of cutting logs into rounds pretty bearable by holding the log at waist high level so you could stand while sawing.

The following day we would go cut another tree, get the logs in, and cut the first day's logs into rounds. The rounds were then stacked by the splitting log. And the third day, we would cut down another tree, bring the logs in, cut rounds out of the logs from the previous day, and finally we would split the rounds from two days ago. I'm not sure why we got so scientific about it? Perhaps we thought the rounds would split easier? Either way, in a few days we had a heck of a jag of wood cut. So much in fact that the stash lasted into the following season.

The head of the river. Looking north towards Rampart Pass.

One day while we were sitting on camp, most everything was done so we were basically just cutting wood. The boss appeared riding his big palomino horse across the meadow. He dismounted by the corrals as we walked over to see what was up? He seemed pleased with our progress and was shocked at the pile of firewood we had managed to accumulate. After looking around camp a bit, checking our work, he filled us in on news from the archery hunt which was still underway.

We sat in the dining tent as he told us that our guide, the reed caller had been out with one hunter that morning. The other hunter wasn't feeling well and decided to stay in camp. The hunter was a crossbow hunter as he only had about half of his left arm. They had wounded a small bull and began tracking him up a steep canyon. Unbeknownst to them, a sow grizzly and her two cubs had found the bull first and had already claimed the carcass.

Ursula, Battle Axe and Red Man packing in the high country.

Once the guide and hunter crested a rise, they stumbled on the three bears taking all parties by surprise. The sow bluff charged the two and ran right by which placed the hunter and guide between her and her cubs. So, the second charge wasn't a bluff! She barreled in and knocked the guide down and bit him on the thigh and arms. The guide managed to un-holster his pistol but the bear was shaking him violently, like a dog shakes a toy, slamming him back and forth on the ground. The hunter kept his wits though and un-holstered his can of bear spray and ran into the fight, placing the can right in the bear's mouth, he discharged the entire can at point blank range, directly in her mouth and nose.

Un-phased by the pepper spray, the sow turned and bit the hunter on the leg, knocking him down. At this point the guide sat up and was pulling the trigger on his pistol but nothing was happening. The trigger wouldn't move on the revolver and the gun wasn't firing. Just then the bear turned to jump back on the guide. At the same moment the guide realized that at some point in the frolic the cylinder had opened on the pistol. He snapped it closed and pulled the trigger hitting the sow right inside the mouth as she was attacking with her mouth open. She turned and walked about fifty feet and tipped over dead!

The two guys gathered themselves and sat on a log. It was said that they both chain smoked an entire pack of cigarettes before retreating the scene as the cubs at that point were barking and raising a fuss nearby. They were both completely orange from the pepper spray but not too badly torn up. They opted to head for camp where a first aid kit was handy.

After making camp and assessing their injuries they were in surprisingly good shape for just being chewed on by an angry sow. Nothing a few stitches and a shot of antibiotics couldn't fix! The problem was we didn't have any antibiotics, just whiskey. And bear bites are notorious for infection as they are always eating rotten, maggot infested meat.

The following day the two rode back to the trailhead to head to town and see the doc. The problem was, once they got to the truck, they found our cooler of beer we keep handy for the ride out day. After five or six road beers they figured the "Saw Bones" wouldn't give them any meds so they bee-lined it for the Silver Saddle Saloon in the Irma Hotel in Cody and spent the night bellied up to the bar. The following morning, they went to the hospital where they both got patched up, made their report to the Game and Fish and the following day the guide rode back into camp to finish the season. The hunter opted to finish his hunt at the Irma!

Meanwhile, I was needed back in the south camp to finish out the hunter who remained. We ended up getting really close on a few bugling bulls but never could close the deal.

The worst part was the boss told me to leave everything except what I needed to guide for a day or so. Including my bedroll, which I naively left behind. Once in the south camp, I was dismayed to find out I was using the boss's old bedroll. Now, the boss in that camp barely showered when we were in town, let alone cleaning up while in camp. He often times wouldn't even take his boots off before crawling into his bedroll. Bloody clothes on and all. Most of the time he didn't bother to take off his hat and he snored like a dying grizzly bear! He never washed his hands and I had several hunters mention it after seeing him eat after butchering an elk with dried blood, fat and guts caked on his hands and fingernails. Hygiene wasn't on his to-do list. I figured it was barely tolerable to sleep under the bedroll, but I wasn't getting in it.

After a few days the Fuzz rode into camp to do their investigation. The guy who rode in was a decent guy who had a fairly good reputation. As I understand it, he is now retired down near the Mexican Border and he always leaves water out for the illegals who cross his property nightly. Anyway, He came in and the outfitter took him to the site where the attack occurred. He had a look around, then cut the bear's head and all four paws off, threw them in a feed sack and they walked out. I remember wondering why, this far in the wilderness they thought they needed to do that? I guess some guides and hunters like to keep the claws and skulls even though it's illegal?

After the archery hunt, the north camp cook had twisted off for unknown reasons. Just up and quit! All we knew was that we were short a cook and that was an emergency. Being that the season had already begun, there were few options other than to just hunt everyone out of the south camp. And during the day we could send the wranglers and camp jack up river to break the north camp. That way we could get it out of there before the end of the season. All that work for nothing!

By this point in the season, I had become friends with the remaining cook. And I still call him a friend to this day. He was just like us, hard living, hard partying, fun loving guys. The only real difference was that he didn't rodeo. But no one is perfect!

Afternoon nap time.

There are unintended consequences of having a bunch of rowdy hooligans in camp at the same time. As an example, let me explain the grocery lists. Really, these camps are run by the cooks. And really good cooks are hard to come by, and he was certainly one of them! Nutmeg and a hint of orange in his French toast batter was amazing! And the guy had a rib recipe that would blow your socks off in town, let alone in camp! I'm not sure what he did but the ribs were so tender and juicy that they would fall apart in the tongs just dishing up your plate! And the Dutch oven peach pies were a marvelous thing of beauty once he figured out to put a horseshoe in the bottom of the pan to keep the crust from burning!

Anyhow, good cooks are hard to find and as a result, certain uh, shortcomings must be overlooked for the benefit of the greater good! After the hunt, before everyone left the cook would write out a grocery list for the outfitter to handle when he got to town. In this case it was for the outfitter's mom as she did the shopping but that's not really relevant. What is relevant however is the cook's personal shopping list that he wrote on the side of the camp's grocery list, and tucked some tip money in with it to cover those expenses. The hunts were eight days. Ride in on day one, hunt for six days, then ride out on day eight. So, it really amounted to a week. Every week the list was the same and I'll never forget it! Especially, because I thought my lists were bad and unhealthy, but I couldn't touch this guy. Every week the list was, ten cans of Copenhagen snuff, a carton (twenty packs) of Marlboro Menthols, a half-gallon of Black Velvet, a half-gallon of Vodka, and a fifth of Crown Royal. And I'm not kidding when I say that he was usually dry for at least a day before the next group of hunters showed up!

Generally, the camp schedule for the wranglers in charge of the livestock was for a morning sort. Meaning the wranglers would wake up a good hour or so before the rest of the camp and they would ride out to find the herd. They would bring them in, sort off the horses and mules who were working that day and kick the rest back out to the meadow after the hunters had left for the morning. It's usually odd to see the stock hanging out around camp during the day.

One morning my hunter had killed a bull right at daylight and we were headed back to camp after butchering the elk. We were going to pick up some pack animals and head back to pack it out. Hopefully, the cook would have some leftover pie from the night before too! On the way into camp, after breaking out into the meadow where camp sits on the opposite side, it struck me as odd to see three mules standing in the trees right in camp. Not thinking much of it, we continued towards camp watching to see what was going on.

One of the old guides who had rode in late, and is a true fixture of the Thorofare brought his own stock with him. One mule in particular was a small grey john mule that was so old he looked bald. A pitifully small mule that looked poor as heck! He was plumb gentle, and always quick to come over and say hi whenever he saw people. But mainly he was hunting treats!

They called the mule Marvin and his name suited him! Nearly bald, and a personality the size of the mountains themselves, Marvin was standing outside the cook tent swishing his tail back and forth and batting his ears to and fro. The cook tent was directly in front of the dining tent and was the focal point of camp. The guide tents were set to the west with the hunter tents to the east. The outhouse tent was directly south and the tack tent, hitching rails and corrals were to the north.

The two other mules stood off just a bit, between the cook tent and the tack tent, but it looked like they had mischief on their minds as well. As we approached, I could see Marvin was sneaking up, little by little, on some panniers that were sitting on the ground next to the cook tent. For convenience purposes, we had a rail hung twelve feet high between two trees right next to the cook tent. We hung food panniers from them so the cook had quick and ready access. Often, the panniers stayed up all night, then were lowered and stayed down all day.

Sounds of cooking and pots and pans clanging came from the cook tent as a steady plume of smoke rose from the chimney into the still air of a bluebird Thorofare midmorning. Everything else was quiet as I assumed the wrangler and camp jack were probably napping? Marvin continued patiently until he was standing directly over the panniers. When the moment was perfect Marvin reached down and stuck his nose in a pannier and began rooting around.

About then the cook noticed the rustling outside and yelled as he charged through the tent flap! That spooked Marvin and his conniving buddies. Marvin's head shot up from the pannier, holding a full loaf of bread in a plastic bag between his teeth and they turned and rocketed out of there like their tails were on fire! High stepping with their front hooves, heads held high seemingly laughing at the cook as they trotted across the meadow, past me and disappeared into the green timber.

The cook was in hot pursuit but he stood no chance as he yelled, "You sonsabitches!" with a cigarette between his teeth, still carrying a spatula.

We laughed for the rest of the season about Marvin, the bread stealing mule. All of us but the cook actually. He held a grudge and later in the year while we were pulling camp I overhead the cook carrying on a full conversation with Marvin who was in the back of the preceding string. I heard the cook cussing him about that bread after a full month had passed.

Marvin's owner is a hell of a hand. That first season I worked in that camp he swore up and down he was retiring after this season. I guided in the Thorofare for about eighteen years after this season and every year I would see him on the trail somewhere. We were always traveling so we never talked much but I'd yell to him, "Are you retiring after this season?" To which he would always smile and laugh and yell back, "Sure am! You?" "Absolutely!" Truth is, he's still probably going in there every season. I heard he was just cooking though? Hell of a guy, and a hell of a mountain hand!

As the season wore on the camp was doing good tagging out clients and I was holding my own with the guys who had been guiding forever. I was gaining a lot of confidence and to this point I only had the bow hunter who didn't tag out. And you could make a compelling argument that he didn't count because I only hunted him one day.

Anyhow, the newest load of hunters got to camp and I was guiding a father/son-in-law combo. The dad was a mid to high seventies and the son-in-law was around his mid-forties. We had had some luck on the first day and the dad was on a 330 bull that he could have, and should have, killed. The problem was he wanted his son-in-law to shoot first as he had killed a few elk in Washington. This was the son-in-law's first hunt.

A decent 6x6 taken under the Trident Plateau.

However, by the second day the dad was fighting a persistent bloody nose. And he was agonizingly slow to get around. He had trouble going uphill, downhill, side hill, you name it, he moved like frozen molasses on a cold day and to a twenty something year old guide this was completely unacceptable. He slowed us down so much we couldn't close in on any of the elk I had put them on.

Eventually, I came to the realization that we could tag out one of them or none of them. Being the snot nosed, inexperienced guide that I was, I decided to "kill the old man off" by walking him up a hill. I figured that would do him in so the next day I could just take the son-in-law out. So, I found a small hill to walk up. And the desired outcome was achieved. The following morning the dad stayed behind to nurse that bloody nose and rest.

I took the son-in-law to a spot that had proven productive for me earlier in the season. A low ridge that divided the main drainage and a tributary that paralleled it before dumping into the main creek. It was a perfect elk crossing spot and there was always activity.

Here we set up at daylight on the top of the ridge and I was able to call a bull into fifty yards just as legal shooting light occurred. But I couldn't get my hunter to see him, so I kept the bull interested by calling a bit more. Soon the bull stepped out at ten feet and the hunter waylaid him with a 300-win mag, straight on. The bull reared up, and fell dead right on his back with his horns stuck in the ground and all four legs in the air.

The following morning was pack out day and the old man left without a word, or a tip. I asked the cook, and he didn't get tipped either, nor did the wranglers. We chalked it up to him just being an asshole and didn't give it much thought.

Interestingly, about two years later I got a call from my dad who had a business in Oregon. He informed me that he got a call from a guy who claimed to be one of my hunters and he wanted my contact information. A few days later I received a letter in the mail with a $500 tip! The dad wrote me an apology letter for the way he left camp and informed me of the events that followed.

He obviously had hypoxia while in camp, we were just too young or dumb to realize it at the time. And the letter mentioned that, but when they arrived in Cody, he wasn't feeling good so he went to the hospital where they promptly life flighted him somewhere to have a triple bypass heart surgery. He also had some complications due to the prolonged hypoxia.

That was a real wakeup call for me as a guide. Prior to this guy, I did not care for my hunters. I forced them to follow at my pace and I killed them all elk. That was the mission! I didn't care about their concerns or even particularly like them, I was there to do a job and that was to kill them a bull. I was of the opinion that even if they didn't like me, it would all be water under the bridge when we whacked a good bull.

I nearly killed this man because I wanted his son-in-law to kill an elk. After this wake-up call, and perhaps some growth and maturity as a guide, I became very aware of my hunter's limitations and tailored their hunts as such. Killing elk was no longer my first priority, safety was, and the experience was second. Nearly twenty years of guiding later I can say that those shifts in priority didn't hurt my tag out ratio much. Mostly it helped me connect and have a better time with my clients. After all, who wants to be stuck in the mountains for eight days with someone you don't like?

Earlier in the year, I had figured out that to ride out of camp between hunts really left you with one day off. Because you spent all day riding out, then had one day off, sort of, because you still had to take care of all your business that day, then the following day you spent all day riding in. So, I enjoyed staying in camp between hunts. On ride out day everyone would be gone by 9am, and if we hustled, we could get the tents cleaned out and ready for the next group of hunters, reloaded with fire wood by noon or one pm. Then we had the rest of the day, the following day, and the next day until about five pm completely off. We just had to cut up a little fire wood every day and we would be rested and all set for the next group of hunters.

As we neared the end of one hunt, we had been having bear trouble every night. Finally, someone noticed that the bear was coming in right at 8pm. Like clockwork, he would show up and look for a snack. We would run him off and the following night he would be back. On this particular hunt, the cook, a wrangler and I stayed in camp between hunts. As soon as the hunters and everyone left, we went about our chores. Once finished, we'd drag out the whiskey for an afternoon snort. That is when we hatched a plan to deal with our evening visitor.

Right at 8pm, as we all sat in the dining tent, still drinking whiskey, the bear came, and we all jumped up and ran out of the tent to confront the bear. Earlier in the evening we had hung a can of bear spray under the cache, then hung a horse bell from the bear spray. Then we wised up to the understanding that a bunch of mules also had bells hanging from their necks. So, we did a quick wrangle of the herd and stripped all the mules of their bells.

When the bear came in, the bell started ringing alerting us to his presence. We snapped to attention and piled out the tent flap! The wrangler had the shotgun which contained cracker sells, a non-lethal round designed to scare the bears away. I had a battery powered spotlight and the cook was there for moral support. The wrangler quickly drew down when I illuminated the bear and made a good shot. The cracker shell burst very close to the bear and sent him retreating back into the woods. We had a good laugh thinking that we really taught that bear a lesson and soon turned in for the night.

The following morning, we awoke to find the can of bear spray had been bitten in half with the orange spray all over the ground. No one had even heard the bear, or bell, or the can go off. We usually rely on the dogs as an early warning system but both dogs had gone out with their owners. So, we hatched a better plan to really teach that bear a lesson the following night.

It was decided the cook would stay in the dining tent to keep up the normal sounds of camp, like dishes clanging and all that, while the wrangler and I would climb into the cache around 7:30

and wait. I was armed with a spotlight and the wrangler with the shotgun loaded once again with cracker shells.

It was a pitch-black night, the only light cast dimly through the stained canvas tent from the propane lantern burning on the inside. The wrangler and I waited patiently, silently, straining our ears for the slightest sound of the approaching bruin. I had set the alarm on my watch to go off at 8:00. We strained our eyes to the south as we thought that's the direction the bear would approach from as the meadow was north. Just as my alarm on my watch started beeping to indicate that it was 8pm, I moved my hand to silent the beeping. Both of us were shocked to hear something spook directly underneath us!

Quickly, we got positioned and the wrangler said he was ready. Now, the bear had spooked off about ten feet towards camp but was standing there like a statue, silently, between the cache and the cook tent. I blasted the bear with the spotlight and instantly we saw that the bear knew we had the drop on him. The wrangler let a cracker shell fly and it blew up right next to the bear as he high tailed it through camp.

You see, we all just assumed that the bear would retreat away from human activity. We expected him to make a hundred and eighty degree turn, make like a fetus, and head out. But he didn't. Rather, he took off at top speed through the center of camp! Seeing that our plan wasn't going quite as expected, and knowing the cook wanted to see the fun, and would soon emerge from the cook tent, I yelled a warning,

"He's coming to ya!"

For whatever reason, be it the chaos or just a misinterpretation, the cook came flying through the tent flap and out into the open directly in the path of the speeding bear who was now in full afterburner mode in his haste to leave camp. My spotlight was shakily following the bear when suddenly the cook and the bear both entered the beam of the spotlight! A head on collision was nearly inevitable! As luck would have it, the adrenaline hit the cook as his eyes widened to the size of saucers! He leaped backwards, landing on his butt while still scrambling to get out of the path! The bear, whose eyes were almost as wide as the cook's, and maybe four feet of separation between them took a ninety degree turn and left camp by going between the cook tent and dining tent, between the empty hunter tents, down through the spring and was gone! We never saw that bear in camp again! The cook ran out of cigarettes shortly after the experience!

Soon we were down to the last hunt of the season before camp pull. I'd been to town once in the last sixty days and was ready to call it a year. The new and last set of hunters for the season rolled into camp in the evening and I was introduced to a smaller Hawaiian guy and his friend. They were my hunters and as we chit-chatted over another first night, spaghetti dinner I discovered our Hawaiian hadn't even seen an elk in the wild before.

Slightly alarmed and a little irritated I pressed the subject, "You hunt deer or any other big game?'

"Nope!"

With a sigh I asked what gun he was shooting and when he told me a 30-06 my jaw almost hit the floor. Don't get me wrong, there's nothing wrong with that gun, it's just a lighter gun than I like to see when I'm a guide and I'm hunting with someone I've never met. I even own a 30-06 and it's my elk rifle! I just prefer the 300 series or better as a guide.

The first day out we didn't have much luck but it didn't take long to realize what good guys these two were. I really wanted to tag them out, finish the season on a high note, and get back to town. The second evening I'd decided to return to almost the exact spot where the son-in-law tipped that bull over backwards.

Just before dark we found the elk and began our stalk. The forest was booming with bugles so close you could feel them. It was the kind of hunt you dream about! The cows were calling and the bulls were going crazy. Spikes and rag horns stealthily snuck around trying to find a stray cow while the herd bulls showed their dominance.

I had zeroed in on a raspy bugle, a very old and mature sounding bull and was closing the distance with both hunters on my heals. I wasn't even calling because all the elk in the forest were and I didn't want to give up our position. Soon we were stuck on the edge of a blowdown where we could see down the hill about a hundred and fifty yards. Moving into the opening would have all but guaranteed us being busted and ruining the hunt. We knew they were right there because of the sounds. You could feel the raspy bugle bounce off your chest we were so close.

Finally, I peeked up next to an old burned-out tree that was still standing. A log was down and laid at its base. I could see antlers if I stayed crouched! I grabbed the Hawaiian by the collar and set him right in front of me and pointed putting my elbow on his shoulder so he could use my arm much like a gun to see exactly where I was pointing. "He's right there, one hundred and fifty yards!" The Hawaiian couldn't see, so he stepped up on the log and was teetering back and forth. Finally, he perked up, raised his gun while balancing on the log and shot. "Ker-Bang!" The elk was down! We scrambled down through the blowdown in the last remaining light of the evening.

We arrived at the bull to find the Hawaiian made a hundred- and fifty-yard shot, freehand, while standing on a round log, perfectly through the vitals! So much for me cussing on the guy with a 30-06 who hadn't seen an elk before! The bull was a giant! A 7x9! Completely palmated on the nine side, more akin to a moose than an elk above the royal. He had mass so great we figured that maybe that bull hit his peak and this was his first year shrinking. What a neat animal! Due to the darkness, we snapped a few pictures, I gutted him in the traditional method, tied his head to a tree so a bear would have to work hard to drag him off and headed for our horses.

As we worked on the elk, I mentioned that I had reservations about him and his gun. He laughed and told me I never asked about hunting people! Turns out he was a Vietnam Vet and had the bullet wounds to prove it!

A typical bull for the area.

From the horses it was an hour back to camp riding straight downstream. It was a dark and moonless night and we rode in silence as we watched lightning strike on top of the Thorofare Plateau once every minute or two. Momentarily, during a strike, it would light up the canyon like daylight. You could see the jagged ridge tops and the intermittent cuts and side drainages during a strike. It was an amazing sight to take in as we made our way to camp. Still to this day, watching that storm light up the plateau is something I remember with absolute clarity. We had been riding in silence and it wasn't until we arrived in camp, and dismounted that we all talked about how neat that was to watch.

The morning came cold and snowy. About eight inches on the valley floor and considerably more, higher up on the ridges. We saddled some horses and a pack mule and rode out to retrieve the elk. During the night I became sick with a cold but we still had work to do. We found our elk undisturbed from the night before and got him quartered and packed onto our mules. We made it back for lunch time and opted out of an evening hunt as we were all soaked tired and as it turned out, sick.

That evening, while the rest of the camp was either out hunting, or napping in their tents. I was sitting by the woodstove in the dining tent drinking some tang that I had diluted with whiskey. The cook had positioned his chair directly in front of the door of the stove. We had been chatting about various things when I felt the heat start to slack off on the stove.

Being in front of the door, the cook agreed and opened it to check our fire. With a cigarette between his lips, a two-month-old beard on his face and an olive-green wool sweater on, he shifted to grab another log. Which he quickly threw on the coals. The problem was the fire had burned down a little too far and the new logs weren't catching fire.

When we crosscut logs into firewood, we always lay down a tarp to catch the wood shavings. Then we dump them into empty coffee cans, add a splash of diesel for fire sustainability, and a bit of white gas just for volatility. The cook shook out some of the concoction on the smoldering coals. Then dug through his pocket for his lighter, still in his sitting position.

"Oops, not that pocket, must be in the other"

Meanwhile, I could hear the hissing coming from the woodstove but before I processed what was happening the cook stuck his lighter down close to the coals and struck it. The results were instantaneous!

A loud, "KaaWOOOF" sound roared from the woodstove as flames shot out completely enveloping the cook! He quickly went over backwards in his chair trying to get out of the fire! After a moment of hesitation to ensure we hadn't started the tent on fire I was hysterically laughing! The cook, staggered to his feet with his hand flat on the side of his face. Soon he removed his hand to show half of his beard burned off and the arm on one side of his wool sweater was burned into little blackish olive-green balls. My laughter was short lived however as the boss came roaring into the tent yelling at us! Through the tongue lashing he said that an eight-foot flame shot out of the chimney, "and nearly burned down the whole god-damned forest!" The white gas disappeared from camp after that for some reason?

Bear sightings were still, at this point in time a fairly rare occurrence as I've already explained. And when they did happen, it was more fun than anything else! It certainly provided some excitement to a bunch of rowdy kids in camp. As it were, we were all huddled around the wood stove in the dining tent in the afternoon. The fresh blanket of snow had degraded spirits a little. After consuming perhaps my twentieth cup of coffee that had been perking on the woodstove for six or so hours the mood suddenly struck me to pay a visit to the outhouse tent.

As I made the hundred-yard trek to the outhouse tent, through the fresh snow something caught my eye when I was a few yards from the intended destination. Brown? Bobbing up and down? I looked closer and realized I was way too close to a grizzly bear who was busy dismantling our toilet seat. I slowly backed away, not having my pistol on me. Quickly, I threw the flap to the dining tent open and walked in. Everyone paused their conversation as I entered and headed for the drying rack near the woodstove where a shotgun was hanging, loaded with cracker shells. Cracker shells are a nonlethal round that is basically a firecracker. It shoots out of the gun, travels a ways, then explodes and makes a big bang. The idea is to put the "bang" right next to the bear so it startles them and they run off. But the fuse is such that considerations for range must be taken into account for maximum effectiveness.

Anyhow, I reached for the shotgun and everyone's eyes got big as the light bulbs went off in their minds.

The outfitter jumped up as the cook said, "Oh shit! Bear in camp!"

The outfitter snatched the shotgun out of my hand and we all piled out of the dining tent. Everyone trotted up the outhouse trail behind the outfitter. Even the hunters brought up the rear excited to see the bear! In a few moments we were a few yards from the bear when the outfitter opened up with the pump action shotgun! The cracker shells hit the bear and were ricocheted up in the air, but no one noticed. The bear beat a hasty retreat and as he started to leave loud bangs started going off behind us! Everyone ducked thinking that someone was shooting but it turned out to be the cracker shells that ricocheted behind us! It was an exciting few seconds before we processed what had happened!

I ended up not filling out that last hunter, to both of our disappointment. Although he didn't seem to mind, he was there to get his friend his first elk and was happy with that. Years later, 2018 if memory serves, I was sitting in the Irma with my wife and struck up a conversation with the table next to us as they were obviously hunters.

Through the conversation we realized that one of them was the Hawaiian's friend who I guided almost twenty years prior. He jumped up and said, "Zach?" when I said yes, he ran up and hugged me. We had a great evening retelling stories of the hunt! Those two sure were fun hunters to have around!

Packing out camp going over Deer Creek Pass in a whiteout. Note the snow shovels alongside of the trail.

By the time the hunters had all left, and the string rested a day at the trailhead, then came back in we had most of camp torn down. The season was officially over and it was time to get the heck out of the mountains! As far as packing goes, it doesn't get much worse than camp pull. Everything is frozen, hard to pack and everything has to go on however many mules you have. Regulation dictates that everything goes too, no caching supplies, nothing. No matter what happens it seems you end up getting to the end and have to fit five loads on three head of pack mules.

This was exactly the case as we packed everything up too. Finally, we had one mule left to pack, a round back red roan molly mule named Wilma who had no withers to speak of. On the ground were eight old army cots, folded up neatly. Beside them was a set of hard, wooden panniers with a single rope that looped over both saw bucks. Army cots are ridiculously heavy and awkward to pack if you can't sling them or plan them as a top pack on certain loads. With no other choice, I stood four cots upright in these wooden panniers and threw them on Wilma, threw a Sierra Box Hitch on it and called it good. Probably eighty pounds a side?

The last mule was packed at 2:00 pm in the afternoon. We all jumped in the saddle and started kicking for the pass and the thirty-mile trip towards a hot shower. When we rounded the bend off the outfitter trail and onto the main trail the Thorofare River drainage had over a foot of snow. It was cold and miserable but the weather had kicked off the elk migration. We had thousands of elk all around us. From twenty yards to as far as you could see, the canyon walls seemed to move as the elk migrated upriver.

This was the only time I've seen the big migration in person. I've seen several smaller ones. But none where it seemed every elk in the country wanted to leave at the exact same moment! The elk were so close we could have hit them with a rock and they didn't seem too disturbed as we passed. It was like we had all called a truce and everyone knew it. We were done bothering them and they knew it. The brilliant colors of the Thorofare were all but gone as the snow covered everything but the steep grey cliffs and the brown elk that seemed to pour out from everywhere you looked.

Eventually, we made it over the pass and were lucky that there wasn't any wind. We were the last ones there as the other camps had to dig through several ten-foot drifts to get over the pass. They were so deep that the mules would disappear as they went behind the drifts. As we dismounted our tired horses to walk the long descent, the last bit of daylight retreated behind the western skyline.

In the darkness, we stumbled down the snow-covered trail using our headlamps for guidance. The high overcast drowned out any moonlight and without the headlamps you couldn't see your hand in front of your face! Eventually we made it down off the switchbacks and remounted.

As we neared the last walk down of Deer Creek, we were crossing a shale sock slide. All of the sudden my sting of mules abruptly stopped. I smooched my riding horse ahead slightly to see if the mules would follow but they refused. Something was wrong somewhere in the string.

Being in the slide, and having nowhere to tie up posed a problem. I was worried my horse would take off for the trailhead if I didn't tie him off. There was one big boulder near enough, so I figured I could tie to that. The problem was my lead rope wasn't long enough but that was quickly remedied by rifling through my frozen saddle bags for a few strings of bailing twine. Soon the twine was securely tied to the boulder, and the lead rope tied to that. From where I was standing, I could only see the first couple of mules in my string in my headlamp. We were on a side hill of forty-five or so degrees, so I opted to take the uphill side as I went back to find what the problem was.

The second to last mule in the string was that round backed Wilma mule. At first it looked like she lost her whole load, including the wooden panniers and maybe even the saddle? But as I approached it became clear that the entire load was there, intact. It was just upside down as the whole saddle and load was now under her belly. To her credit, she didn't panic and cause a huge wreck. She just stood there waiting on me to come help.

As I stood on the uphill side, Wilma's back was waist high and I couldn't really see a good way to fix it. I went around the string and came in from the downhill side but that was even worse! The footing in the loose shale made it hard to stand up straight and I was eye level with Wilma's belly. So, I returned to the uphill side and reassessed the situation.

Not having a lot of options, the best and quickest way to hopefully fix the load was to right it, then untie the hitch and retie it. But the only way to right the load was to literally crawl onto Wilma's back. Put both knees slightly off center of her spine on the uphill side, grab the cots through the mantie tarp that covered them and lean back and hope for the best! With any luck she would stay standing like she had been so far. But Wilma had proven to us she wasn't a riding mule. Several times she showed us that she didn't approve of humans on her back. However, there wasn't many options, so I carefully committed and got one knee on her back with the other still on the uphill shale slide. She shuffled a bit in order to brace herself and once she was good and stable, I made the slight jump all the way onto her back. I grabbed those cots and jerked backwards as hard as I could! The saddle was loose enough, the entire load came with me and as quickly as I started, I landed on my back underneath Wilma.

I scrambled carefully out of the danger zone to find Wilma still standing like a rock and the load almost perfectly centered. I jerked a few more times from the ground to get the load perfectly centered, then reached under the wooden panniers to find a latigo. I gave a few quick tugs to tighten the saddle back up, then retied the box hitch as best I could from the side.

Finally, we were back underway and eventually we made the trailhead around midnight. By the time we were unpacked, saddled and fed it was 2am. I headed for home in my old trusty Ford with a beer between my legs. That was a wrap on a good season, my first season in the Thorofare!

Building a new Cache in camp. Just getting the Circus to approve of building this was a year long process.

A snowy, cold Thorofare day.

| 5 |

Ambushed by Bullwinkle

The predawn darkness was so black you couldn't see your hand in front of your face. It was a classic crisp fall morning. Severe clear on a moonless night with a stable high-pressure system stationed right on top of us. Everything was eerily still. The grass in the meadow was frosted over hard and made crackling noises as our horses made their way up the trail.

The only light came from high above. You could see what seemed to be the whole Milky Way galaxy overhead. I kneaded at the hand warmers I had in my gloves and raised my shoulders a touch so my oversized collar on my conifer camo coat was above the earflaps on my insulated scotch cap. As we rode, I took in the quiet of the morning. It was almost like meditation as we made our way up the trail.

All I could see was the grey blackness ahead giving way to pure black. I knew the trail we were on well enough to know we were entering a band of green timber that paralleled the river bottom meadows. I was headed up-stream to a spot I had heard the other guides in camp talk about before.

Although I had never been there personally, as this was my first hunt in this particular camp, I had studied the maps and google earth before we packed in, and most of all listened to the guides that had hunted the area. I knew we had another forty-five minutes at a minimum of riding to get where we needed to be.

Beaver ponds in the meadows in the Upper Thorofare with Yellow Mountain in the distance.

I gave my horse, Cricket a little bump on the reins and he stopped at the edge of the timber. I turned in my saddle and reached up and gave a double click on my hat mounted head lamp. This activates the red-light function which won't blind, and therefore potentially spook the horses behind me. Over the years I have learned to listen to the footsteps of horses. Usually, I can tell where my hunters are without having to constantly turn around in the darkness and use my light.

The crackling of the grass in the meadow was just enough noise that I wasn't sure that both of my hunters were right behind me. Dude horses have a way of abusing inexperienced riders. They will walk slow, then trot to catch up. Walk under low branches or rub a guy's leg on a passing tree if they get the chance.

My light flashed on, and I could see my two hunters both giving me the thumbs up in the glow of the red light. Another double click and my light was off. I gave Cricket a little kick and we continued into the blackness.

As we continued, I could occasionally hear the "ding" of a cowbell in the distance. We hang bells around horses and mules' necks in order to aid in finding them after they are turned out in the mountain grass. I knew we were approaching the picket meadow, where we turn the stock loose because of the occasional dull dings of the old cowbells.

As we exited the dark abyss of the green timber, I could see it was greying up a little on the southeastern horizon. You could just barely make out the rugged and jagged pinnacles that surrounded the valley we were ascending. Another quick double click on my headlamp reviled two hunters, two dude horses and everything appeared to be in order with their reins and saddles.

We skirted the picket meadow so as not to disturb the horses and mules that were turned out. When we reached the upper end of the picket meadow, we ducked back into the trees for a few hundred yards before arriving at a wash site. It wasn't a wash out; the spring runoff had flooded an area taking all of the dirt and plant life and washing it down stream. Leaving only rocks and gravel and trees.

The sound of twelve hooves crunching across the gravel and rock soon gave way the swishing and trickling noises of water which I knew to be the side creek that we wanted to cross to get to our spot.

By now it was late enough that I could see my hunter's silhouettes in the predawn grey. I gave the roan a little kick and he stepped out into the flowing current of the creek. It is about twenty feet across and I could hear my hunter's horses as they waded the barely knee deep (to a horse) creek behind me.

At this point I knew the trail headed right by an old camp site. It's long been abandoned but it was actually the first camp ever in Wyoming's Thorofare area. Of course, this was back when the commercial camp sites did away with the old method of free roaming and camping outfitting in the area.

Once out of the creek you are basically in the old camp's picket meadow so I neck reined Cricket off the main trail and out through the short willows and grass and right into the old campsite. I could see the outlines of the old A-frames leaned against the trees and old uprights for tents. There is still a "bear proof" rusted steel box on the ground.

We rode right by what once was a fire pit but bears had been digging in it and the rocks were scattered about. As we rode through the hair stood up on the back of my neck. I thought it must be the eerie history of the camp that I had read so much about or the stories I'd heard from the old timers that made my senses come alive?

As time passed and I guided several more seasons in this camp I would come to loath that old camp. More often than not, when I've gone through there I have run into bears. A lot of locals still use the camp and I don't know if they don't keep it clean or what? But seven out of ten times you'll meet a bear there. It is in a place that is the equivalent to the Long Island Expressway for bear traffic. Maybe they just always lay over there? Or maybe I have bad luck?

Anyway, just as the guys had said, Cricket, who had been through there many times knew right where to go. A trick I enjoy using when I'm new to an area is to take a horse that has been in there many times before. They know the trails better than we do and a good horse will get you there even if you only sort of know the way.

As we picked our way through the old camp Cricket perked his head up just a touch and snapped his ears straight ahead. I recognized he knew what the plan was and let some slack in the reins. The big roan gelding angled out of camp and picked up the old outfitter trail out the back side of the camp. We cut through a stand of short fir trees and crossed the Thorofare River and started up the embankment on the other side. At this point, nearing the upper reaches of the Thorofare drainage the river is actually a small creek. Ten feet across and less than a foot or two deep.

Just as we crossed the creek and I was checking on the hunters the screech of a distant bugle pierced the stillness of the cool morning air. Everyone froze in their saddles trying to figure out where the sound was coming from. Just then another bugle, closer. Up the river and on the side of the canyon. I instinctively pointed as we continued to sit motionless in our saddles. Another bugle! Across the river and upstream. I whispered to my hunters to follow me and stay close. Then gave Cricket a slight kick as he turned and continued up the trail.

As we rode on for another few minutes the bugles continued to penetrate the stillness of the crisp autumn air. Cricket was climbing up a steep but short grade on an old overgrown trail. Just as shooting light arrived, we stepped out around a large bushy evergreen and I could see our meadow. I knew by the bugling that this was our spot. I eased out of the saddle and tied Cricket to a tree, then tied my reins up on my saddle horn.

The meadow was long. It stretched maybe a mile and a half up the valley with a dog leg in it. Although it was off the main river a few hundred yards, on a side hill it was gently sloping with belly high grass and intermittent springs. A few of the springs were beat out into wallows. The old outfitter trail skirted the trees on the uphill side of the long meadow. Picturesque to say the least. Perfect elk habitat.

I nodded to the hunters to dismount and grabbed the first hunter's horse by the lead rope. I led his horse to a tree and securely tied him off. Slipped around the other side and pulled his rifle from the scabbard and handed it to him as I motioned with one finger to stay quiet. By the time I got to the second hunter's horse he had his rifle out and handed me the lead rope and I found a third tree to tie off to.

I motioned for them to follow me and we crept up to the edge of the meadow where we could see. I pulled my 10x50 binoculars from my chest mounted case and gave the meadow a quick look. The verbal sparring continued between several mature sounding bulls as we watched and waited. There was no movement. Just the vapor of our breath raising and dissipating in the crisp morning air. The bugles continued back and forth. Then a third would join in. Then a fourth bull. This was activity like we used to see in the pre wolf days, I thought to myself.

I had just made a mental decision to stay high, on the upper end of the tree line of the meadow and begin easing forward. With the frost on the grass, I thought staying on the trail would be the quietest option. I was just getting ready to move when we felt a deep, throaty, and raspy roaring bugle. Whatever he was he sounded like a really old dominant herd bull.

I estimated him to be a couple hundred yards from us in the timber between the creek and the meadow. I turned to my hunters and they were smiling ear to ear, looking intently across the meadow. By the look in their eyes, I knew they were trying to will an elk into view.

I whispered to follow me and pointed down the meadow, there appeared to be a point of trees that would conceal us and let us close another hundred to one hundred and fifty yards on the elk. This point essentially would put us a third of the way up the meadow right smack in the middle of it. We crept slowly but the grass was too frozen by the frost. Too crunchy. So, I angled deeper into the trees and into the fallen pine needles of the forest floor. We took our time and moved methodically and silently through the trees until the trees ran out, giving way to a full view of the meadow.

Spot and stalk hunting is my favorite kind of hunting.

We could see in all directions now, except for behind us. I motioned for one guy to sit with the view up into the meadow and the other to sit where he could see ahead and down into the meadow. Once we were settled, I checked the rubber band on my bugle and fished a cow call out of my coat.

I wear my cow calls on a necklace type strap that keeps them easily accessible. Normally in this situation I would have cow called but it was early and the big roaring bugle was so close you could feel it. I figured I was in his "fight zone" I gave one last check to my hunters and licked my lip before I inhaled quietly and let go of a bugle.

The sound of my power bugle ripped through the morning air. It wasn't until I was about two thirds through my first bugle that I heard a sound no one likes to hear in the woods. It was abrupt, loud and most alarmingly it was directly behind us. "WWOOOOOOFFFFF!!!"

My body immediately kicked into autopilot mode. Instinctively, I thought I knew what it was and knew we were in for it. I could hear the forest floor erupt with the thunder of sticks popping and branches breaking and the sound of a large animal's feet thumping through the trees behind and slightly below us. There was no question it was headed our direction.

Continuing on instinct or reaction I jumped to my feet and yelled "HEY BEAR!" as I jerked my .44 Magnum revolver from its holster. Both hunters were scrambling to get to their feet in a startled fury.

Although it was shooting light, it was still very low light under the forest canopy. As such, all I saw coming at us was grey legs and a brown body. I was scrambling to get my pistol up and get my hunters behind me. Just as my sights came into view and I closed an eye, simultaneously pulling the slack out of the trigger.... It was over.

A big Shiras Bull Moose trotted out not more than twenty feet from us. He trotted on by, out into the middle of the meadow and he kept going right up the center until he was out of sight.

Legs trembling, I sank to one knee in an effort to display calm and control for my hunters. I had to will a smile on my face before turning to check on my guys.

"Exciting elk huntin' here in Wyoming ah" I whispered as they processed what had just happened.

We spent the next few minutes gathering our wits back as we all retold the story to each other. We had blown it. We didn't hear another bugle after I yelled at the moose. In hindsight, the "WWOOOOOOFFFFF!!!" sound was actually a perfect "OOOOOFFFF!!!" sound that moose make all the time.

Perhaps I jumped the gun? Call me a pessimist if you want, but in my defense, I've seen two moose in the Thorofare my whole life, including this one. Moose aren't known to frequent this far up river. Conversely, I've seen hundreds of bears in this area. The possibility of a moose making that woofing noise was the farthest thing from my mind. Oh well, it's only day one.

Anyway, we waited a while hoping for another bugle. Whispering back and forth about the moose. After about an hour I decided to still hunt the upper edges of the meadow for a while. This proved futile and we called it a morning hunt around ten am. We headed back for the horses and rode on up through the country we had just hunted.

Once we were about a mile inside "virgin country" I reined Cricket off the trail once again. We headed a short distance across a clearing and into a stand of trees in the middle of the next meadow to tie up the horses. We walked out through the clearing to the top of a mound that sat by itself in the middle of the clearing. Maybe thirty feet high and fifty yards diameter. We sat down and had some lunch and glassed the surrounding area.

My plan was to wait until the wind changed in the evening and hunt a slide area that appeared to have good cover and feed. We discussed it at length as a group and everyone was on board.

The biggest problem with waiting however, is patience. Not my patience, I have plenty. A guy who has spent upwards of $10,000 by the time you figure processing and travel sometimes has patience issues. Guys need to understand that you can't pound elk in this type of country. If you do, they'll just pack up and you won't see them again until someone else makes the same mistake you did in the next canyon over.

As the day passed, we all got to know each other better. A couple of blue collar, heartland corn farmers. I knew I was in good company when they rolled out the Obama jokes before 11:00am. Most of the time we just briefly see the new clients at the trail head. I always make it a point to say "hi" but there is a lot of work to get done for the hands.

Cricket and Larry poacher packing an elk out on a late season cow hunt.

We have to pack in food and supplies for the hunt on top of all the hunters gear so there isn't much time to shoot the bull at the trailhead. Once all the hunters arrive, we get them mounted up and started up the trail with the outfitter. Then we get back to saddling and packing. Once everything is loaded, we all tie our string of mules together and ride in.

Once we get to camp, we have a repeat of the morning drill only in reverse. Unpacking, unsaddling, doctoring and getting all the stock fed and turned out for the night. Once those chores are done, we have to bear proof the camp. Get all of our food up into the cache. The cache, pronounced, "Cash" is just a glorified tree house that each camp has to store food out of reach of bears.

Anyhow, back to the story- about 4:00pm I began to really methodically glass out the slide we were to hunt that evening. Not only was I looking for game but I was also studying the way the topography worked around the area. I knew once we got into the green timber, I would be on my own to make sure it was an effective hunt and not a hike.

One hunter was getting antsy and was squirming around and asking a lot of questions. It was really hindering my glassing so I lowered my binoculars and sat still hoping, willing the wind to change quickly so we could start our evening hunt.

The wind showed no signs of switching yet. Not that I was surprised, it wasn't due to change until about 6:00. So, I opted for an old trick I used to employ on other clients to get them to quiet down and keep their mind on something. I got out my bugle and gave a bugle. A little bigger and more dominant than I usually like to call but I figured I would try to get something to answer. Or not? Either way it would make the hunters think we were hunting again.

I had finished my bugle and just started glassing again when way off in the distance behind us came a faint reply. I paused and looked at the two hunters. They heard it as well. I rolled over and began glassing the hillside behind us. I bugled once again, and a reply came within a minute. Having a better direction to zero in on we glassed high on the ridge above us. Finally, we spotted him. A respectable

6x6 thrashing a tree with his antlers. I bugled again and cow called as loud as I could.

Finally, the bull began making his way down the hill and towards us. After about an hour and a half of bugling and cow calling, we knew the bull was within range. We just couldn't see him on account of the green timber. We could hear him thrashing trees and breaking branches, we just couldn't see through the timber enough. I was beginning to worry that he would do what a lot of elk do and hang up a couple hundred yards out.

I blasted a few long and drawn-out cow calls, figuring it best to avoid a confrontational bugle hoping to lure him in closer and avoid a hang up. After about two and a half hours of calling with this particular bull we picked up some movement through the evergreens at the upper end of the meadow. I gave my hunters a general direction of where he was, and they readied themselves. Another cow call and the bull trotted into the meadow angling straight towards the stand of trees our livestock were tied in.

"Is that a black wolf?" I heard one of the hunters say.

I immediately began looking around but it turned out what my hunter saw was an almost black elk. Our bull had been in a wallow we couldn't see and he was covered in wet mud from head to toe.

"No! That's the bull!" I whispered. "Get him in your scope and make sure that's what you're seeing"

My hunter soon agreed he was on a bull elk. A quick glance told me he was pointing his gun in the right direction.

"When I stop him, you nail him right through the heart."

"Okay" came his reply.

In a few moments, when the bull was clear of all the trees and out in the open, I chirped on my cow call. The bull stopped and looked right at us, breaking his sight away from our horses.

"CRACK!" Came the shot and the bullet sailed true to its mark. I watched through my binoculars as the bullet hit the elk just high and aft of his elbow. The bull stumbled and tipped over, right out in the middle of the meadow.

We all took in the events of the last few hours for a moment before I took a quick glance at my watch.

"Oh crap, it's an hour and a half before dark! We better get to work."

A view of a typical Thorofare dining tent.

As it was a clear walk through the meadow, I sent the hunters to the bull while I trotted down the little rise and across the meadow to our horses. I tied them all together, jumped on Cricket and smooched him out across the meadow towards the elk. I pulled into a few small trees to tie up the stock twenty yards from the elk. Cricket was snorting when we arrived. Obviously, he wasn't going to take meat today and I didn't have time for a fight so I decided not to push my luck.

By the time we got through with some pictures we had an hour of daylight left. I butchered and packed the elk in fifty-six minutes which was a new personal record and is certainly only attainable when the hunter wants a European mount as you don't have to fiddle with the cape.

I had one hunter on his mule, Mike, and the elk on his partner mule, Ike who were a big pair of sorrel john mules. I put the other hunter on Cricket, and I took point on foot with Mike following. The two riders fell in behind me, Cricket first. I wanted him close because Cricket will abuse a hunter with the best of them. All of that, just as darkness fell on the Thorofare.

We made it back to camp an hour and a half after dark. I flipped the door to the dining tent open and asked for help hanging the quarters on the meat pole. Everyone was eating supper so their enthusiasm was questionable but we got the elk hanging and the horses unsaddled and turned loose before heading in for dinner.

When I was walking into the dining tent the two hunters were immersed in the story of the day's events. As I walked in and unzipped my coat and hung it near the wood stove, I heard one of them say, "And that was the tallest bear I ever saw coming through the trees at us!" The tent erupted in laughter as they concluded their story about the moose.

Over Rib-eye steaks, potatoes, corn and pie we recounted the day's events. Everyone seemed to be happy so far, there were a few other guys who were successful on their opening day hunts as well and everyone listened as they retold their stories from the day. After dinner we all headed to bed to get some sleep for the upcoming days of work.

The next morning, we would be back at it and eventually kill another elk. It was about as uneventful as horseback wilderness hunts get. Happy hunters and a happy outfitter were alright with me for the first time being in that camp. It's hard to sing aloud a favorite camp because they all have different things I enjoy. But this camp became my home camp for about six or so years until I moved to Alaska and stopped guiding.

Years after this hunt I ended up buying Cricket off the outfitter. He was one of the toughest horses I've ever swung a leg over. He had a surfer dude attitude about everything but meat and mountains. A mountain he would stick his head down and powerfully devour. Point him up the mountain and he would go, go hard and go until you told him to stop. But his drawback was meat.

Cricket and I headed up a ridge near Cody.

A lot of horses won't tolerate packing meat. Cricket was not one of those. He didn't have a clear set of rules. But I came to find out, some days he would refuse to pack it, and other days he wouldn't bat an eye at the bloodiest mess of meat, hide and antlers you've ever seen. It just depended on how he felt that day, I guess? One time I did find out that when he said no, he meant it. Like, he'd tear down a twelve-inch-thick tree and meet you back at camp, meant it!

I eventually accepted his quirkiness and did my best to work around it. I figured if a twenty plus year old outfitter horse made it that long with this quirk, who am I to be a judge? Like the old saying goes, don't saddle broncs you can't ride!

Cricket was awesome until he was about twenty-five years old. We were paying a kid to feed stock one winter and he wasn't watching for mold in the hay. Cricket got into that hay and ended up catching the "Wheezes" which scared his lungs and basically made him unusable anywhere but flat ground. Shortly after he was placed into retirement in my pasture in Cody, Wyoming until he died of Colic around the age of thirty. Solid mountain horses don't come around every day but Cricket will always be a huge part of my good memories in the mountains.

Topping out somewhere in the Wiggins Fork. Once a full season of guiding is done, there are few General Areas open. Wiggins was one of the exceptions and we would head over to fill our own freezers sometimes.

| 6 |

Twistin' Off

Summer was drawing to a close and the leaves were starting to turn yellow when we set camp. Running over Deer Creek, it was a thirty-three-mile ride. However, I was working a camp that had two camps this year. Not only two camps, but a new outfitter only in his second year with the camp. I didn't know much, but word around town was the guy had been fired by most of the outfits in the Thorofare. The scuttlebutt was also that his parents had purchased the camp for him.

For whatever reason the boss hatched a plan to split the mule herd and run out of two different trailheads. At the time, I was oblivious to the ramifications of that, so I signed on anyway.

What we soon figured out was the route we were taking into the north camp was significantly longer, and due to the trail conditions through the topography, significantly slower traveling as well.

The first hour, or hour and a half, were spent riding down the highway as the corrals were several miles from the actual trailhead. That's not a huge deal when you're headed into camp, but it's pure torture to hit the road after being away from civilization for eight or so days and still have an hour and a half, or so of riding. Compound that with the fact that by this point all your packs have had time to loosen up, and there's no way to keep your mules in line. They are just as excited to get done as we are, so they start walking next to you, fanned out six or eight abreast rather than in line. Add some traffic or darkness and you can see how this becomes inconvenient to say the least!

The North Camp. A small camp by Thorofare standards. Note the saw bucks on the log near the tents used for cross cutting logs into firewood.

Once you were on the trail, there were several gates that you would have to stop at, open, ride through and then close if no one was behind you before you could climb back on and continue. All of this so far occurs on mostly sage brush covered, gently rolling terrain. Just to make it extra nice the soil composition is predominantly alkali. The repeated pounding of eight mules per string, plus a riding horse, and usually we traveled in groups of three or four strings, let me tell you from experience, you didn't want to be riding drag! The dust was terrible!

After a few miles of alkali, you cross a river and head into a timbered canyon that ran twenty or so miles in the general direction of camp. This canyon starts out in sparse cottonwoods and timber and sagebrush. The alkali slowly gives way to basalt rocky conditions from lava flows that occurred eons prior.

It's a wicked good deer migration hunting spot! Especially if you manage to not get bit or scratched by one of the hundred or so grizzly bears who have come to rely on the gut piles as a food source. All occurring precisely as they enter hyperphagia just prior to denning up for the winter. Other than all that, it's pretty perfect!

Once on the side hill the trail becomes a mess of ins and outs as it traverses cut after cut, drainage after drainage and gully after gully. While pulling a string of mules, a crack the whip effect starts to happen as you ride around sharp corners. The only way to stop it is to check up your horse a little so they round the corners slowly which gives the mules in the back time to get through the cut. The consequences of continually slowing your horses down are that it makes it nearly impossible to maintain a pace of approximately three miles per hour.

If you can hold three to three and a half miles per hour you only have a short ten-hour ride into, or out of camp. Just those cuts cost us, by my calculations two hours. So, it's a twelve-hour ride if everything goes perfectly, which almost never happens. Packs slip, a mule breaks away or any number of other factors can slow you down more. We had been averaging in the neighborhood of fourteen hours to complete this trip.

Anyway, after several more miles, and solidly in the forest the trail gets better. Well, until you come to another gate. Once through the gate there is a bridge that spans a narrow, but very deep ravine that is solid rock. Once across the bridge there's another gate. The area around the bridge is fenced because horse and mule wrecks are so common, at least they won't get too far away when they all break apart. And hopefully they'll stay on the bridge or on the ground. That wasn't always the case though.

There's a legendary story of one infamous outfitter who for some reason preferred to run his string at night. He'd just crack a few glow sticks, strap them to a few mules in his string and ride into camp in the dark. Being dark he couldn't see his packs and the results were that a lot of those mules were too sore or spotted up to be a lot of service for a reasonably useful lifespan. They all ended up broke and gentle though! I'll give him that!

As the story goes, one night he hit the bridge in the dark and there was a bear, or something, maybe a Bigfoot, who knows? Anyway, something was trying to cross the bridge at the same time. From the downriver side of the bridge, once through the gate there's a ninety degree turn onto the wooden planks that span the coulee. The coulee is roughly forty feet deep I'd guess? Allegedly, he had his string tied hard and fast to his saddle which is a big no-no for reasons I'm about to explain. As he turned the corner and his horse was on the bridge one of the mules spotted the bear or Bigfoot or whatever it was and pulled back. Which pulled a mule or two, plus this outfitter and his horse through the 2x4 railing. In the fall at least one horse was killed, the outfitters riding horse, and was laying on the outfitters leg trapping him in the stream of water. Eventually, the outfitter weaseled his leg out, cut his saddle off the dead horse, and climbed out with his saddle. They say he walked the remaining twenty-some miles into camp in his cowboy boots.

I can't swear to every detail, but that's the gist of the story. And based on what I saw, and other details I'd heard about the guy, I believe it's far more fact than fiction. I only have two questions, the first is I don't know how the guy didn't die? That's a steep wash and it's a long way to the bottom. And second, I don't know how the hell he got out? It's a solid face of smooth, slippery rock.

Nowadays, the bridge is pretty decent. The Forest Circus finally spent some money and fixed it right. It must be eight feet wide now with big timber rails down each side and they fixed the approach so it's not that sharp ninety degree turn. Back in these days however, it was barely wide enough for a fat mule with hard panniers to cross without rubbing both sides.

We were a new outfit, with a lot of new mules. And not many of them were broke enough to cross a bridge. I had too many wrecks to count there, until I figured out how to manage the wreck. The first step was to admit that you were going to have a wreck every time you crossed that bridge! From the approach end you could barely see the gate on the other side if you stood in your stirrups. I would make damn sure it was closed, first. Then I'd hit the bridge at a trot, let whatever was going to happen, happen and sort the wreck out on the far side. It worked pretty well until the mules had crossed it enough to not be scared of it. Unorthodox? Perhaps, but it worked for me!

After the bridge, and a few miles more you pass the turnoff to a different outfitter's camp, then on up the trail farther there's an old camp in a meadow. It used to be a layover camp the old outfitter used so his clients didn't have to make it all the way in one day. It's pretty well abandoned the last few times I rode by, which has been years ago now.

After the layover camp it was several more miles up to a gentle pass that drops off into a tributary of the Thorofare River. You ride a few miles down, then cross that canyon and ascend the opposite hillside which puts you on another pass.

The second pass is breathtakingly steep, and solid rock. Completely and thoroughly treacherous! By this point your packs will be fairly loose as the stock lost weight in the previous twenty-five miles, give or take. It's always best to stop and check everything before potential problems arise on the steep descent into the valley below.

Once on the valley floor, it's an easy and flat five or six miles to the mouth of the drainage then another mile up the main canyon into the north camp. Don't get me wrong, it's a gorgeous ride with spectacular scenery. But it is brutal on the livestock, hands, and especially the hunters. And it only took about fourteen hours on a good day!

The main problem with the northern and southern camps was that they were only three miles apart, in the same canyon. You can roll over Deer Creek and have a nice, flat, downhill ride on great trails all the way into the south camp. And another hour gets you to the north camp. The decision to run two trailheads must have been purely egotistical? Short of that, I can't think of a viable reason to do this? And as soon as we had our first freeze, no one wanted to run pack strings over that steep, ice laden and snow-covered rock. Suffice it to say, there was almost what amounted to a mutiny from the employees, and the outfitter relented. We all rode out (and back in) over Deer Creek from that day on.

That all seems pretty reasonable, we had a problem and we fixed it! But that's not how it works really. See, the outfitters are permitted trailhead corrals or space. So, it wasn't as simple as changing trailheads. The outfitter eventually had to surrender his permit for the layover camp in order to be allowed to run everything out of the Deer Creek trailhead. Add to that, there wasn't ample room at the Deer Creek trailhead so the Forest Circus decided to not really do anything except force the surrender of the layover permit and give a reluctant nod to allowing the use of Deer Creek. Meaning, they left it to the outfitter to figure out his own corrals. The only catch was, the corrals couldn't be permanent. Which meant that the outfitter had to use portable corrals which is a considerable amount of time, energy and money to get all set up. And that's before you consider hay and water storage. Suffice it to say that the Circus isn't renowned for their ability or willingness to help fix a real problem. But I digress.

Taking a quick breather on top of Deer Creek Pass.

We had set camp and cleared the meat pole, cut firewood, dug a hole, set the outhouse tent on it and set up the corrals by the time the first batch of hunters were scheduled to arrive. However, just a day or two before the hunters showed up one of the other guides had a horse wreck. The guide came out of the scrape with a broken nose and a lost tooth. But the horse came out of the accident with a broken femur.

These types of situations never easy and never good for the camp. The guide didn't care about his own injuries, but he did care about the horse as it was one of his personal riding horses. He took the horse way away from camp, a half a mile or so, and put the horse down with his pistol. At that point, we thought that the unfortunate situation was over. But it had just begun.

Our cook that year was an older, wore out guy who had a reputation for being a good cook, but not a very good hand overall. He took personal offense to the events leading up to that horse's death. After a few days of building up anger and frustration, the cook and the guide had it out between the cook and dining tents. It never got physical because they were both pointing guns at each other the whole time! The guide had a Desert Eagle 50, and the cook had a 12 gauge. Thankfully, it didn't go beyond the cook leveling his shotgun at the guide, and the guide responding by pointing his gun at the cook. They hollered back and forth, the rest of us were pretty hesitant to get in the middle to break them up due to the cannons both were holding. It was a tense few moments to say the least! Eventually, cooler heads prevailed and both of the knuckleheads put their guns away.

A few days later, the other hands and the boss rolled in with the hunters. I was hunting a couple of guys from Florida who worked for NASA. They were pretty good guys. Both younger, capable and had a good attitude.

We had a couple of new guides and as the hunt started one was having some trouble finding elk. It wasn't that the guide didn't know what he was doing, it's that he was too honest with an overbearing hunter. The guide had admitted that it was the first-time hunting in that camp and they weren't seeing or hearing much. Conversely, I knew the country and how to get around on old trails because I had been there before. We had been in bugling elk every hunt so far. However, often when a hunter hears reports such as this from their guide, they start questioning everything the guide does and adding their opinions a little too often. I'm not saying that I blame them, they paid good money to hunt with a good guide and all that. I'm just saying, if there's ever been a great time to lie, it's when you're a brand-new guide to a new camp! If nothing else, it will keep the hunter's confidence up so that's one less thing the guide has to worry about!

We had been hunting a couple of days and the normal camp protocol was in the morning the wrangler would bring the stock in, while the hunters had breakfast. The guides would also eat a quick bite, then go saddle the hunters and guide rides for the day. Meanwhile, the hunters would get ready while the cook would lay out lunch supplies for everyone to build their lunches. About then the guides would be done saddling, come into the dining tent and build their lunches. Then everyone would take off for the day.

However, after the altercation between the cook and the guide, who happened to be my tent mate and as such, I was guilty by association. While we were saddling stock, the cook was hustling the hunters through their lunch building. He would then take all the food back to his tent, shut his lantern off and go back to bed. We ended up not being able to make a lunch for several days.

I had a big bull spotted across a canyon from one of my favorite places to hunt, but didn't want to charge over there to kill him because we had several bulls bugling between us and him. Seeing as how I had two tags to fill, I didn't see the sense in blasting a bunch of elk out of the canyon to chase one 330 bull on the other side. We had been working right there, trying to knock one down before making the big assault on the bull across canyon.

The second morning broke with a slight dusting of snow on the ground. My hunters and I were perched on my rock on a ridge dividing the main drainage and the side drainage with the bull on the opposite side of the canyon. I bugled once and the mountain erupted in song of the elk! Bugles above, below and to the sides of us rang out continuously. Soon we eased off the rock and began stalking a bull a few hundred yards below us.

Eventually, we got into some cows and had to sit down under an evergreen along an elk trail. Cows were all around us as we sat quietly, holding as still as possible as we knew it was just a matter of time until the bull showed himself. After a few toots on my cow call a bull stepped out of the green timber twenty yards below us. The hunter made a good shot and soon we were caping and quartering a nice 6x7. He was a smaller bull but had a cool crab claw on his G-1 that made the seventh point.

We headed to camp to grab some pack mules and returned to find the carcass undisturbed. We loaded the elk and were back in camp before dark. One down! Now it was time to concentrate on that bigger bull across the canyon I thought!

I was only in my third-year guiding, and I couldn't see past the end of my nose, at the time. But I had noticed over the last two seasons that while I could get my guys on elk, and tag them out just like the older, more experienced guides I wasn't killing big bulls like they were. My average bull was probably between 290 and 310 6x6's. But these experienced guys were consistently killing 330 bulls.

I might have been a cocky kid back in those days but I wasn't stupid. So, I moved my stuff into the older guides' tent. They agreed to let me stay on the condition that I didn't snore, so I just started listening to them. I was an Oregon brush hunter, new to the spot and stalk ways of the big mountains. And what I learned from two guys in particular was that they were always high. Really high. Often, up with the sheep. And they had good binoculars and were patient.

I was excited to have spotted this bull in the type of terrain the older guys talked about. I had a good read on him because I'd saved a bunch of tip money the year before and bought a Swarovski 10x60 spotting scope and a good set of Leopold 10x50 binoculars. This was the first hunt I was going to be able to chase some big bulls!

That night after a rib-eye steak dinner with salad, mashed potatoes and gravy and green beans all the guides huddled to make a plan for the following morning. As we all talked about where to go it was obvious that our new guide needed to at least let his hunter hear some elk. That would improve both of their morale. I suggested he come up the bottom of the canyon I was going to be in. There was a meadow halfway up and if he didn't come above the meadow, he wouldn't mess up my hunt, as I was going to be in the rocks going after that big bull.

As we talked the outfitter pipped up and said, "We have too much country to put two guys in the same drainage."

The new guide had to find somewhere else to go because I wasn't walking away from the bull we had spotted. The outfitter wasn't wrong, but it was needless to stop our plan in my opinion. It wasn't going to hurt anything! Soon the plans were made, and we all retreated to our tents for the night.

As daylight broke the following morning I was on my rock, glassing across the canyon to find our bull. Soon we found him a few hundred yards from where we'd last seen him so we jumped on the horses and rode as far as we could around the bowl. When we got to the subalpine, rocks and cliffs we tied up and proceeded on foot.

When we were three quarters of the way around the canyon, staying high, above the thermals that the older guides talked about all the time we took a quick sandwich break for lunch. Well, the hunters did. I still hadn't figured out how to get a lunch from the cook? As we sat, I caught movement below while my hunters were eating. I stuck my face in my binoculars to see the outfitter and his hunters riding right up the drainage, exactly where he said we didn't need two guides. By a stroke of luck, they busted the bull at five-hundred yards, jumped off their horses and shot him.

To say I was shocked would be an understatement. I was boiling mad! What kind of counterfeit outfitter runs over his own guides? And it was even worse because he did it wrong and just got lucky! That bull should have winded him! And I shouldn't have told him about that bull! Soon my hunter and I returned to our horses and made a halfhearted hunt back toward camp.

That evening I had been avoiding him in camp, still so mad I knew I'd cuss him if he looked at me cross eyed. But dinner was on and the new cook in the north camp had some famous stuffed meat loaf everyone talked about. I strolled into the dining tent to get a plate.

The outfitter was sitting in a camp chair, legs crossed like a girl, looking at pictures on his brand-new digital camera. At the time, those cameras were new.

"Hey Zach, you want to see what a real bull looks like?" he said. Probably not meaning it like I took it.

I turned and backhanded the camera he was holding out for me to look at. Knocking it out of his hand and onto the dusty floor. Without thinking, and honestly without planning it because all the hunters were in the tent as well as the guides, wrangler and cook I stuck my finger in his face and let him have it right there in front of god and everybody!

He sat there nodding his head as I cussed him for running me over, and reminded him of what he said about having two guys in the same drainage. His nodding made me all the madder too because if some employee said to me, what I was saying to him there would have been some serious consequences to say the least.

Nothing happened though. He just sat there and let me finish. Then he apologized to me and my hunter. And said he was in the wrong.

After that I was left feeling like a jerk. Not sorry for what I said, just sorry for saying it in front of everyone. I thought that was the end of it so I didn't see a need to hold a grudge. We had dinner, the meatloaf was good, a little over hyped though, and we turned in for the night.

Mules hanging out in the corrals after a snowy night.

The next day I went to a side canyon nearby and we climbed up to the top to begin glassing. Soon we had a bull spotted. He was a spike on one side with a six on the other. He was a cool bull because the spike was as tall as the six-point side. But instead of coming to a point at the end it was a softball sized club! I begged my hunter to shoot him as he was a "unicorn," or unique bull, but he wasn't too interested having got his hopes up for that bigger 6x6.

By the time we got back to camp and had dinner the hunter changed his mind and agreed to go back the next day to see if we could find him again. We discussed all this in the dining tent and I believe the change in heart came because of peer pressure from the other hunters. Either way, we had a bull spotted and knew where we were going!

Just like ground hog day, the following morning we were atop the ridge looking for our bull when you'll never guess who rode over the ridge and shot our bull right in front of us? You guessed it! The outfitter! The same guy who had just told me he was wrong for doing that two days before. He sat there all night and listened to our plan, then ran us over, cut us off and killed the bull we spotted and were hunting!

I told my hunter to follow me and keep up at all costs as I headed for our horses. I swung into the saddle and hit a lope down the mountain. When I got there the outfitter and his hunter were just riding up to the bull. I aimed my horse right at the outfitter's horse and we plowed into him at a trot. His horse stumbled but didn't fall and the outfitter was hanging onto the saddle horn as I jumped off my horse and grabbed the collar of his shirt helping him with his fall. I swung a leg over him and figured a knuckle sandwich or two might teach him a lesson! Soon we were rolling around the meadow before the hunters pulled us apart.

Cussing and swearing up a storm, I remounted my horse and trotted off. I rode into camp, getting there just before the wrangler turned the mules out for the day. I grabbed four of the best packers we had and saddled them. Then loaded my stuff and my hunters' stuff and we rode out. A few miles down the trail, I was surprised to see the wrangler trot up behind us with his own packer in tow. I haven't been to that camp since.

Something about that trip still haunts me to this day. The outfitter deserved what he got, and then some. Of that I'm convinced. But in reality, I signed up for a job and didn't do it. I didn't complete it. The whole camp was in a ruckus on account of me. The clients and other employees didn't deserve that. And I never quit a camp again. I just was a lot more careful who I worked for from then on.

Another average 6x6 for the area.

After this season I decided it was time to do something with myself. I had always been intrigued by aviation so I began flying lessons out of the local Cody airport. What I hadn't figured on was how I was going to be able to afford to fly and rodeo at the same time. Quickly, I learned I couldn't. I drew up a budget that would allow me to continue flying, and not working until the next hunting season. When I had completed the budget, I found I was $20,000 short. As luck would have it, I had the best winter and spring I'd ever had rodeoing. I won a touch more than the $20,000 by the following June and that's when I quit rodeoing. Well, quit for the first time. But that's a different story!

I ended up pursuing all of my aviation ratings and ended up taking nearly five years off of guiding. That's about how long it took to go through all the schooling and become marketable for a job flying.

Deer Creek Pass from the Deer Creek side.

| 7 |

The Bubba Mule Part 1- Outlaw Horses

By the time the water came down, leaves started turning yellow and those all too familiar frosty mornings started rolling around I had signed on to a relatively new outfit. The crisp smell of fall was in the air and the anticipation of those first autumn bugles were on everyone's mind. This particular camp is historically significant if you've followed the old trapper tales from the Mountain Man era of American History. It is situated twenty-seven miles from the road, bordering Yellowstone National Park's eastern most boundary. Complete with an old trapper cabin and everything. Well, it was complete with a trapper cabin until a tree fell on it a couple years after this story, knocking it all down except one wall.

The camp was newly purchased by an acquaintance of mine from back in the rodeo days. The guy was, at one time, one of the craziest bull fighters around! Fear wasn't in his vocabulary either. And he was a bonafide cowboy! The kind of guy that would get you into a wreck, and you would know the wreck was coming but be too scared to let him think you weren't as game as he was.

And I don't mean that disparagingly either! He was the one to ride the worst horses in the herd. Take the worst hunting spots, pull the greenest strings into camp. As such, we all respected him as a leader! Other than being pretty high strung, and everyone being scared they weren't cowboy enough to pull off the next task, he was a good guy to work for! We all respected him and would have, and did a few times, follow him to the gates of hell.

The Bubba Mule hanging out in the horse pasture.

I had signed on from start to finish. Camp set through all six hunts to the camp pull in late October. Hopefully, before the big snowstorms hit and started closing the passes. By the time the following story occurred, we had completed a few summer trips and although I had not previously seen this portion of the Thorofare, I had been into the camp early for the camp set. We cleared the outfitter trails, and I was able to learn a lot about the topography of the area.

I had been away from guiding for nearly five years, so I made sure to sign on early enough to get in and learn the country before we started hunting again. I hadn't been on a horse, or even hunted for myself that entire time. I was fresh out of the Alaska Bush where I had been flying for a small charter outfit delivering literally anything that you can either fit into an airplane or tie on the side of one. From people to sled dogs to 55-gallon drums of fuel, to cases of hot pockets, soda or Tony's Pizza Rolls, we flew it. I had recently quit the job because I was having way too many near misses to feel good about my long-term survival prospects. So, I came home and blew the dust off of my gear and got ready to return to the hills.

We were in the final phases of packing in our camp. By this time, we had already made the first two trips and had most of the essential supplies in and set up. Tents, cook stoves, wood stoves and all of those sorts of items were there. This trip was supposed to be an in-and-out, where we topped off the camp. Propane tanks, plastic sheets for the roof of the tents, perishable foods, all the things we had forgotten on previous trips or didn't have enough of. Feed! Lots of cake for the horses and mules.

Seems we are always bringing in lantern parts and pieces, extra tent stakes, and things like that. Originally, we were planning on riding in on day one and riding back out on day four. It was just myself, another guide and our wrangler. The boss was staying out to tend to business in town and we had left the camp jack and cook in camp to take care of the place while we were gone.

It's a dangerous situation to let either a cook or camp-jack out of camp. If they quit, you're hard pressed to find a replacement! The cooks are usually more reliable but far too important because they are hard to replace! You don't want to end up between a rock and a hard place when the hunters are rolling into town! The camp-jack on the other hand is easy to replace, but a pain in the ass to do so. Usually, they are younger guys and the likelihood of them hitting town, heading to the bar and shacking up with some bar fly with the aroma of stale energy drinks and cigarettes is a lot higher. There's been more than one who's disappeared between ride in and ride out day never to be seen or heard from again. The outfitters are aware of risk. So it's easier to let them soak in the hills for two months than to have to sweat them being in town.

The author's company Cessna 207 unloading "Bypass Mail" to the village of Kwigillingok, Alaska. Kwig is roughly 460 southwest of Anchorage.

Lucky for us, between the first couple trips and a few summer outings our new pack mules had, for the most part, figured out what we were doing. Unlike every other camp I had worked for, each hired hand had their own "string" of pack mules. Usually, six of them but we always seemed to have a few interchangeable mules that we could shift around between strings, but for the most part everyone had their six mules.

By this time, we had figured out their pecking order and could arrange them so it kept the mule squabbles to a minimum. But we'd learned the hard way. There were several blow ups, breakaways and slipped packs on the few summer trips we had done in the front country.

We had the brown string, sorrel string, paint string, and we called my sting the "grey string" because they were mostly all grey. Except for one little bay mule I kept in the back. He was a small headed, long eared little fella who stood about 12 hands. He wore "00" shoes and wasn't afraid to stand up for himself around the larger mules. We called him Bubba and although he was pretty inexperienced to the packing game, he had proven already that he was level headed and dirty tough. His main drawback was when you were loading him, sometimes he would blow up and try to kick at you but we learned quickly how to ease around him and get him packed without too much protest. Let's just say that he wasn't going to get to carry the eggs in without a lot of work.

Mules are interesting creatures, once they understand their job they don't tend to complain much. They even have their own form of "trail justice" if one of them is causing trouble on the trail. The others will bite or kick or jerk on their lead ropes to put the mule who's acting up in its place. Once the mules know the drill, they'll toil tirelessly for you, so long as you know their pecking order. If Fred was used to following Wilma and you switched them, they'd spend all twenty-seven miles trying to pass each other on the trail. More than once, this resulted in big wrecks due to the mules getting hung up in blow-down timber and what not.

On one trip in particular, I learned a valuable lesson about mules. I had let the boss tie my string together and he got the order wrong. Just one mule was out of place and she kept trying to pass the mule that was usually behind her. I figured they would figure it out and decided to be lazy and continue just so I would not have to deal with the pain in the neck of retying everything. About six miles up the trail as we made our way through a small stand of blow down, I looked back at the perfect moment. The mule stepped out of line to try to pass the mule she was following. I looked in time to watch as a small Christmas tree, about twelve to fifteen feet high which was laying on its side with the top of the tree pointing opposite our direction of travel. The tree was laying at an angle with the top about waist high off the ground. As the mule approached, walking alongside the trail, the tip of the tree slid perfectly between the panniers and the lash rope.

As it happens, when you pack a mule, there is always a gap between the bottom of the panniers and the lash rope. As the lash cinch is under their belly but the panniers don't sit that low. This creates a triangle, so-to-speak with one side being the mule, the other being the bottom of the pannier and the last side being the lash rope.

The top of the tree slid perfectly through this gap, it happened quick enough that even by stopping, the string would take several more steps before being forced to stop. Seeing the wreck starting, and since I was riding a big, stout 16 hand paint horse, I turned sideways in the trail. That was my only option to try to stop the impending runaway. As the mules continued forward, the tree began to stand up as the root ball was still in the ground which started to spook all the mules in the string. I was absolutely certain that the tree was going to stab the mule in the guts! As the tree stood up, the whole string spooked and lurched forward into me and my horse. But the horse held his ground which stopped the run away before it could get started.

I yelled for the guide behind me to help because I was worried if I moved the horse the runaway would start again. But soon came to find out the mule was anchored to that tree now. We ended up having to cut the tree above and below the mule with a small hand saw I carried on my saddle just to get her free. As luck would have it, the tree went between the pannier and the mule and as it stood up, went between the saddle pads and out the back never once even touching her! That was a lucky mule! And another one of the countless lessons you learn to never repeat after making poor decisions to gain experience! I swapped the mules after that and never let another person tie my string together for the rest of my career in the mountains!

It seems like every hunter who ever booked a horseback wilderness hunt does some research on the perspective outfitter's livestock. "Does he have good horses?" is a question I've been asked by nearly every client I've spoken to. Don't get me wrong, nearly every outfitter has gentle, sure-footed livestock for the clients to ride. What the clients usually fail to realize is the work involved to get a horse or mule to a point where they are trustworthy enough to take an inexperienced rider into such formidable terrain without getting someone hurt.

Good, solid, broke, mountain horses and mules bring a premium on the open market. Depending on various factors, I would estimate that any animal trusted to keep a client safe will bring a minimum of $5,000 at the sale barn. If you have eight clients in a camp at any one time you need three "dude rides" per client. That's $120,000 worth of horse flesh just to go hunting before we even start talking about the pack stock. Financially, that is too expensive of a burden for an outfitter to bear so they don't just go out and buy these good horses. They'd rather make them themselves.

Being that the majority of the employees who work in these camps have some equine savvy, and most have a cowboy'ing background, it doesn't take much of an imagination to figure out the outfitter's solution to this expensive burden.

A small mule squabble happening on the trail. You can see the grey has her ears pinned back. Usually, its best to let them sort it out between themselves.

Also, remember that a bunch of young cowboys and sometimes cowgirls seem to get some sort of ego boost from riding a bad one. This creates an environment where an outfitter can go buy several head for $500 and start sorting through them. The real bad ones usually start in the pack string. Once they get some fire knocked out of them by way of heavy packs, they'll get tried again with the saddle. Often, all that happens in the camp by one of these young whipper-snappers who crave a little added danger or ego boost.

It's fairly common for outfitters to also be horse and mule traders in the off season. Now, people need to understand that the equine trading business is about as greasy as it gets. Generally speaking, they make used car salesman look like choir boys. With few exceptions, they all lie to each other in an effort to buy for the lowest price or sell for the highest. There's been a lot of horses bought that look great! They travel well and seem calm and gentle inside the sale ring. Only to find out later that the selling party drugged the horse to relax him enough to get him sold at a high price. To be fair, there are exceptions to this rule. And I don't want any of my friends who are in the business to take offense. But those are exceptions. Certainly not the rules.

I had a friend buy a fancy looking horse out of the sale barn in Billings one time. The horse was a big, good-looking black and white paint. On the ninety-mile trip home the drugs wore off and that fancy horse that he bought for a few thousand dollars nearly totaled out his horse trailer! The horse kicked and pawed the whole inside of the trailer, popped a bunch of the welds on the roof, dented all the side walls and otherwise just destroyed the inside of the rig. Without the drugs that horse was plumb wild. Lucky for this friend of mine, he too was an experienced horse trader so he pulled over, drugged the horse some more and got him home. If I remember correctly the horse ended up being renamed, "Satan" and he ended up going back through the same sale a few months later. True story!

I'm not saying I don't have an ego; I'm just saying that I never once got a boost of ego by riding some ignorant animal that outweighs me by five or six times in the middle of the mountains. Riding buckin' horses back there, thirty miles from a road, is fairly dangerous. There are trees, rocks, low branches and blow down, oh and no 911 emergency services. In town you can control the environment a bit. You have round pens and if you mention to your buddies that you're going to snap out a few bad ones you'll have more help than you can shake a stick at. Mostly because they all enjoy watching a good wreck. Not to mention emergency medical services are at your fingertips.

In my opinion a guide is supposed to guide. The most important thing for a guide is to keep his clients safe. Second is to make sure they have a good time. Lastly, to provide an opportunity at some game. How effective can a guide be if he can't look at his surroundings while riding up the trail because he knows he is sitting on a ticking time bomb? Ready to break in two at any moment? If I can't dig a can of Copenhagen out of my pocket while riding up the trail without having a wreck, well that's just not my idea of fun. It definitely isn't providing a good service to paying customers.

The first outfit I went to work for, I didn't know any of this stuff happened. So, my naiveté kept me safe, and lucky that first year. As the years went on and I worked for other outfitters I got an education pretty quick. In fact, once I had some experience I got to where I would flat out tell the outfitters before I signed on that I won't ride bad horses or mules. I'd even threaten them a bit by adding that I expected "X" amount for guide wages. If I'm training horses and mules, then I need "X" amount more to cover the horse training wages. That seemed to work well and I still have that same conversation every year I work for a new outfit. It isn't one-hundred percent fool proof though.

Nowadays, I have my own stock. Daily wages increase a bit by having your own horses but not enough to justify feeding them all year. The little bit of money that I lose on having my own stock pays dividends in reduced stress. It saves a lot of dumb conversations with outfitters, and lastly, I'm not ever trapped inside a camp. At least I could get myself and my gear out of there if something really went sideways.

On this particular morning, I rolled into the trailhead around 4:30 am. The sharp bite of fall was in the air and the sky was glistening with stars high above. Not a cloud in the sky. I usually beat everyone there by a good half hour just because I lived thirty miles closer to the trailhead than they did. I always pulled a small goose-neck trailer made of pipe that had the loads of food, gear and supplies that we had made the day previous. All carefully weighed out to the pound. I would unlock the tack trailer which stayed at the trail head, then start catching and tying up all the mules and horses. Normally, the rest of the crew would roll in when I was about half way done catching.

When the boss and the rest of the crew rolled in that morning, they had a bunch of new stock in their trailers. As everyone was going about their business of catching, saddling and packing the boss yelled for me to throw my saddle on this one. I walked over to find a big stout good looking Dun colored horse I didn't recognize.

"Where'd he come from?" I asked with suspicion in my voice.

"I just picked him up out of the sale, he should be a good bastard but go ahead and throw your saddle on him and see if he'll cross the creek."

I turned to go get my gear, cussing under my breath. I just didn't have a good feeling about this one. What kind of "good bastard" doesn't cross water?

I had told the boss that I don't ride bad horses and he'd been true to his word on not asking me too thus far. So, I gave him the benefit of the doubt and decided to be a team player. The horse was fine as I saddled and bridled him. He stood quiet, tied to the hitching rail as the sun was peaking over the mountain tops on that cool autumn morning.

Once he was saddled, I untied him and led him away from the work area and all the other stock that was tied up. I walked him in several circles, both directions and he still seemed fine. So, I carefully "cheeked" his head around and swung up in the saddle in one smooth motion. There he stood, calm and quiet. I thought to myself that maybe he will be a good bastard as I gave him a little kick and pointed him toward the river. He wasn't too excited about getting out of sight of the rest of the heard but that's expected.

He did what was asked and soon we were approaching the river. He stepped right out into the water and acted like a good gentle horse, so we waded around a bit, he seemed to have a pretty good handle on neck reining, so we headed back to the corrals. No problem!

Soon we were tying our strings together and making the last preparations to leave the trailhead. I was second out of the trail head, following the other guide who was riding one of the old dude horses. Right off the bat my horse didn't like following his string of mules and was trying to trot to catch them and pass them up.

His attitude and reactions to my commands were spiteful, even ignoring me a lot. Once the trail narrowed down some he was almost panicking as he pranced up the trail trying to break into a run. His head movements became wild and jerky and his pace was so inconsistent he was really jerking on the string of mules we were leading up the trail. Obviously, the horse was in an environment he had not been in before and was having trouble coping with the situation.

On top of that, the guide in front, who had guided in the camp for the previous owner was from back east somewhere and he wasn't much of a hand at anything other than killing elk. I'll be honest that I didn't care for him much, but it would be dishonest to not acknowledge that he was a pretty good at killing elk.

His "un-handiness" is relevant here because he crawled on a good horse, one that a hunter should have been riding, and didn't bother looking back. He also had the best string of mules because he didn't know much about handling a string. We always had to give him the best and easiest stuff.

When we left the trailhead, he had just taken off and was leaving me and the wrangler in the dust. I've run enough miles in the mountains with both good and bad livestock, good and bad coworkers to know that everything is a lot easier if people are team players. If you stay together, what might have been a big horse wreck can usually be mitigated just by having help. He wasn't that kind of guy though. Usually, when the work started, he was nowhere in sight.

Perhaps three miles in, the trail starts to side hill away and above the creek. It starts to cliff out, small cliffs that are more like rim-rock outcroppings. If you fell off of them, you probably wouldn't die. You most likely would be injured however. The trail then alternates between steep rock slides of large flat reddish colored rock and areas where the trail is cut into these short rim-rock type cliffs. It was becoming more and more apparent that my horse was not thinking about what he was doing. He was just staying borderline panicked and for the most part unresponsive to any commands. He wanted to trot to catch up but trotting with a pack string is a good way to have all your packs come loose. I was trying to make him walk faster but not run. The dun horse wanted to trot though, so he ended up prancing slower than he could have just walked.

I freely admit that at the time, I wasn't handy enough of a horseman to tell a horse to walk fast but not run without double queuing them? At least with the way this horse was acting. So, as you might imagine, we were both getting frustrated with each other and that turned into anger the longer we fought. Soon, he was stepping off the trail and onto the slippery, loose rock slides. We nearly fell down two or three times before we reached the next set of rim rock.

When you're in the mountains you have to figure things out and if you try something that isn't working, you have to either force it to work or try something else. That's just the way it is. You can't weenie out and give up. You can't back down. You can't get your iPhone out and Google the answer. You just have to figure it out yourself or with the help of your fellow riders. Assuming you have them with you.

Having said that, I am smart enough to realize when I'm getting out of my depth. Especially with horses. So, it would be a lie if I didn't admit to trying to think up a reason to split my string between the wrangler and the guide and get back to the trailhead and get a different riding horse. It would also be a lie if I said I wasn't scared that this horse might do something that I wasn't quick enough to correct that he could get me or him hurt.

A lot of the times you can tell why a horse is being ignorant by their mannerisms. Sometimes they are acting a certain way because they're confused. Occasionally, you'll run across one who's being ignorant because they want to hurt you but that's pretty rare. One horse might act like a fool because they are being asked to do something they've never done before. They have to trust and be confident in the rider to understand that they are not being put in danger. If they don't trust the rider and the rider doesn't have an answer, things can get hairy quick. But it's not really the horse's fault most of the time.

Still other times you can watch a horse act pretty ignorant but you can tell they are trying to think their way through the situation. That's fairly normal when you ask them to do something new. The dun horse on that day was being stupid and not thinking at all. He was zeroed in on one objective, to catch and pass the string in front of him and he threw all other thought and logic out. He wasn't minding where he stepped. He wasn't listening to me and he wasn't aware of what he was doing.

Making all that worse, I was tense and horses can feel that. Those horses know what you're thinking when you're riding them. The tenser you are, the more on edge they are. So, I was doing myself no favors at this point but being calm on a horse who's freaking out is easier said than done.

As we proceeded, prancing up the trail, we arrived at a point where the trail was meandering in and out of slides and rim rocks and back and forth between little runoff drainages and cuts. We were rounding a corner and the trail started descending off the side-hill back down towards the creek bottom. There was a small Christmas tree, maybe three feet tall, growing on the side of the trail. Another fifteen or twenty yards past that there was a large old growth evergreen pine tree. Both on the downhill side of the trail.

Just then the dun horse stepped off the trail with a hind foot and started to go down. My boot on the uphill side hit the ground, still in the stirrup. I was able to step off while keeping the lead rope to my pack string in my hand as the dun horse went over backwards and did a complete somersault, crashing down the rock slide only coming to a stop when he landed in the creek.

My lead mule, Molly was an older, really trustworthy mule and the trail was narrow so I tied her up to the small Christmas tree and trotted down to the dun horse, who at this time was standing up in the creek. I admit to being disappointed to find not a single scratch on that horse.

I checked my saddle for damage and there somehow wasn't any so I led the horse up to the big tree on the trail and tied him up. I made the decision, come hell or high water, that I wasn't riding that horse another step. Not now, not tomorrow, not ever!

By this time the wrangler was tied up and coming to lend a hand while the guide who was up front was long since out of sight. I told him I wasn't riding that horse another step and blurted out a comment about threatening to shoot him.

The wrangler was a young kid, barely twenty and this was his first job in the mountains so he didn't have much to say. He just stood there with a blank look on his face as he peered out from beneath his wide brimmed and flat shaped, cheap cowboy hat.

As we stood along the trail, I noticed two of my pack mules had propane loads. One was the small bay mule named Bubba. I forget the other mule's name but for whatever reason I decided Bubba was going to help me out. I carefully walked back through my string and untied Bubba and brought him up to the big tree.

With the help of the wrangler, we unpacked and unsaddled Bubba. We stashed the propane in some green pine needle covered shrubs that are often found at the base of pine trees a few yards off the trail.

Then I began unsaddling the dun. As I grabbed my saddle to slide it off the horse's back, I was in a poor position. I had all the weight of my saddle up about chest high and my back was facing the abrupt drop off of the slide when he suddenly reared up trying to strike at me and the wrangler.

When the dun reared up to strike his shoulder caught my saddle and momentarily lifted most of my weight off my feet. As he ascended in his rare, I was pushed backwards off the embankment, saddle still in hand. Luckily, he missed us both but now I was flying through the air.

Soon I hit on my back in the middle of the rockslide and watched helplessly as my feet went over my head as I rolled down the embankment through the rocks. When the horse reared up his halter broke with a loud pop that sounded like a gunshot! The dun's lightning-fast front feet missed both the wrangler and myself, but they made contact with that old tree. To this day there's strike marks in that tree alongside that rockslide! They are head high to a person who's horseback!

When the dun realized he had broken free, he turned and took off straight up the steep rock slide. I remember watching him make huge, powerful strides as he continued straight up the mountain. He was sinking to his knees with every stride as the rocks gave way and tumbled down the hill right at us.

I quickly started making my way back up to the trail to do something. I didn't know what? But I was going to be ready as I scrambled to dodge falling rocks and debris. As dust filled the air and the chattering of falling rocks of all sizes, from golf ball to the size of basketballs plummeted down the steep embankment. I quickly decided to leave my saddle behind as it was slowing my ascent.

The dun had put us and the whole string in the middle of an avalanche of rock! Dust and debris continued filling the air as rocks streaked by while the dun continued up the slide. I continued to scramble up to the trail hoping the big tree would provide some protection as I climbed.

Quickly, aided by a burst of adrenaline I regained the trail and got to the big tree, I could see the wrangler was alright and, on his feet and out of the way of the falling rock.

About then the dun horse, obviously still completely panicked, had reached the top of the rock slide, about one-hundred yards above us. He was standing with his head facing toward a fifteen-foot cliff, trapped from further ascent. In a quick glance I saw that my string of mules hadn't moved. I was thinking of heading up through the rock slide to retrieve the horse once again, when we saw the horse wobble. Then he just sat down like a dog and flipped over backward.

From the base of the cliff to the trail was about a hundred yards. From the trail to the creek was another fifteen or twenty. We watched as the dun did flip after flip down through the steep rock slide. At times he was high enough off the ground to drive a car under him. As he tumbled down the hill, he was headed right toward my string of tied up mules. As he tumbled, he would land on his rump then flip into the air and land on his head and neck. He continued gaining speed, air and force as he flipped down the hill.

Rocks and debris were still flying and the dust cloud thickened as he crashed down the slide. The mules were watching the action and knew he was going to hit them. I watched as the two lead mules, Molly and Dolly lowered themselves and leaned into the hillside in order to absorb the blow of the horse flipping and tumbling in their direction.

The dun horse came flipping and crashing right through them. It knocked the mules just a few steps down off the trail, breaking lose my quickly tied lead rope on the tiny tree. Molly powered through though and came right back up on the trail and got the mules out of the way as best they could.

As I waited for the dust to settle, I was certain the dun had killed himself! He had to be dead after tumbling off a rock slide that big and steep. But to my surprise, the dun was hanging with his head facing downhill and his rear feet tangled in that little Christmas tree alongside the trail. Just lying there breathing.

I scrambled over to my string and led them off the slide and tied them up in the trees twenty yards up the trail. I gave them a quick once-over to make sure none were hurt in that massive collision. They seemed no worse for the wear. Sometime during the ruckus, I remembered the dun's back feet were hung up in that little Christmas tree so I grabbed what was left of the broken halter rope off the big tree and headed over to assess the dun's situation.

Pure disgust washed over me as I stood over the dun. He was just lying there. As I looked him over there were no obvious broken legs or anything. Except for a few cuts around his legs, he appeared to be fine! Still unsure of his health however, I decided we needed to move him. I used the lead rope and flipped it over his back feet.

At the time I was still pretty sure the horse was going to have to be put down so it made sense to get him as far off the trail as possible. I looped the rope around both back feet and pulled as hard as I could, rolling the horse over on his other side, freeing his feet from the Christmas tree. I pulled hard enough that when he came free I kind of plopped down in a sitting position on the trail and watched as he slid and tumbled the rest of the way down into the creek. He made a pretty good splash as he plummeted into the creek head first while I sat there out of breath.

Now, "Murphy's Law" tells us that any horse that meant something, or was worth something would have broken a leg or sustained some mortal injury in a fall like that. I was just regaining some composure when I noticed the dun struggle to his feet. He just stood up like nothing was wrong, walked over to the creek bank and started grazing on the tall grass that was along each side of the creek.

I stared in disbelief momentarily, then rage began to well up in me and I began seeing red. I had lost my composure and jumped to my feet and took off at a run down the slide toward the horse, I un-holstered my pistol as I went trotting down through the rocks. Determined that I was going to shoot that horse in the face!

About then the wrangler caught up to me and grabbed me by the shoulder. At the time it was a surprise, but during the chaos he had retrieved the satellite phone from his horse and had called the boss. He handed me the phone.

"You know what this son-of-a-bitch just did to us?" I barked into the phone.

The reply was quick and sharp, "If you kill that horse, you owe me $700!"

That was all the sense I needed talked back into me in order to regain some composure.

"Besides, you don't want to fight the bears that will be on his carcass the rest of the year" the Boss said.

He was right, and I'm not the kind of guy that goes full on barbarian. As I re-holstered my pistol, I told him that I was turning the horse loose and he could come find him if he wanted him. And I did. I took the mangled remains of the halter off and walked back up to finish saddling Bubba.

Bubba turned out to be a non-event. Not without some experimenting first though. When I swung into the saddle it was immediately made clear that Bubba wasn't ready to lead us up the trail. He didn't know what it meant when I pulled on the reins, and it spooked him a little if my feet touched his sides. But all in all, he was alright. I just had the wrangler get in front of me and ol' Bubba acted like a pack mule and followed the mule in front of him.

About the time we were leaving the wreck site I realized I had a rolling sweat going. My shirt, and undershirt were soaked all the way through. I took my button up shirt off and just rode in my tee shirt that was soaked. The spot where the wreck happened was three or four miles into a twenty-seven-mile ride. We left the trailhead at 9:00 am and when we left the wreck sight it was 12:45. It was going to be a long day!

The first mile or two after the wreck went fine, but as we proceeded, and the adrenaline wore off I became more and more exhausted. That rush earlier had turned into an energy dump now. Pretty soon I was fighting to keep my eyes open and eventually dosed off in the saddle. I woke up as we entered the meadows, a good twelve miles from the trailhead and looked around.

What was a bluebird day had quickly changed into overcast and it was starting to rain. I didn't think it was a good idea to try to get more clothes on while in the saddle on a green mule so I yelled ahead to hold up. We both jumped off, put on our Outback oil cloth slickers and were soon back riding towards camp.

On a normal trip we expect to hit the meadows in four hours. Then the pass in six. Camp in about nine hours. This trip we hit the meadows at 5:00 pm which was a good four hours behind schedule. As we plodded up the increasingly sloppy trail, I looked behind me to see that dun horse following us. I shook my head in disgust and decided to pay him no mind as we continued. After all, we didn't have any extra halters. So, there wasn't a lot we could do but hope he wouldn't try to get between animals in our strings.

As we exited the meadows the ticking sound of rain falling on my oil cloth slicker was only drowned out by the slopping sounds of hooves splashing up the trail. We started gaining elevation pretty quickly. Soon the rain gave way to snow as the temperature dropped. At length, we reached the top of the 10,000ft pass in a full-on blizzard.

It was getting dark as we dismounted our horses and began walking down the back side of the pass. After the long descent, we remounted our riding animals. It's an hour or so down to the Park Service cabin, then up and over a smaller pass, then another forty-five minutes to an hour into camp.

We ended up arriving in camp around midnight, several hours after dark. We unpacked and unsaddled in the rain and snow mix weather, kicked the stock loose and hoisted the food panniers up into the cache for the night. Dinner was quick and we hit the rack. I was exhausted. I had been so hot that day that I sweated through all my clothing, then later froze my rear end off in a blizzard.

The horse wreck really rattled me too. It's been a long time since I'd had an adrenaline dump big enough to force me to take a nap on a moving mule's back!

Going over Deer Creek Pass inside the clouds.

| 8 |

The Bubba Mule Part 2- Bob Got Screwed

The events that led up to this Medevac started four days prior when we packed in the archery hunters for their hunt. As usual, the hands had left the trailhead a few hours behind the hunters.

The pack strings almost always travel much faster than the "dudes" so the morning drill is always to get the hunter horses and mules saddled first thing. As soon as all the hunters arrive to the trailhead, we get them on their horse and usually the outfitter leads them to camp. This accomplishes a few things, first and foremost, when we are packing thirty-five head of mules in the morning, we don't need anyone in the way. And being in the way around some of those pack mules is a dangerous situation for eager and enthusiastic hunters who most likely don't have much livestock experience. And secondly, it's always good to give the slow pokes a good head start so we can eat dinner at a decent hour.

Generally, the pack strings overtake the dudes in the meadow when they stop for lunch and to stretch their legs about four hours up the trail. The dudes stop a lot. The strings can't.

On the other hand, the pack strings are loaded at the trailhead, tied into their respective strings, and we set out for camp. It's difficult to stop for any period of time with a string due to the nature of the mules. If you stop for long, they'll start grazing and trying to walk around.

A Medevac helicopter waits in the meadow as the crew preps a patient. Note: my hunter and I are riding across the meadow returning to camp. Several years later I worked for this company on the fixed wing side of the operation. This picture was in the company calendar.

They inevitably start jacking around and get tangled up in the other lead ropes, rub and loosen each other's packs and so on. Stopping with a string for long is a sure-fire recipe for a wreck, at least it was with these particular strings. Often when pulling a string the guides will not stop or even get off their horse until we reach a pass that we must walk down, or we arrive in camp.

On this trip I was in the lead with several strings behind me. We had left the trailhead on time and I was just starting to think about digging my first sandwich out of my saddle bags when we topped a little rise in the trail. Ahead of me I could see the boss and one of the hunters riding toward me.

The look on the boss' face told me something was seriously wrong. I pulled up on the reins and stopped in a wide spot in the trail as they approached. The hunter who was with him was in serious trouble! He was a very large man, about six feet tall and well over 250 pounds. The boss had him tied onto his saddle and the hunter was drifting in and out of consciousness.

As they got closer, I noticed that the hunter had crapped his pants and it was running out of his pant leg, down his boots and dripping onto the trail. After witnessing that scene, I figured that sandwich could wait a while.

The boss told me he had to get the hunter to the hospital and declined offers to help. Being in aviation and having studied it, as well as having some experience with other altitude sensitive hunters, I figured that he had hypoxia and told the boss so.

"How do we fix it so this big sombitch can ride himself?" he said.

"Unless you have an oxygen bottle in your saddle bags, best thing you can do is get him to the hospital."

We quickly decided that I would have the rest of the hunters, who were waiting a mile up the trail, fall in behind my string and follow me into camp. That way the string behind me could help keep an eye on them. As we parted in opposite directions, I shouted back to the boss to take care of his guy and not worry about us. Famous last words, right?

Quickly, I arrived at a wide place in the trail where the hunters were waiting among the cottonwoods and willows near the river bottom. I quickly briefed them as to the plan.

"Guys, I'll do my best for you but we can't stop every two hours to pee or put a coat on and all that crap, we have to ride" I told them, "It's two and a half hours to the meadow, we'll stop for ten or fifteen minutes there. Plan on eating your lunch in the saddle, other than that, if you kinda' have to pee I don't want to hear about it. If your teeth are floating, let me know and we'll stop. Fair enough?"

Not twenty minutes later as we rode up the trail one of the hunters, Bob said, "I could kinda' use to piss"

I said, "Well we ain't stoppin' for kinda', Bob. Can you make it a little farther?"

He agreed and soon we were arriving at the meadows. Knowing I had guys who needed to go to the bathroom I planned on stopping at the bottom of these mile-long meadows.

Just when I began looking for a place to tie up, we spotted a bear grazing just a hundred yards from us. I decided to push for the top of the meadows before stopping to avoid any potential trouble.

At the top of the meadow, I found a suitable tree in the center of the grass with no other obstructions nearby that my string could get messed up on. I tied up and started helping the clients dismount. I went through all of the client's livestock, checking cinches, reins and anything else that could cause problems later on. I looked over the stock for sores and when I was done, I started rounding guys up to get back on.

Away from the group of clients I noticed Bob standing by a tree. Bob was an older guy, in his mid-sixties I'd guess, but a high mileage sixties. He stood maybe 5'8" with a thin build. An easterner with just enough grey hair to have a thin comb-over.

He was standing with his back to us, leaned slightly forward. He had one hand above his head bracing himself on a tree. His red and black plaid wool shirt spared us from his bare ass but I could see he had his wranglers pulled all the way down around his ankles. Like my two-year-old does when he is potty training.

I stood and watched and waited for him to get done. And I stood some more. And then some more. Finally, I walked over to see if he was okay. Approaching from behind, I could not see a stream. He was just standing there with his pants down and his wiener in his hand.

Jokingly I asked, "Is everything coming out okay?"

Bob didn't say much until he got his pants up. Then he confessed to me that he had forgotten to take his prostate medication that morning and now he couldn't pee.

"I'll stop on top of the pass and you can give er' another whirl up there. But we need to keep moving."

My fifteen-minute stop had already turned into a forty-minute stop and about half way through another guide with a pretty green string decided to keep moving. So, we watched as he disappeared into the trees at the top of the meadow before we even got Bob mounted up and riding again. Soon we had everyone else back in the saddle and we were kicking for the pass.

Halfway to the pass Bob demanded we stop again, so we did. And again, we all watched as he stood against a tree, pants at his ankles and couldn't pee. Forty-minutes later we had talked Bob into getting back on his horse and we continued on.

On reaching the pass we had another forty-minute show of Bob standing against a tree. Pants at his ankles. Not peeing. Just standing there holding his "little smoky." Once that was done, we started our walk down the steep section of trail on the back side of the pass. In total there were eight hunters. I led us off the pass and down to the area where we climb back on our stock.

At the bottom I stood and waited for everyone to catch up. By this point I had sent the rest of the other strings ahead of me so they could get to camp as some of their mules were acting up while we waited on Bob. After an hour Bob finally showed up. I asked if he was okay and he assured me he was, using a condescending tone. He told me he had stopped and take a dump. When I asked, he admitted again that he couldn't go.

"Well, get on your horse Bob, we aren't getting any closer to camp standing here" I stated as I turned to head back to my string.

"Hold on, I still have to piss" he said.

So, again we waited for another forty-minutes while Bob stood next to a tree. With his pants around his ankles.

Finally, without peeing we got Bob mounted and were headed toward camp. As the trail descended the back side of the pass it eventually ends up paralleling a small creek inside Yellowstone Park. After a few miles of riding along the creek the trail crosses the creek, exits the Park heading east and starts up a blow down timber, fires of '88 hillside towards the next small pass. From the top of the second pass, it's about a fifty-minute ride into camp.

Once over the second pass, and down off the back side the trail meanders through a small meadow. When we arrived Bob, once again had to pee. So, we all stopped. And waited. Again.

It was getting dark and at this point my mules had been packed coming on twelve hours. I could see that all the hunter's horses and mules were tired and restless as well. We waited as it was the same thing again.

About thirty-minutes into another one of Bob's displays I reached my limit. I had myself half convinced that Bob was "putting us on" because he was tired and sore from the long ride.

I kicked my right foot up and over my horses' neck and slid off the side no handed, Lone Ranger style. My pony didn't care and continued grazing. I handed my reins to another hunter and marched back to have a word with Bob. As I was approaching Bob saw me coming and before I could say anything Bob wailed out, "Just leave me here, you guys go on!"

That pretty much confirmed to me, a young, tough, invincible, know-it-all guide, that Bob's problem wasn't that he couldn't pee. It was that he was being a pussy! And I told him so.

"Get your ass on your horse right now! And quit being a pussy!" I roared, "We are a half an hour from camp, there are seven other grown-ass men who have been waiting on you all day! Either you get on that horse or I'm tying you on him! Right now, Bob!"

I stomped off and grabbed his horse and led him over to Bob. "Pull your god damn pants up Bob! Get on right now, quit being a pussy!"

Packing another one off of the, "Bread Loaf."

Bob crawled on and reached for the reins I had in my hand. I snatched them away and led his horse up to my sting before handing them back.

"You ride right behind my string and I don't want to hear another peep out of you until we get to camp!"

And on into camp we went. Bob, riding quietly behind my string. When we were a hundred yards out of camp and dusk was turning to dark, the boss came trotting up beside me. He told me he had rode his guy back to the truck, wrestled him into the front seat and drove like hell to the emergency room in Cody, dropped him off then drove the forty-miles back to the trailhead and long trotted into camp.

I briefed him on how our day went and explained what had happened with Bob. Which explained why our nine-hour ride had turned into a now, almost fourteen-hour ride. I told the boss that my opinion was to get a helicopter in to pick Bob up in the morning which he dismissively waved off with a scowl and a wave of his hand.

Once we were in camp and had all the stock tended to, we all sat down to the traditional first night in camp, spaghetti dinner, complete with garlic bread and a salad. Bob was a no-show. The following morning, we hunted, then came in for lunch and Bob was still acting like he was in bad shape.

We tried to talk him into a helicopter ride to town but he refused. He said he felt constipated so another guide who had a pretty robust medication kit found Bob some Ex-Lax. We loaded the poor guy up with about triple the normal dose of laxative. In the days that followed we all noticed that Bob wasn't ever seen near the outhouse tent. One morning when the camp jack went into his tent to start his morning fire it was discovered that Bob had been pooping in a five-gallon bucket inside his tent! The bucket was normally reserved for the camp jack to mix wood shavings and diesel into fire starter. Anyway, he was crapping into the bucket inside his tent, then emptying it into the outhouse tent. Not a lot of stuff grosses me out but this one got me. And the camp jack was pretty dismayed about the violation of his bucket!

As the hunt continued, and Bob was still using our bucket to crap in, we all began noticing a pattern to his stories around meal time. He was one of the kind of guys who made sure everyone knew what a mighty hunter he was. To the point he packed in his hunting photo album and left it on the dining tent table. He would talk at length about how he hunted here and there and killed whatever.

It annoyed the other hunters and camp staff to say the least. We all began noticing a pattern to all these hunting stories he told, something happened and he got screwed over. Some outfitter did this and that in order to screw him. I noticed he never said anything good. About anything!

Meanwhile, since I'd cut Bubba out of the pack string a few weeks ago he had been turning into a pretty good riding mule. He liked to kick though and he had been nailing me every morning I had used him so far. Although young, and sort of mean he was doing a good job and seemed to be figuring out what I meant when I pulled a rein one way or another. A total plow reining mule as any hope of him learning anything about neck reining was a bridge too far at the current moment. But ninety-nine percent of mules are like that, so progress was good.

You just had to watch it a little while getting on him. He was still getting used to the feel of a rider swinging into the saddle and he wasn't afraid to protest a little. You didn't have to "ear him down" every time anymore though. So, one morning I decided to promote him to hunting donkey.

I was guiding a one-on-one client this hunt who was a successful businessman from the southeast. He was a good guy but was a real slow traveler due to being a shade, umm... short for his weight. However, slow he was, he was a lot of fun to hunt with. I have had a lot of fun with guys who aren't as capable. They generally understand their limitations and their expectations reflect that.

Any guide worth his salt knows to design the hunt based on the hunter's capabilities. So, when I make comments about someone's appearance in this book, just know I am using them as a descriptive term to more accurately paint the picture in the reader's mind. Not to judge or demean them.

The previous day while making the evening hunt we had spotted some elk in a far-off basin. They were in a pretty bad spot, nestled along the Yellowstone Park line. In order to get there, you had to bushwhack up a steep ridge that was a mix of small new growth piss firs. Making matters worse, you have to traverse through an area where the Yellowstone fires of 1988 had come through. It was a massive area of blow down timber, good, knee-high grass and plenty of good cover for the elk. It also happened to be right on the Yellowstone Park line.

Although I had some reservations about our capabilities, we made a plan and headed up there in the morning darkness late in the hunt. I was riding Bubba and we had my client on an older big draft cross mule we called Minnesota.

We managed to jump game trail to game trail until we reached a meadow roughly two-thirds of the way to the top of this mountain. We tied up and made the excessively long hike up through the blow down timber until we could peak over into the little basin at the top of the mountain where we had seen elk the previous day.

There was a northern peak which was almost entirely inside the Park, and a southern peak which was outside the Park. About eight-hundred yards of blow down burned timber with sporadic pockets of new growth green timber lay between the peaks creating a small basin.

It is an exceptional place to rifle hunt due to several factors. Visibility, resident elk, and so on, but the average shot up there is around three-hundred yards. That made the archery hunt a lot tougher in that area due to the lack of cover between where you crest the ridge line to where the elk usually are.

Basically, when you peek over the ridge the elk are either there or they're not. You can't maneuver very well up there because of the lack of concealing cover. Proximity to the Park line is always on your mind because a poor shot will almost certainly result in unrecoverable game.

It took so long to get up there this morning that we had essentially lost the entire morning hunt. We decided to take a nap in an area of rocky outcroppings and wait for the evening activity. It was a perfect bluebird day. Laying on the rocks the sun penetrated our cloths and warmed our bodies.

We could see the Tetons to the southwest, just a sliver of Yellowstone Lake due west and virtually all the country we hunted in this particular camp to the east. I spent the early afternoon glassing a few of the other guides who were out on various prominent ridges a few miles away. We chit chatted about the fast-food industry that the hunter was involved in and had a pretty mellow afternoon.

While basking in the afternoon sun I was in a semi-conscious half sleep. The kind where you are partially aware of your surroundings. As I lay there on the rocks with my hat over my eyes the silence was gradually pierced by the distinctive "whop, whop, whop" of a helicopter flying down the canyon toward us.

From our perch high above the valley floor, we both looked on through our binoculars as the skillful pilot flew down the canyon far below us. The pilot was slowing and descending as he flew toward our camp.

We looked on as he overflew the camp and banked around to face the nose into the wind. Soon he was hover taxing just above the treetops moving slowly towards our camp. The pilot skillfully set the Bell 406 down in the meadow near camp. As he descended below the treetops and out of sight, I breathed a sigh of relief that their passenger was finally leaving camp.

We found out later that finally, on the fourth day of the hunt the boss pulled the plug, so-to-speak on Bob's parade. He called the life flight helicopter and didn't give Bob a say in the matter. Something I had advocated for from the first night. The report was the flight crew stuck a catheter in him right in camp. I forget the details but however much fluid the human bladder is supposed to hold, they drained two and a half times that out of him. Strapped him to the board and got him to the hospital in town. Good riddance pretty much summarized my thoughts.

Months later, after he made it home, I received a letter from the outfitter board wanting my side of the story. Which was simple, the dude forgot to take his medication, then sat in a saddle for thirty-some miles. Nothing ever came of it and even later I found out that he also tried to call the Game and Fish on me. Poor Bob got screwed again!

Later that evening after the helicopter had left, high above the valley floor hidden in a rocky outcropping, my hunter and I were awaiting the evening wind shift. As we waited, we noticed we had a few bad little puffs of wind. I had been cautiously calling with a bull inside the Park when those dreaded puffs hit the back of my ears. The calling we were doing was with a herd bull who was bedded just inside the park.

Once that happened, I decided to cut out a little earlier than usual to make sure we had enough time to at least get back to our mules before dark. When we started back for the horses, once on the front side of the saddle there are many cuts and small canyons. A few avalanche chutes as well. Some of those cuts were washed out from the spring runoffs so deep they were a very serious chore to cross. Given our limited ability to move quickly, it was imperative that we found the correct ridge that led down to the small meadow where our mules were tied up. Everything was blow-down and new growth Christmas trees standing anywhere from an ankle grabbing one foot high to ten or so feet. The farther we descended the deeper the cuts were and the harder they were to cross.

As you might have guessed, this stellar guide missed the ridge by one cut! By this time, I had once again misjudged how long it would take to get off the peaks. Blacker than the inside of a cow, darkness enveloped us! The result was the illustrious guide and hunter unknowingly descended into more and more blow down. At the time, it was too dark to be sure, but I was pretty certain of my mistake when we got to what I judged to be an even level with the mules. I was second guessing myself though, so we descended further. Soon we could hear the creek running a few hundred yards below us. Just across that creek was a large meadow and in that meadow was the main trail that led to camp.

I told my hunter that we'd made a mistake by missing the ridge. It obviously wasn't reasonable to ask him to go back up through the blow down when we were so close to the trail. So, I instructed him to go to the creek. Cross it and assured him he would be in a meadow. The trail is in the meadow. Find it. Stand in it and don't move. He agreed and we parted ways.

I hit a quick pace angling to cross the ravine and gaining elevation at the same time. Eventually, I was in a blow down area so thick I was walking on logs five or six feet off the ground while using the tops of the piss firs as handles for balance. It didn't take long before I wasn't sure where I was in relation to the mules. I wasn't sure which way to go. I was out of options and ideas.

As a last ditch "Hail Mary" I hollered out, "Hey Boys!" which was what the wrangler would always yell to the mules to get them into the corrals at feed time. Through the silence of the pitch black, I heard a mule brae. I took off in that direction but soon lost the bearing. I yelled again. And heard the same mule brae again! This went on perhaps ten times before I found them. Right where I left them on the edge of that little meadow. I whispered a profound, "Thank you!" to Minnesota as I got situated to ride back to camp.

Salty, one of my favorite mules to travel in and out of camp on, Crossing Eagle Pass.

As I readied myself to swing into the saddle, Bubba kicked me in the thigh, once again! After some choice words, I got in the saddle. I pointed Bubba to roughly where we came from that morning with Minnesota's lead rope in my hand. We didn't go fifteen-yards before I knew Bubba had messed up. So, we stopped and I tried again. Nothing but more blow down would appear in my headlamp. We were on Bubba's third or fourth attempt to head down when all of the sudden Minnesota pulled back sharply and unexpectedly. He did it quick enough, he jerked his lead rope out of my hand. It caught me completely off guard because Minnesota is such a good old mule. He has more experience in the mountains than ninety percent of the guides!

I jumped off Bubba, carefully to not get kicked again and set out to catch Minnesota. But that old mule just turned and walked away from me. Whenever I got close, he would speed up a little, but he never broke into a trot or run. I decided to just keep him from running so I stayed just close enough behind him to keep him in view of my headlamp. I continued to follow as he walked right over to the game trail we came in on that morning and started down the hill. Minnesota walked us, leading me and Bubba all the way down to the meadow. To my surprise when walked into the meadow that big mule just stopped and let me walk right up and catch him. Don't ever let someone tell you mules aren't smart!

I gave him a pat on the head and a scratch on the ears while we waited for our hunter. I yelled once and figured he was right here close. After a bit we headed up the trail a ways hollering for the hunter and receiving no response. We went down the trail with the same result. Soon I was sure we had a lost hunter so I dug my radio out of my pack and called camp. They reported that my hunter had just arrived in camp without me or a mule.

When I got to camp that night, I was diplomatically trying to explain to my hunter why he made a bad decision when he suddenly cut me off. He said he knew it was a bad decision and he apologized. He said when he hit that meadow he was scared and the only thing that kept him from being scared was to keep moving. Fair enough!

| 9 |

The Bubba Mule Part 3- Just John Wayne Em!

It was the peak of the bugle hunts where a guy could sit on a hill and watch herd bulls breeding cows up and down the canyon. We had spotted some elk the previous evening in a little side drainage that ran mostly east to west but was doglegged so parts of it were to the east northeast. We made a plan and returned to camp for the night with high hopes for the following morning.

I was guiding a father/son pair and we had been having a great time. Bubba was a regular as a guide ride at this point and had learned most of the trails around camp. He remained a tough little fella and didn't seem to mind his promotion to riding mule.

You just had to watch him in the morning because if you let your guard down while saddling, he would zero in and make another precision strike, as in kick you and almost never miss. Needless to say, I was limping a lot those first few hunts. To his credit, however, you didn't have to cheek him every time you wanted to get on anymore. Maybe half the time! Progress nonetheless!

We rode out of camp an hour before light and as we rolled around the ridge the elk were bugling away. Squealers, Growlers and everything in between. It was reminiscent of the old days guiding on the other side of the Trident Plateau.

Eagle Creek Meadows.

We tied up in the grey light and began a stalk to the edge of an oval-shaped meadow that provided a good view of an old burn. Above the meadow there was a prominent rock feature that we also often liked to hunt from. As dawn broke and the temperature dropped several degrees as it does in the morning. We were glad to be positioned in a good spot and through the crunchy meadow grass encrusted in frost. As the first birds began to chirp as daylight breaks, cows and bulls were spread across the hillside.

Soon a bull stepped out that we deemed a mature 6x6. I tooted on the cow calls, and he closed the distance from six hundred to three hundred yards over the course of an hour. With the gunner lined up, and a solid rest across a log we waited until we had a good broadside shot. As the sun began to peak over the jagged canyon walls the gun roared to life. "Bang!" And the hillside erupted as elk bee-lined for the dark green timber up country. The bullet found its mark and soon we were standing over a superb bull estimated around 320-inches. I left the elated hunters and struck up a trot back to gather our mules.

Soon I returned with the livestock, with only a mild limp from being kicked by Bubba. After a good picture session, we were butchering an elk on the mountainside. Bubba was tied nearby facing us. Occasionally, he would peek out from behind his tree to see what we were doing and snort at us. Generally speaking, pack mules have experience packing and by my logic at the time, I figured Bubba a good candidate to carry some meat. Especially because I can keep pace with the mules on foot when we head back to camp. Usually, a hunter can't. For convenience purposes, I wanted to use Bubba for this elk.

One other noteworthy item was that at this point in time I was fairly new to something we call poacher packing. Poacher packing, simplified for the purposes of this book is when you tie the meat on your riding saddles. And on this day, I hadn't completely worked all the kinks out of the endeavor. As such, I had a few difficulties while settling into this learning curve.

Soon we were caped and quartered and ready to pack the meat. I brought Bubba up to a small tree in the middle of this moderate blow down area and tied him off short and high.

Before messing with the meat, I got some ropes ready and dangled them off the saddle horn. It was a fifty-foot piece of rope that I used for slinging pack loads so it was plenty long with plenty of slack. Soon I hoisted a hind quarter up towards the saddle horn and put a double wrap and a half hitch on it to hold it until I figured out the best way to tie it off good. Bubba was standing like a rock and giving no hint of protest, so I moved behind him to the other side. The hunters observed from a safe distance, rifles nestled in the crook of their arms, still technically on bear patrol.

Looking up at the Trident Plateau.

Just as I reached Bubba's offside, he exploded into a fit by rearing up and then trying to kick like a bronc. As he kicked, he launched himself forward, past the little tree until he hit the end of the lead rope which caused his head to be jerked back toward the tree and his rear end to swing around. Then, he continued the process and soon he was basically bucking in a circle around the four-inch-thick tree that was flopping back and forth like one of those inflatable figures you see at car dealerships!

At some point in the frolic the quarter came loose and fell to the ground. But then the dallies of rope came tight on the saddle horn as he spun around the tree effectively making a hundred- and fifty-pound hind elk quarter into a crack the whip sort of projectile. Roughly ten feet of rope had slipped between the saddle horn and the hurling quarter of bloody meat.

Sensing the danger of my position I opted to tuck tail and run. As I dashed across the blow down logs and timber, I made a split-second judgement that if I could make it over a giant fallen log ahead, I'd be to a safe area.

The log was about three and a half feet thick. The kind you have to swing a leg over and sit down before swinging the other leg over. But I didn't have the time. I tried to jump over it. Just as my feet left the ground to start my hurdle the quarter of elk meat smashed into the small of my lower back! My head involuntarily snapped back as the weight of the hurling hind quarter bent my body into a backwards "C" shape. Then I was pounded belly first into the log just as Bubba's hind legs swooped over me and landed harmlessly on the other side.

Soon Bubba came to his senses and calmed down while I was searching for all the air that had been forcibly evacuated from my lungs. Other than a big bloody spot on the back of my wool vest, I'd come out unscathed. Upon further review, and in light of new evidence to the contrary, I decided that it wasn't that important to pack Bubba. So, I opted to pack the two dude mules and we all walked to camp, just a touch slower than I had wanted. But we made it safe and sound for the most part. I'm just glad that log didn't have any stobs on it!

Later, that same hunt and same hunters, we awoke to snow. A lot of snow. Six inches in camp! We woke up late too because the wrangler never brought the horses in. Usually, you can count on thirty-five head of mules and horses trotting into the corrals with bells around their necks to wake you up. This morning, not so much!

We were all starting to stir from our bedrolls and began wondering where the wrangler was when suddenly the tent flap opened and he gimped inside, covered in snow, and looking defeated. He told us of the events of the morning, and I had to smile. The boss had him ride the dun horse to wrangle on to see how he was. On this cold and snowy morning, the dun decided he didn't like his job anymore and a few hundred yards out of camp he flipped over on our wrangler. Then hauled ass out to the herd with the saddle still on!

A dangerous situation to say the least! To have a horse flip over on you when you're alone, in the dark, thirty-ish miles from a road is a good way to never walk again. The wrangler was darn lucky to have some snow for padding when the dun flipped over on him, so other than being a little sore he was alright. On hearing the news, the boss agreed with me, and the wrangler's assessment and that horse went to the trailhead after the hunt never to be seen or heard from again. Hopefully, he was loaded on a semi and sent to Mexico! Being turned into dog food would be the most productive thing that horse had ever done with himself.

Anyway, we were running behind and didn't have horses. It was snowing and cold and I didn't wake up on the right side of bed. Highly annoyed with the morning events, I gathered my hunters and decided to walk out of camp towards the Yellowstone Line. I wanted to see if the snow had pushed anything into the area. I was the only guide who left camp that morning as snowflakes the size of silver dollars were falling hard and fast. The boss made a late morning hunt I found out later, but everyone else opted to "hunt the wood stove in the dining tent" that morning. As we ascended the ridge of burnt and blowdown timber, all conveniently covered in snow, we paused for a breather. I put my arm up to support myself as I leaned against a tree. Just then a slight puff of air hit me behind the ears.

The morning was dead still and calm. The kind of quiet that only happens when big snowflakes are falling hard. I knew that puff had ruined our hunt and as I turned to my hunters one was cleaning the end of his scope out. It was completely filled with snow. I just happened to glance up the hill as the fog and mist parted enough to see the silhouettes of two big bulls just standing there! Big ones!

We scrambled to get into position to shoot. The visibility was about two-hundred yards in the heavy snow, fog and mist. The yardage was purely a guess as there's no chance of a rangefinder working in those conditions. My hunter, now frantically trying to clean his scope enough to see through it asked how far?

"Two-hundred yards" I said.

He jacked a round into the chamber and leveled his 300-win mag.

"Take the one on the left. He's the biggest one" I said!

BOOM! To my dismay the hunter made a perfect shot laterally, it was just about eight inches low. He wounded the bull in the leg.

"Shit, he's three hundred yards! Three hundred!! Hit him again!"

BOOM! And the bull limped out of sight. I thought he hit him again but was unsure as the elk would obviously be limping from the broken leg, he received on the first shot.

We raced up the hill to where they were last seen only to see divots in the snow instead of good tracks. It was snowing so hard that it was filling in the tracks that fast! I knelt down and blew into a track and as the snow flew out of the way it reviled blood in the track. My fears were confirmed too, because those elk were bee-lining it for the Yellowstone line. We had to catch up to them!

We began the process of tracking and after about two hundred yards we jumped the wounded elk as he was bedded in a small cut. BOOM! And the bull fell like a ton of bricks. Then immediately jumped back up and took off!

"Hit him again!" I said.
"I'm out of ammo!"
"Reload then!"
"No! I'm out of ammo! All my bullets are in my saddle bags!"

We found out later that the shot that briefly downed the bull actually penetrated the back of his ear, at its base. The bullet exited the ear, cut a groove down the bull's face and popped out an eyeball.

At this point we were in the cut, less than a hundred yards from the Yellowstone line. There was no time! We had a critically wounded elk that was going to be wasted if he got across the line. I had no choice but to grab my hunter and take off at a sprint after him.

We bailed off into the cut running as fast as we could through knee deep snow and blow down timber. We caught up with the wounded elk and stayed above him trying to turn him down the hill. But the bull knew where that line was and kept coming towards us. At about fifteen yards I jerked my .44 magnum and thrust it into the hunter's hands! He quickly pulled up and dropped the elk dead. A mere twenty yards from the Yellowstone Park Line. We were standing between him and the line. It took several minutes for the other hunter to catch up and he was excited to find us looking over the 370-bull laying on the ground in front of him. Both of us, still gasping for air after that wild chase!

We took our time with pictures and butchering and we even packed the quarters two-hundred yards down the hill towards a trail. I was taking extra precautions to keep the bears from finding it. A good trick I always liked to use was to always keep plastic bags in my hunting pack for bloody tenderloins and back straps. On this morning, I didn't have any with me because a few days prior I had used them on another elk. I guess at the time having a whiskey when we got back to camp was more important to me than refilling my pack? Anyway, I flopped the valuable cuts of meat in my pack anyway and we left the kill sight headed for camp.

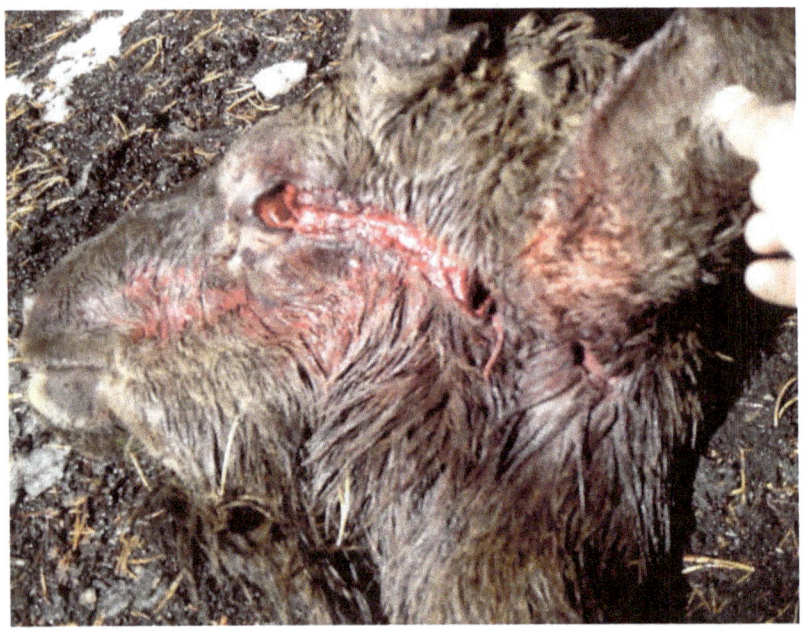

You can see the groove the bullet left down the side of the elk's face and the hole in his ear. Although morbid, it serves as a lesson of inches and the importance of accuracy.

Rather than return the way we came I opted to drop down the ridge to the trail I mentioned earlier. Eventually we hit the trail, followed it east and headed for camp. We were all soaked and our clothes were heavy with moisture from both the inside and out. We took several breaks on the hike back to camp. The meat I had in my pack was heavy enough that I was happy to take a few breathers. Especially, when there was something to sit on near the trail! After about two hours of trudging through the snow we wandered into camp.

As soon as we arrived, I saw the horses were in. I asked the wrangler to saddle a pack mule and be ready. I was going to grab dry clothes; saddle my horse and we'd go retrieve the elk. The wrangler was excited to go as he had mostly been stuck in camp. Eager to learn the ropes of guiding and to see some country he was ready when I was done with my costume change. He even had a riding horse tied next to my hitching rail. And seemed to be gimping a lot less than he was first thing that morning!

Soon I was saddled and we set out to back track our tracks from the morning. It was already warming up enough to begin the melting process of the snow. We had only made it about seventy-five yards out of camp when my heart sank. We came across a set of extremely large bear tracks that crossed our foot tracks from earlier. Tracks so big my size 13-pack boots didn't touch the heels or the toes of this bear's back paw print.

His tracks told the tale too. He circled two or three times and started tracking us backwards. He had paused to lick the logs I'd sat on where my blood-soaked pack had been. We continued on until we left the trail. Still following the bear's tracks which were following our tracks. Soon we crested the little ridge that enabled us to see into the cut where I'd stacked the quarters and antlers. I had a sinking feeling that the woods were about to get more crowded than I preferred. As we crested the rise and peered down, we spotted the bear standing atop the quarters. He was the largest grizzly I've ever laid eyes on. Brown to the point he looked like an Alaskan Coastal Brown. He didn't even look at us as we crested the ridge fifty-yards away.

The wrangler was behind me as I yelled "Hey bear!" But the bear just kept eating. I stepped off my horse and fired a round into the air and yelled again. But the bear just glared at us out of the corner of his eye, then turned to face us so he could watch us and continue eating. We yelled some more to no effect. He just started growling and swaying his head back and forth between bites. I looked back and saw by the look on the wrangler's face, he wasn't ready for a fight. To be honest, I wasn't either. Discretion being the better part of valor, I swung back into the saddle and we headed back to camp.

On our arrival back in camp I explained to my hunter what had happened. I told him his meat is gone but we will recover the antlers in a few days. He was gracious and thankful. Concerned about our safety and all that. A more deserving guy for a bull that big is hard to find! His dad however was not so level headed. And at that point in my life, I didn't have the patience or wisdom I believe I have now. After a short and blunt conversation, being told to go get the antlers himself or to shut his yap, the dad scampered off to his tent.

A few hours later the boss rolled into camp with his hunter and they had a bull down as well. But they had to leave theirs on the mountain too. Soon my hunter's dad cornered our young boss and gave him an earful. At the dinner table that night we were discussing the plan. My style of not forcing the issue, and being safe wasn't sitting well with the boss-man after getting his ass ate by the dad.

"Zach you gotta' go whippin' and spurring and war hooping and John WAYNE those cock suckers!" The boss exclaimed as he slapped a hand down on the table!

"You gotta' just bail off in there! That son-of-a-bitch will run off I guarantee it!" Flailing his arms around wildly.

And let me tell you I have "John Wayne'd" more bears than most people have ever seen. I know how to do it. And although I don't claim to be a bear biologist, I knew this bear meant business. None of that foresight mattered to anyone now, as such, a plan was hatched that the boss and I would go, "John Wayne" the bear first thing in the morning. Then I would help the boss get his bull when we returned from the, uh, "John Wayne'ing"

I was totally against the operation and protested right up to the point I was comfortable not making the situation worse. I had no choice but to agree to the idiocy, and the morning plans were set. We waited for daylight before departing to retrieve the antlers. Once we had sufficient light, the boss and I long trotted out of camp with nothing but our pistols. Like a couple of idiots.

I was riding Bubba mule and had a pack mule in tow while the boss took the lead. Soon we reached the point where the bear tracks departed the main trail and headed up to where I stashed the quarters.

The boss turned and whispered, "how far?"

In a louder than normal tone, "Two-hundred yards, in the cut. Can't miss it, there will be a giant-ass bear waiting." I replied sarcastically.

We let our mules walk the rest of the way in, all senses on high alert. Soon we reached the crest of the cut with the quarters and bear about fifty yards below us.

"Holy shit that's a huge bear!" he whispered to me as I pulled up next to him nodding in agreement.

Without another word the boss let out a blood curdling war hoop, and we spurred our mules in the belly to commence our charge down the hill at a full run.

The cut was maybe two-hundred feet across and fifty feet deep. It was full of four to six feet tall saplings and piss firs with a few assorted larger trees, and a lot more down timber.

At the time we killed the elk I thought it was a good place to hide the quarters. What I learned as a result of this experience is that hiding quarters in bear country isn't a good idea period! But in the event, you have no other choice, they need to be placed in the wide open where you can see them from a long ways away. Or better yet, poacher pack the whole she-bang out on the first try and you won't ever have to be in a situation such as this one!

Anyhow, we war hooped and made a hell of a racket as we plunged into the cut, thundering our way to the quarters and antlers. I was a horse length behind the boss as he slid his mule to a stop, leapt from the saddle and tied to a tree. I followed his lead and tied Bubba up. I still had my pack mule's lead rope in my hand and was headed for another tree to tie to when the boss marched off towards the quarters.

"Hey you cock sucker get out-a-here!!!" As he fired a round into the air intending to scare the bear away.

At the sound of the shot, my pack mule pulled back, so I had to regather him and tie him off. As I stepped out from behind my mules. I heard a shriek and the boss came running past me going the opposite direction with the bear in hot pursuit!

There are a few traumatic experiences in my life that have a mental picture, or snap shot in time, if-you-will, associated with it. And this is one. As the boss came running by, his belt buckle was eye level and his legs, one forward and one back in an excessively long stride. His arms were in the classic running position with his pistol in the hand that was up high. His chin was slightly up and he was screaming for me to shoot!

The bear was less than an arm's length from him when they raced past. It all happened so fast there was no time to shoot. It probably would have done more good to pistol whip him anyways? But none of that mattered because when they went by, the mules panicked and Bubba, true to his nature, tried to kick the bear with both hind feet. The problem was that I was between him and the bear! Perhaps he wasn't kicking at the bear and his timing was just perfect? Either way, it didn't matter much.

I didn't get the chance to see where the bear went because when Bubba kicked me, I became entangled in his legs and when he recoiled them, he sucked me underneath himself! Eventually, I was kicked out from under Bubba and launched under the pack mule. The pack mule, then trying to get out of the way stepped on my boot breaking several toes and two other bones higher in my foot.

I didn't feel it due to the adrenaline though and bounced to my feet. The boss and I somehow ended up back-to-back against a tree, between the mules, pistols at the ready. I took point and the bear had briefly retreated into the piss firs. He made a chuckling type of growling sound that was really eerie. The noise told us that the fight for the meat wasn't over as far as he was concerned. As the boss was reloading his spent cartridge, we suddenly heard the sharp snapping sounds of the bear popping his jaws. But we still couldn't see him.

Before the gun was reloaded the piss firs exploded as the bear made another charge. All that was visible was the tree tops violently shaking and swaying back and forth as the bear charged down the hill again. I thought I was ready but when the bear appeared, neither of us got a shot off due to the unbelievable speed the bear came by! He must have broken every stick in his path during the charge because it sounded like a freight train bearing down on us!

The bear continued past us and ran up on the hillside of the cut and turned and sat down like a dog atop a log. He was popping his jaws and swaying his head back and forth low to the ground. Growling and making that eerie chuckling and growling sound all the while.

The boss snapped his cylinder closed after replacing the one spent cartridge and we held our ground. By luck, in the heat of the battle we ended up right by the antlers which I had stashed against a tree about fifteen yards from the quarters. With the bear growling, and another charge seemingly imminent, the boss glanced down and says, "That's a hell of a big bull, man!"

All I could think to say was, "Thanks."

I reached and grabbed the head and antlers with one hand, pistol at the ready in the other. Swung them at the pack mule and they landed on his back awkwardly. I then took watch as the boss had a little "Judge" pistol, and those things are only good at being a boat anchor, while I had a .44. The boss put a hitch on the antlers quickly with a lash rope and we were ready to scram.

The trees I had my pack mule and Bubba tied too were arm's length apart. I jerked the pack mules lead, keeping the rope in my hand, and the same hand on the horn of my saddle. With my free hand I jerked Bubba's lead rope and he took off like a rocket.

I somehow managed to swing into the saddle, trick rider style as we took off at a dead run. Purely as passengers, those mules were quitting the country! We lit out of there like fat kids chasing an ice cream truck! The boss had a small jump on me and everything ran! Full speed! Getting the hell out of there!

As we ran, the boss yelled over his shoulder, "Don't fall off!"

As we ducked and dodged tree branches and low limbs I knew the pack mule would be better on his own so I pitched the lead rope back to him and watched as the tail of the rope perfectly looped around his neck and landed on top of the antlers! This was fantastic because now he wouldn't have to deal with a dragging line that he could step on. And it was just luck that put it there! We ran, and the mules negotiated in and out of trees and down logs until we exploded from the timber, took a 45-degree turn onto the trail and continued racing towards camp.

About a hundred-yards out of camp we got them pulled back into a trot. But there was no going any slower than that. With the reins tight, Bubba's head high, he fought the twisted wire snaffle bit. High stepping with his fronts, foam forming around his lips as we snorted up the trail towards safety. In a moment we came trotting into camp. The pack mule still following right on Bubba's heals. I'm not sure what we must have looked like, but by the look on everyone's faces in camp, they knew we had a hell of a wreck.

We both came to a sliding stop in the muddy ground around the hitching rails. Instantly, the boss was barking orders at the wrangler and cook. "Grab my rifle off my bunk and get the shotgun too!"

The cook and wrangler scampered off to follow orders. While the other wrangler walked up to Bubba who was still snorting at anything that moved while dancing around the hitching rail area. He stepped to the side as Bubba pranced out of the way and snagged the pack mule's lead rope.

"Here's your fuckin' antlers boys!" I said as they looked on, eyes still as wide as saucers.

By then the other wrangler was handing me a shotgun which I slung over my shoulder. The cook handed the boss his rifle. Then the wrangler handed me another pack mule and we gave the mules their heads and left camp at a trot.

The recovered head. The bears always tear up the side of their face it seems.

Up country, looking for the boss's bull we decided we weren't "John Wayne'ing" anything. He said he was just going to shoot a bear off the top of the carcass. Luckily, when we arrived at a glassing point a hundred yards out, the crows and ravens hadn't even found the elk yet!

We just rode in, got him packed and left easy as you please. It was quite refreshing! The whole time I knew my foot hurt, but I hadn't had time to give it much thought until now. As we walked down the steep canyon, leading our mules back to the main trail, I knew something was pretty wrong.

Back in camp after pulling my boot and socks off, the lower part of my foot was black and swollen. Luckily, I was tagged out so I hobbled around camp for three days resting before the end of the hunt when we would ride out to get the next set of hunters. I didn't bother going to the doctor because I knew that they wouldn't be much help. Or perhaps, the opposite of help had they wanted my foot in a cast. That would have stopped my season and put everyone in a bad way. So why bother? Especially when I figured I could walk okay if I just pointed my toe straight out, parallel with my shoulders. That kept my toes from flexing which was the cause of most of the pain. I guided the rest of the year with that broken foot.

Truth be told, camp was quiet the rest of the hunt and we didn't get into much of the details of what happened near the Park line with the hunters.

We did however call out via satellite phone and told the head bear guy at the Fish and Feathers what had happened and asked what we should do? The head guy back in those days was a pretty good guy. He told us, "If the bear is that bad just kill him... but not maliciously!" Which of course meant to not hunt him. And truth be told, my curiosity about that bear had been satisfied and I wanted no part of him! I didn't even care to see him again! Weeks later I did see him though, we glassed him on another carcass. Still fat as a pig and looking shiny and sound. That was one heck of a scary bear!

The Park Service liked to put a couple of unarmed, granola eating Rangers in the A-Frame cabin we rode past on our way in and out. Their purpose is to patrol the Park Line for any less than honest hunters who might not have the willingness to abide by the rules. It came to light later that they were in the area that day and heard all the commotion. Later, they went down to investigate, with their trusty bear spray. Word, was they had a heck of a run in with our bear. So, the Bear guy at the Fish and Feathers apparently knew of the Park Service's run in and that's why he said what he said.

After we glassed the bear on the carcass, I didn't see him again that season. Although, that might have been because I stopped frequenting the Park Line after that? And I had one particular mule who had sworn a vow to never return down that trail. No sense in poking the bear if you know what I mean!

From the day of the bear encounter forward, Bubba decided there needed to be some changes if he was going to continue being a riding donkey. And he was serious! Mostly, he was no longer willing to set foot on the trail that led to the place where that traumatic event took place. And there was no amount of convincing that could be done. He had quit the lower country all together. One day I even resorted to jumping on a hunter's mule, dallying Bubba's lead rope off and attempting to drag him down the trail. It didn't work and eventually we found him back in camp.

Not only that, but now every bush, stick, squirrel, chipmunk, grouse or anything else on the trail that moved, or that Bubba thought might move, became a life and death situation. Never mind balking and snorting. Bubba could jump, whirl and be going full speed the opposite direction if anything moved in his view. And he proved it so often he became nearly impossible to guide on. He was fried. Completely and totally ruined!

Hoping we hadn't ruined him completely; we gave him a few weeks off before trying again. But that was a wrap for him. Bubba ended up being demoted back to a pack mule and later sold to someone who doesn't go to the mountains. We hear he is excelling at being a town mule. He lopes around arenas smeared in show shine last I heard and the new owners love him.

As for the hunters, I have kept in touch with them on and off throughout the years. They returned for another hunt in that camp but I was working for a different outfit at the time. One night, in town we had a few drinks over dinner and once the Dad understood what all happened, he made it known how he felt. Several apologies and heartfelt thanks was good enough for me! I would hunt those guys again, any place and anytime! Great folks to be in camp with, minor miscommunications not withstanding!

Bluebells on the Thorofare Buttes in early July.

| 10 |

Surrounded on Hat Pass

Late in the afternoon, from a glassing point high above the Thorofare river valley floor, I sat with my binoculars in my face. I was looking up at a United Airlines 757 descending for its 7:00 pm arrival into Jackson Hole. I'd spent countless hours looking down from an airplane window at the mountains below. Longing to be horseback, where the world moved at three miles an hour. I enjoyed it enough that I had been using my vacation days to guide hunts for the last few years.

Now I was looking up longingly. Sick of smelling like I'd gone eight days without a shower. Tired of having sore feet and cold hands! Ready to be in a world that moved faster than a horse! The lure of on-demand heat and hot water were winning the battle inside my mind, I was ready to be done for the season.

Thus far, it had been a good season! I had filled out all but one hunter, and he had missed one. We had been safe, not much bear trouble. The weather had been holding out well with no snow yet. That kept the local elk around which kept the hunting good. Morale in camp had been good all year!

Never the less, by the time two solid months of hunting is drawing to a close, you're ready for a break. Regardless of how much you enjoy it, two months without modern amenities is a long time. But first, I had to finish off this last hunter. And we had one more day to do it assuming we didn't see anything this evening.

V7 on top of Deer Creek Pass.

As the sun sank below the western ridges, we retreated from our glassing point high in the rocks, near the tree line. Briskly, we walked back to our horses and led them down the steep mountainside. Once off the steep stuff, we mounted and headed for camp. As the horses walked the trail in the dimming light, I was day dreaming about dinner. Tonight, was prime rib night! Potatoes, gravy, beans, pie. One of the good dinners! And most were, as we had a fantastic cook that year.

As we rounded a bend in the trail the hair stood up on the back of my neck. The old camp was straight ahead. The same one I talked about in "The Tallest Bear I Ever Saw" chapter. As we approached the camp I looked as hard as I could into the growing shadows around the camp. Straining to pick up any movement through the rapidly darkening forest floor in the grey light of the evening.

I was especially keyed up because I was riding a horse that had been leased to the camp. And the company who leased these horses was pretty notorious. Don't get me wrong, if you ordered ten dude rides, they would always deliver ten very solid and safe dude horses. The problem was that outfitters usually ordered ten dude rides and five guide rides, for example. These folks would show up with eighteen horses.

"We just threw these three in as extras! No charge, of course!" They would say.

Extras? What kind of fools did they think we were? Actually, they knew precisely how big of fools we were because I worked for six different outfitters who used that company and they did it to everyone.

As it were, there was a stark contrast between the sleepy eyed, gentle dude rides and the fire breathing guide rides. The guide rides would give most amateur horsemen the vapors. But you could usually get around them if you expected them to be cold backed and need a good "topping off" every morning. There was one bay in particular that I had ridden for two or three years in a row. We called him "V7." V7 was the brand on his shoulder so he was easy to spot. He was a guide ride for several years and he was fine. Actually, a joy to ride. Having some semblance of wisdom at the time, I knew what would happen if I bragged on V7. So instead, I gripped about him! I would roll my eyes whenever the boss told me to ride him. Eventually, they figured it out and V7 was off to greener pastures in someone else's dude string. I kind of miss that bay!

As for the extras, the free ones? You better have your hammer cocked to get around them. And more often than not, you'd end up flying through the air and landing on your head several yards from where you thought your horse was supposed to be. Generally speaking, if you see your stirrups slap together above the saddle horn, you're going to get drilled into the ground in short order! It didn't take but one of those experiences for me to prefer to try to shave a wild cat's ass in a phone booth rather than throw my saddle on one of them.

Of course, those folks were just smarter than the outfitters. They knew that if they dropped off three extras, by this time next year they could lease those same three as guide rides. I never went to their ranch but I heard they ran around a thousand-head of horses! So, a fairly big outfit. I had guided with several of this ranch's ex-hands and every one of them was crazy. Very heavy handed on horses. All of them truly believed they were John Wayne. A few had even adopted his gait.

Anyhow, I wasn't sure what this lease horse would do if he saw a bear, but he had already tried to buck me off several times this season. So, I was ready. Both hands on the stiff leather reins, heels low, sitting ready for whatever was coming.

As we passed abeam the camp my hunter was ten yards in trail riding a little mule, we called Bubbles. Once we were most of the way past the old camp, I glanced back to check on my hunter. He was still there, about ten-yards back. That's when I caught movement in my peripheral vision. Towards the back of the camp, I saw a silhouette of a grizzly, with the classic hump, walking through the camp toward the old fire pit.

I briefly thought about mentioning it, but I decided against it as we were well out of harm's way, or so I thought? I turned to face forward and continue my daydream about dinner when I heard the loud fart that an equine is prone to as they tense up and do something strenuous.

"WHOA!!!" yelled the hunter as the thunder of hoof beats neared. I turned in time to see Bubbles at a full run! She had seen the bear and decided to quit the country and run for her life! Bubbles is a short, little grey appaloosa cross molly mule with short legs and a jug head. And she was moving like a fat girl headed to the buffet! A move I was unaware that she was fond of doing at the time.

Not having much time to do anything but watch, Bubble's stubby little legs brought her crashing right into the rear end of my horse, who was also very alarmed at the moment. The collision resulted in my horse panicking and starting to scatter off!

I yelled, "Don't fall off!" as the hunter's knee hit mine as Bubbles pushed by us on her way to camp.

My horse started hogging along next to Bubbles, trying to buck, but not having much talent, I held on and watched the hunter and Bubbles streak past! As my horse crow hopped it caught me off guard briefly and I lost a stirrup, but was able to find it quickly and get my foot back in place.

I looked up in the commotion to see Bubbles running across the picket meadow of the old camp headed toward the creek. The hunter was yelling hysterically, both arms out stretched like he was on the bow of the Titanic in the movie.

"DON"T GET OFF THERE'S A BEAR RIGHT BEHIND US!!!" I screamed.

Instantly, the hunter got his arms down and got a hold of the saddle horn, not bothering with the reins. Purely a passenger! About then my horse was done crow hopping so I trotted alongside the hunter and reached for a rein. The plan was to pull Bubbles up alongside me and start turning away if she didn't give up her running. But my horse didn't like my idea and began crow hopping and hogging off alongside Bubbles once more.

The hot-mess express continued across the length of the picket meadow and soon we were at the creek crossing. With several hundred yards of river rock for footing. Once on the rocks both Bubbles and my horse quit acting like idiots. We crossed the creek and continued down the trail towards camp. As darkness enveloped us, we were still chuckling about what that bear must have been thinking as he watched us cross the meadow. Soon we were back in camp still laughing about our evening ride.

The following morning broke cold and snowy. We had drifted off to sleep the night prior to the sound of wolves howling up and down the drainage. Our luck with the weather had officially run out and the wolves just made the hunting a lot harder. Low clouds hung in the valley floors limiting visibility to a few hundred yards. The clouds obscured the hillsides about two-hundred vertical feet up as snow lightly spit from the low overcast. It was grey and gloomy. Cold and miserable!

Due to the weather my plans for a morning hunt in the high elevations were dashed, so we opted to return up river. As we neared the creek crossing where our livestock ended their hysteria the previous evening, a bull appeared through the snow and fog. Maybe a hundred feet off the valley floor, about two hundred yards ahead.

I jumped from my horse and tied up as the hunter jumped from his. I grabbed his led rope as he unscabbarded his rifle and took aim. BANG! And the bull disappeared into the grey snowy morning.

After the shot, it began snowing so hard binoculars were useless, as were range finders. In fact, the snow was falling at such a rate that when we went to look for blood there must have been twenty head of elk there that we never saw! We spent the rest of the morning looking for any sign of blood or an elk who was walking funny, dragging a leg, anything abnormal. To no avail however so we headed back to camp to warm up and dry out.

Once back in camp the hunter decided he wanted to be done. Tomorrow was ride out day and he wanted to be rested. But as the day went on the sky began to clear. Soon we regained our visibility and the snow had quit. Blue sky was cracking through the high overcast and my spirits were raised.

Don't get me wrong, a wounded bull is a dead bull in this country. Whether by the hunter's choice or otherwise, once we have one wounded the hunt is officially over. We spend the remainder of the trip tracking, or we call the hunt completely. Very few hunters protest when that sort of thing happens, but occasionally they do. When that happens, the guide is obligated to keep the clients happy. So, we go on many, long and strenuous hikes if you know what I mean? It's weird too, because I've never been able to spot another bull after a hunter wounds one. And we hunt really, really hard!

That wasn't the case here though. I was convinced it was a clean miss. And I was watching that barrel swing back and forth like a flag in a stiff breeze when the hunter was trying to aim! It looked like the top of a small tree when a bear has an itch! Plus, I'd done all my due diligence with the tracking. Clean misses are okay! It happens.

After some convincing in camp, I talked the hunter into one last "Hail Mary" hunt. We would ride the main trail out of camp up to the pass, then loop back around checking the basins as we descended a different ridge. It's a solid hunt that I have killed close to ten bulls on over the years.

He agreed and about 3:00pm we were close to summiting the pass. We had ridden up from the bottom through mostly green timber. The fresh snow had weighted down limbs and branches into the trail. As we traveled there was no hiding from it, you just got showered with snow as you or your horse bumped the limbs causing the snow to fall all over you.

By this time in history the bear population was so dense we would see at least two a day, per group. And the bears knew we were killing elk and leaving gut piles. So, they had been tracking us everywhere we went. At this point, most of the guides had gone to shotguns for protection and I was no different. I still kept my .44 on a cross draw on my hip, more of a weapon for a wrestling match rather than a primary self-defense tool. Even the crustiest guides who were the last to finally carry pistols had turned to a sawed-off shotgun for protection.

Riding horseback through a blizzard in the Thorofare. "Go guiding!" They said. "It's fun!" They said.

I carried my shotgun in a short scabbard that I attached to my saddle horn and the front cinch. That way, with the folding stock folded I could draw it like a pistol. A giant pistol, but you get the idea.

My saddle bags were frozen, and everything from the cantle to the saddle horn was solid snow that had crusted over and refroze. The top of my scabbard was so full of snow I could barely see the handle of my street sweeper.

Once on the summit, we would leave the main trail and circle the base of a cliff along a steep hillside. Then cross a solid rock slide and pop back out on the ridge. It's a treacherous eight-hundred yards, but after that it's a nice easy descent that you can ride the majority of the way to the bottom.

As we arrived at the base of the cliff face the snow had crusted off on the top, making what amounts to a snow cliff on either side of the narrow ridgeline. As we got close to the cliff, I spotted a sow grizzly with three yearling cubs feeding on the rockslide a few hundred yards ahead. Basically, blocking our intended path.

"Oops! We can't go any farther until they clear out" I thought.

And since there was a lot of good elk country below and behind us, I decided to tie our horses in a short stand of white bark pines on the ridge top. At that point the bear was just slowing us down some, but not hurting anything so I didn't see the sense in raising hell and running them off.

Soon we were sitting in the snow glassing down country. Sitting about ten-feet below our horses, still waiting for the sow and cubs to move off the rockslide. The sow had the trail blocked. No way around her with the frozen conditions. Riding up and "John Wayne'ing" her, or shooting would have ruined the hunt so we decided to be patient.

As we sat on the ridge, as mentioned, in front and behind us were snow cornices. Basically cliffs. In front the bear had us blocked, so really the only way we could have gone was the way we came in.

During our glassing session and frequent looks to keep track of the sow and cubs just a few hundred yards from us I happened to look back the way we came. I was astonished to see another grizzly bear a hundred yards away, walking up our tracks, right towards us!

My hunter chambered a round and I ran the ten-feet back to the horses to retrieve my 12-gauge riot gun. I pulled it from the scabbard and it came out in a puff of snow. Quickly, I ran my hands over it to knock off the snow that was encrusted over nearly the whole upper half of the gun.

As I returned to the hunter, I cranked a shell in. The bear still hadn't seen us and was about twenty yards now. I yelled, "Hey bear!" and he paused, looked at us, looked at the horses, and then peered over the cornice. Then back at us, and began walking towards us again, seemingly unfazed.

I yelled some more, but he kept walking. He would stop, look over the cornice then look back at us, then keep walking up the trail. At that point I decided to unfold the stock on the shotgun. Believing at the time that accuracy was going to help. Unfortunately, I found the release button frozen from snow that had fallen off trees that hung over the trail on the way up. I couldn't get it open and when the bear reached fifteen yards, I gave up and stayed ready to shoot.

I instructed the hunter to back up slowly, shoulder to shoulder with me. Be ready to shoot but don't shoot unless I shoot first. Soon we were at our horses who were also watching the bear.

The bear hadn't made an aggressive move. He was just walking and that's the only reason I let the situation deteriorate that far. Remembering we were now pinned down with bears on two sides of us and cliffs on the other two. I told the hunter if he gets much closer, we're going to have to shoot him. But like I said, don't shoot unless I do, and when I do, make yours count.

Before long the bear was standing twenty feet away with a confused look on his face. Completely nonaggressive however. The hunter asked how much closer we were going to let the bear get. As if it was on que, the bear turned his head, yawned, and then continued walking. Now right on the lip of the cornice, clearly giving us as much room as he could.

"Did that son-of-a-bitch just yawn at us?" The hunter asked in disbelief.

"Yeah, and I don't think we can shoot a bear who yawned at us?" I said.

"I agree, I guess?"

And just like that, the bear walked ten-feet away from us, right on by and headed for the rockslide. I'll never forget looking in that bear's eye as he passed, with my shotgun aimed right at his face. He just casually got around us, then returned to the trail and disappeared behind some rocks that lead to the rock slide never looking back. Those bears have no respect, I tell you!

After that we decided to return to camp the way we came. So, two hunters of mine left that year without an elk, but at least one had a pretty neat bear encounter!

The horse pasture during a blizzard. There is a bear squatting to go to the bathroom in the distance. Near the green trees.

| 11 |

Swayback Horses

It was a bluebird afternoon with no wind as I reigned in my good grey horse, Klondike, on the summit of Deer Creek Pass. The birds were chirping, and the chipmunks were chipping as the last of the summer wildflowers, with their red, blue and purple colors glistened in the sun. I stepped off and tied my string to the piece of bailing twine I had on my saddle in preparation for the long walk off the notorious pass. My right hip flexors were sore so I kicked my leg a little to shake it out. When I did that, I noticed my left knee had a twinge as well, deep in the joint. I sighed in anticipation of the pounding my joints were about to take on the long descent. A descent that I'd made roughly ten times a year for the last, nearly ten years.

I had been guiding for just a few years now, or so I thought. I struck out at what I felt was a good pace but soon noticed all the other guides were out walking me. All but one, and that was the old guide who was on his twenty-fifth consecutive season that year! They were leaving me in the dust and that had never happened before! Man, I felt old!

Anyway, we were coming out after camp set and headed to town for the first load of hunters. After watching all the young bucks walk faster than me off the pass, I was glad to not be coming back for the archery. I had about twelve days off and was taking the family on a quick vacation!

Larry and I in the high country after a big snow. I stand 6'2" and this picture really shows Larry's size.

That summer had been a long one. I'd run a lot of miles getting some of my older horses in shape for the fall. My best, and oldest horse was a big feather legged black gelding named Larry. Best we could figure, he was in his mid-thirties. 17.5 hands of grade, but predominantly Percheron. He wore a size 5 shoe and was as gentle as they come.

A quick author's note, I don't care if 17 ½ hands isn't a real measurement and you really shouldn't either. We all know what a hand measurement is. Larry was 17 ½ of them. A big horse and that's the point! What is not the point is understanding when horse people change their math just because a horse hits a certain size. Even if it sends a few of you horse Nazis screaming for the hills. You're just going to have to deal with this author's lack of equine prowess!

Anyhow, I'd known Larry for years as he was the boss horse of the herd in this particular camp. He was usually tasked with taking fat hunters in and out. A few years prior, he had lost a step so we gave him lighter duty as he was prone to a sore back after one particular fat hunter sat on him like he was sitting on a chair for twenty-five miles. It really did a number on his kidneys and you had to really watch him because he would get sore quick with the wrong person on him.

We had the one guide who had been in the camp twenty-five consecutive seasons who said Larry had been there the whole time. The story was that Larry was a bucking horse in the rodeo and belonged to a famous bareback rider from Kaycee, Wyoming who bears the same name. Once he came to the camp he was broke to ride and used as a guide ride for several years before earning the trust of the outfit. Once that trust was earned, he started taking dudes. And as a big horse, he was always stuck with big hunters.

A few seasons prior to this story we noticed a big tumor that appeared to be cancerous on the head of his penis. About the size of a man's fist. When the boss saw it, he mentioned that Larry was going to the kill pen at the auction at the end of the season. That didn't sit well with me but I understand the thin margins these outfitters are forced to operate with. But to just dispose of such a good horse seemed like a piss poor thing to do to me? Larry had earned a better demise than that.

Luckily, I had pasture space and I offered the boss $500 for him. Which was roughly market price per pound at the time, less the diesel to drive him up to Billings. I had been keeping an eye on the old horse and watching that tumor. I admit to having zero medical knowledge but my gut said that the tumor wasn't cancer. And I noticed it was not interfering with his urine stream. So why not?

Larry, Cricket and Klondike on a late season hunt.

A deal was eventually struck where I bought another horse from the outfitter for $500 and Larry came for free. I figured I'd be the lightest rider he had carried in a decade and I ought to get a year or two of light use out of him before we had to put him down. Occasionally, he could take my wife on some day trips as well. And she's certainly lighter than any hunter! The point was, he'd be mostly retired and could hang out in my pasture. So, at the end of the season, I loaded a big roan called Cricket and Larry into my trailer and brought them to my house.

Before we knew it Thanksgiving was upon us and my parents had come to town for a visit. My dad is a retired veterinarian so we went to the barn and gave Larry a good look. To my surprise, Dad agreed with what my gut told me so we hatched a plan to knock the big guy down and cut that tumor off his penis. Soon dad had scrounged up some equipment and drugs from the local vet who he'd made buddies with and we were ready!

We pulled a weight tape around the big goliath but it was about ten inches too short to get a good weight! And the tape maxed out at seventeen-hundred pounds! So, dad made an educated guess and we knocked the horse out. For those that don't know, knocking a horse out can be dangerous for the horse if a guy doesn't know what he's doing. And I wouldn't say that I know what I'm doing! But Dad sure does!

First thing, when you inject them, the horse will sway back and forth a bit, then take a few steps backwards, sit down like a dog and then flop over on their side. More than one horse has killed themselves by being knocked out and flopping over. Their head can hit the ground hard enough to kill them. So, whoever your "Shank man" or the guy holding the lead rope is, he needs to be paying attention and keep that lead rope tight. I nominated my dad for the chore because, well he's the vet and who better to keep the horse safe?

We got through the process of getting Larry knocked out safely. But as he sat down like a dog, something went flying through the air and landed ten feet away! It was the majority of the tumor! Dad was focused on his job on the lead rope and didn't see it, but everyone else did based on the, "Whoa! You see that!" and the "Holy crap(s)!" that erupted from everyone!

My job, as nominated by the vet was to approach from the back of the horse, lay across his body and get both hands on the penis to keep the horse from retracting it back inside the sheath. One of my buddies who's a good hand with horses, and also happened to be a biologist with the Game and Fish was the guy nominated to stay on the horse's head in case we miss-figured the dosage of the anesthesia. Dad was our knife and suture man for obvious reasons. And my wife was our nurse who was tasked with handing the doc whatever he needed. Since she's a nurse in real life, it just made sense. And finally, my mother-in-law was nominated to run herd on my boy who was just old enough to be walking around getting into mischief! It was a family event!

Larry and my wife, Jessi ready to go for a spring ride. She has to use the fender of the trailer to get on.

Anyway, as we got Larry laid down and his massive head situated on a dog bed to ensure he wouldn't damage any nerves in his face while he was immobilized. Dad fished our prize out of the sheath. I grabbed and squeezed as hard as I could with both hands while laying over Larry. And let me tell you, whatever muscle horses have to retract their penis back into the sheath, it is strong! I suppose the self-preservation of one's genitals isn't exclusive to humans?

Soon the nurse handed off the scalpel and Dad cut the remaining tumor off. Then began suturing Larry up. When we had nearly completed the job, we had a quick discussion of whether or not we should put in one more suture. However, we decided to leave it open so it could drain. In less than an hour we were done and not long after that, Larry was up and at-em! About a week later I received a bill from the vet for $350. And I honestly don't recall if I ever paid it!

By the time winter was over and spring rolled around I noticed the tumor was coming back. Coincidently, it was back at the exact location where we had decided to not suture. Dad came to town that April and we did it again except this time we used a branding iron to cauterize the area around where we cut the tumor off.

"Like light brown toast! Light brown toast! Not burnt toast!" Dad kept saying as he dabbed the red-hot iron on Larry's penis. If watching smoke rise off a penis while listening to the sizzling and smelling the burning flesh won't make a guy cringe nothing will! Anyway, now you have something to think about in the future whenever you wonder about horse penises or you hear someone say, "Light brown toast." You're welcome!

And yes, I got another bill from the vet for another $350. I believe I paid that one but disputed the first due to the defective surgery on the first try?

The second surgery ended up being the ticket and the tumor never came back! I had a good horse, albeit slow, but Larry was the embodiment of the cliché, "There might be other horses as good, but none are better." A "Once in a lifetime horse." A babysitter! He loved kids and would meet my young son at the gate every day when he got home from school.

For the next couple of years Larry was on light duty. He went on some summer trips, he duded my wife around the mountains some and he even went on a couple close in, late sheep hunts. He was doing good and seemed to be enjoying his job but I hadn't taken him into the Thorofare since I owned him.

This particular summer I had Larry in the best shape I'd ever seen him in. He was slick and shiny and appeared to be half his age. We had been a hundred or two miles just scouting and enjoying the mountains that summer so one day while we were in Boulder Basin, I asked him if he wanted to go to camp. And I'm not a weirdo, horse whispering, skinny jeans and helmet type of horseperson, but I believe he wanted to go by the nudges he was giving me. So I decided to try it. I planned to take him in naked and give him two days off before using him. He had certainly earned it!

So, when the hunters arrived, I tied Larry on my string and watched him close as we headed to camp. Larry knew where we were going the whole time and he stomped right into camp without a bobble.

After the two days off I saddled him up and we went down country to find some elk. Larry was excited! He stomped out of camp like a colt! About a mile down river, we ran smack into a bear at twenty yards. The bear didn't want to leave the trail, because they have no reason to fear humans. I smooched Larry up intending to get inside the bear's pressure zone but Larry pinned his ears down and took off like a shot! We chased the bear and gaining on him at first! His front legs overextending like he was going to strike that bear!

Meanwhile, I was hanging on for dear life trying to slow him down. Which eventually we did and returned to the trail to find my hunter laughing!

"You're over thirty man! You shouldn't be chasing bears!" I said to Larry while patting him on the neck.

That night as we returned to camp Larry stopped and looked up the hill. I smooched him forward and he took another step then stopped, looking up the hill again. So, I let the reins slack as I looked and soon three wolves trotted out into the meadow a hundred yards above us. Once they passed, we headed for camp. That horse sure knew the mountains!

Prior to all that, while on the vacation I talked about earlier, my phone began to ring. On the caller ID I knew it was a satellite phone based on the excessively long set of numbers showing on my smartphone. It's never good to hear from camp on the satellite phone in the middle of a hunt! There's no reason to call unless something bad was happening.

The black wolf Larry spotted.

Apprehensively, I answered. The boss was on the other end as expected, and he explained that one of our new guide's had quit. Adding that since I was the only one in town and with access to a phone, I was nominated as the new head of the Human Resources Department for the camp. My first task was to find us another guide.

Historically, finding guides was easy, and finding good guides was just barely harder than that. However, times change as they say! Under the Trump Economy the oil patch was back in full production, as such most of our local guiding aged males were working seven days on and seven days off on an oil rig somewhere between Wattenenberg, Colorado and the Bakken, making the big bucks. And this was the case this year.

After some thought I remembered I knew a young kid. Well, I knew his girlfriend. And had seen him around a bit. A horse hand, and all he wanted to do was cowboy. I thought I remembered him saying something about guiding last season in a camp I used to work in but for whatever reason, it hadn't worked out.

After a few messages on Facebook, I got a hold of his girlfriend. She gave me his phone number and I gave him a call. He confirmed to me that he worked half a season in one of the camps farther down the Thorofare River. He voiced some displeasure with the outfitter and I agreed, having firsthand knowledge of the guy. Naturally, he inflated his experience guiding, which I fully expected. Wouldn't trust a guide who didn't!

As we talked, I soon decided he was our guy and I didn't give the kid a choice, I told him he was coming with us because we were in a pinch. He laughed as he agreed, told me he would quit his job and the plan was set.

A few days later the family and I rolled back into Cody with just one day before we had to start the first rifle hunt of the year. Remembering my first few trips to the mountains, I went to the Kid's house to make sure he hadn't flaked out on us.

Being the nice guy that I am I offered as much advice as I could to the youngster. As we went through some of his gear, I could see he was a little short on some things. So, I decided to help. We loaded up in my pickup and headed for the local sporting goods store. Once that was done, I gave him a coat and a few other hand-me-downs. They still worked well but I didn't use them anymore. You see, now-a-days all the cool kids wear incredibly expensive camo gear sold out of California!

I also took the opportunity to explain "Huntin' camp math" when he bummed a dip from me. Huntin' camp math goes like this, if you chew a can of Copenhagen a day, and you're going on an eight-day hunt, how many cans do you need? To which the correct answer is anything over ten! Not eight! What if a horse yanks on your reins when you are riding with an open can in your hand? What if you win a fight with a bear and need some extra to calm down? What if you lose a can?

Anyway, huntin' camp math is critically important to a successful and pleasurable time in the mountains and it applies specifically to chew, smokes and whiskey. Sometimes batteries as well? Anyway, I didn't want him bumming off me in camp. So, I gave him the speech! When we were done, I told him I'd pick him up at 4:00 am the next morning and to come with grit teeth!

The kid really was a good horse hand and the pack in was uneventful. That evening in camp we gave him the one-on-one hunter. Then we decided to send him into a side draw just outside of camp. He certainly wouldn't get lost there! It was great elk country, and it would build some confidence.

This is actually quite common for new guides who don't know the country. Since we ride out of camp in the dark, and they don't know any of the trails, it's a no brainer to send them to an easy spot. Let it get light so they can get their bearings, and in no time at all they'll be functioning quite well.

The evening of the first day I returned to camp with my two hunters and asked how it went with him. He told me of three big bulls on a ridge across the canyon that he thought we could kill if he knew how to get up there. Well, I just so happened to have two hunters, and a willingness to share my knowledge of the trail! So, we planned to ride out in the morning to what I figured was the ridge he was talking about.

Rex and Winchester poacher packing an elk back to camp.

The following morning was cold and snowy. I kneaded at my frozen reins as I steered my horse off the main trail about a mile upstream from camp. As we ducked into the trees to pick up the partially hidden outfitter trail, I stole a glance back at my hunters and the kid and his hunter. They all seemed fine. It had snowed about a foot the previous night, so all the trails were invisible due to the fresh blanket of powder.

That didn't matter to the old riding horse I had that day though. We called him Rex and he was almost as big as Larry. He had more experience on those trails than me and as soon as I bumped the reins he knew exactly where to go. Don't ever let someone tell you horses aren't smart. Those old mountain horses know more than we do. And they know trails we don't. All it takes is some trust and patience and they will show you.

We periodically stopped as we ascended the ridge to let the horses catch their breath. It was brutal traveling conditions for the livestock as the snow was getting deeper the higher we climbed. Rex had it especially bad because he was breaking trail in the deep snow so we took it easy on them and just eased our way up the ridge.

As we approached the top of the ridge, a few far off bugles sounded. So, we stopped just shy of the crest of the ridge and tied up in some short white bark pine trees alongside the trail. The snow was thigh high as we trudged our way to the ridge to peer over.

After a good long look and a lot of discussion with the kid we decided we were one ridge too early, so we headed back to the horses, remounted and cut cross country as we traversed the high subalpine bowl. Now the snow was deep enough that our boots and stirrups were dragging as the horses walked. I estimated our elevation to be around 10,000. It was a clear, calm morning as the sun began to top the rugged ridges to the east, with the temperature hovering near twenty degrees Fahrenheit.

We all rode in silence as the horses made their way through the deep snow to the other side of the ridge. Soon we were tying up in another short stand of white bark pines. Almost immediately after peaking over the ridge we spotted a bear working the same hillside we were on. We kept an eye on him as he was just a few hundred yards below us.

There were elk tracks in the snow wherever we glassed and soon the kid had spotted a bull. Within minutes we were all looking at a very nice elk at four-hundred yards. He was fast asleep, laying on a short knob facing down the hill. It was difficult to tell exactly how big he was because the bull wasn't moving. After a good long look, and going solely off of main beam length we all agreed he was definitely a shooter.

Not that it mattered now, but the kid realized that we were still one ridge over from where he'd seen the elk the day previous. And when we looked, that ridge was covered with hundreds of elk. All staging for the last big climb before they would leave the Thorofare on their migration to the low country for the winter. Just a quick scan of the skyline revealed over twenty respectable, branch antlered bulls and more cows than you could shake a stick at. And, in the time of the grossly mismanaged predators, alarmingly few calves.

A bird in the hand is better than two in the bush so we decided this bull needed shot first. And since the kid was the one who spotted him, it was his hunter's bull to shoot. We began looking around for a good firing position, a rest or anything to help. The hunter claimed to be comfortable taking a four-hundred yard shot and began doping his scope.

The kid was like I used to be. In a hurry and wanting his hunter to shoot right away. I held my hand up to signal him to shut up, and he did. The bull was unaware of our presence, we could use the time to make sure we were going to make a good shot. It was also the hunter's first elk hunt and hopefully first elk. So, we needed to get it right.

Our movement had to be limited due to the open terrain we were in, not to mention there were five of us. Not having a rest close by, I began digging a hole in the snow with my hands. Soon the kid figured out what I was doing and joined. Before long we had a seat and a place for the hunter's feet, with a backpack to rest his gun on. He crawled in and got steady.

With the clear blue sky above, and a few hundred elk on the ridgeline in the distance, and not a breath of wind between us and the target, it was go-time! We soon noticed the hunter's breathing has increased as he got the bull in his scope.

"Stop!" I whispered. "Just look at him through your scope. We have time."

The hunter did, and as his breathing relaxed, I told him to dry fire a few times until he was comfortable. Which he did once. He gave me a thumbs up so we had him to chamber a round. I was shoulder to shoulder with him and this time couldn't detect a change in his breathing.

"Okay, whenever you're ready, aim small, miss small, follow your shot through" I whispered.

The .338 roared to life as we watched through our binoculars. The vapor trail streaked across the cut and struck the bull in what appeared to be the brainstem! The bull's head tipped forward, sticking his nose deep in the snow and he didn't move again.

As we were watching just after the shot, I peeked out from behind my Swarovski Binoculars to see that bear standing there, looking at us from twenty yards! With all the excitement of the elk we had completely forgotten about that damn bear!

I jumped up and yelled at him, but to our dismay the bear whirled and headed right toward the elk. I don't think he knew the elk was there, he was just getting away from us? His chosen direction was going to be a problem however.

We all jumped to our feet and ran, as best we could in the deep snow, for the horses. Once mounted, we trotted down the ridgeline paralleling the bear's course, from a few hundred yards above. Once we hit the spine of the knob our elk was on, we pointed the horses and headed straight down. Like a fat kid on a seesaw, we descended the ridge to get in front of the bear. Who gave us a confused look, then opted to just sit down like a dog in the snow and watch us.

We tied up near the elk, with the bear still watching from a hundred yards. He seemed content to just sit in the sun, right out in the open and wait for us to do whatever we were going to do.

Once we arrived at the bull, we realized he was still breathing. Badly hurt, we figured he would expire on his own shortly. While we waited, we got our gear ready to butcher and made sure the hunters had their guns loaded and were watching Mr. Bear.

The bear, waiting his turn while we worked on the carcass.

As we discussed the situation someone saw the kid had a long, "Arkansas toothpick" style knife on his belt. It was then somehow decided that stabbing the elk in the heart would be a decent course of action. Hey, it sounded reasonable at the time? With the hunters returning to bear patrol at my insistence, I put a foot on the bull's main beam, between the G3 and the royal. The other foot bracing for balance. One hand on the antler that was in the air, and with the other I pulled a front leg up towards the bull's head.

I gave the kid a nod and he dropped to a knee and began sinking his knife into the bull's chest being careful to miss the ribs. As the knife sliced into the bull, the bull who we thought was paralyzed suddenly was not paralyzed! He lunged forward trying to regain his feet and lift his head.

Before I knew it, I was standing between the elk's antlers as the bull yanked his foot out of my hand and somehow in the struggle had gotten his antler out from underneath my boot. I had no choice but to get a hold of both antlers. As the bull struggled, we only made it a few yards before I was slammed, back first into a big, old growth tree. Holding onto the antlers with all my might, I was stuck between the bull's antlers and a tree. I knew letting go of one of the antlers would most likely result in me being impaled somewhere on my body. Knowing I had no options, I just held on as the bull feebly thrashed around.

I freely admit that the thrashing bull was pretty feeble. He was badly wounded and weak. But let me tell you from personal experience, even a feebly thrashing bull is scary when you find yourself stuck between his antlers and a tree and you're on the low ground!

About then the hunter showed up, rifle in hand and put a round into the bull's chest from a broadside angle, with me between the horns and the tree, with the bull's nose right beside my knee. The bull struggled a bit more and flopped on his side as I made my escape. Jumping as far as I could to get away.

I bounced back to my feet after making my escape and it was all over. The bull was laying on his side, with the kid's knife still stuck in his side up to the handle, covered in blood. My hunters' eyes were still wide as saucers. So, I asked them to get back to bear patrol with a nervous laugh and thanked the other hunter for saving my life!

Not long after we had the elk caped and quartered and poacher packed. I gave the kid directions on how to hit an easier trail on the way down and sent them on their way.

The "Kid," his Hunter and the bull. Note the blood in the snow and the disrupted snow from when the bull tried to get up.

As we rode back up to the ridge, we passed the bear who was still sitting there in the open waiting for us to finish. I've had a few bears do this and I don't mind bears who are patient! I'm sure he claimed the gut pile after we left and had a good winter.

That particular bull ended up scoring over 360 inches. He was the Wyoming Outfitters and Guide Association's Typical Bull of the Year that year. That's pretty darn good for your first bull!

Meanwhile, my hunters and I rolled around to the next ridge to see if any elk were left. There wasn't. In fact, we tried to hunt it but we ran into four different bears all looking for where the gunshots came from. That made for six different bears in that area in just a few hours!

My two hunters were brothers from the upper Midwest. Roughly, late sixties or early seventies. They had been to the camp before but hunted with a different guide. Anyway, after wading through a slew of bears we thought it was a good idea to quit the country and go find some virgin ground.

That night we returned to camp for taco night. Taco night had become my favorite dinner during that time as the cook we had for the last two years couldn't boil water without screwing it up! We had often resorted to tabasco, horse radish or cayenne pepper to get some flavor in the meals. She was too busy chain-smoking cigarettes, ducking off to smoke her reefer, then washing it all down with a bunch of whiskey to be bothered with menial details like tasty food.

That's not at all a stretch either. We ended up putting horseradish on almost everything she made just to get some flavor. On top of it not being good food, she was also famous for not making enough food or cleaning up too fast before everyone was done eating. There isn't much worse than working your butt off all day and getting back to camp in the dark to find very little food left, and it be cold! Or have to have granola bars and apples for dinner!

Manners matter, and I'm a firm believer in those ethics. However, manners are the first thing to go when people are hungry. It didn't take many occasions of being short on food before the guides started piling into the food line with the hunters. Rather than waiting until all the hunters had their food before going through the line, which is the mannerly and ethical thing to do. We all figured if a paying customer complained that would hold more weight with the outfitter than if we did? Regardless, the problem persisted as long as she was in camp.

When I heard she hired on for the second year I did offer my unsolicited opinion to the outfitter. To no avail however. I even offered him three other names of cooks in desperation but he wasn't interested. The cook's secret weapon was that she was married to one of the wranglers. So, if you fired one, you lost two. I get the logic, I guess? Anyway, tacos were easy! Dump a pack of seasoning in some burger! How hard is that?

That evening after dinner we were all sleeping when the cracks of thunder sounded through the canyon. We went to have a look and thunder clapped every minute or so while heavy snow fell at a rate that was accumulating about a foot an hour. Thunder snow is a rare weather phenomenon and it was cool to see it in the woods! The old guide and I thought it was cool anyway, everyone else stayed in bed! When we returned to our tent, we shook the snow off the roof and dosed off for the night.

We awoke before daylight to a crack that sounded like a gunshot. We went to investigate and as we stepped out of the tent, we found ourselves standing in snow that was above the knee! We went back in the tent and carefully shook the snow off to prevent a collapse. Then went to assess the rest of camp. The tack tent ridge poll had snapped under the tremendous weight of the snow, collapsing the entire tent. One hunter tent had a side rail suffer the same fate, we put a temporary fix on that and then went to the 18x32 dining tent and started carefully shaking the snow off of that.

Luckily, the dining tent held as we got the snow off. If that would have collapsed, we would have had a heck of a time getting it fixed because of all the essential items located in the tent, as well as its size.

Both hunters and guides helping to Stock up on firewood after the storm. No mechanical equipment is permitted in the wilderness. All trees are fell and all wood is cut with a cross-cut saw.

The boss quickly recognized the situation and called for all hands-on deck. It was decided that no one was hunting that day and we all were going to secure the camp and then cut firewood. And that's what we did all day. When we shook the snow off the tents the snow berms got so tall, they would cave in the four-foot sidewalls of the tents. Which forced us to shovel out a path around the tents as soon as we shook off the roofs. With eleven tents in camp, and only two small shovels, it was a big job.

Everyone chipped in and helped though! All the employees, and hunters worked all day to get the camp safe and secure. Everyone except one father-son team of hunters who were being guided by another one of our newer guides to the camp. Those two sat in their tent and burned wood all day. Only appearing when it was meal time so they could eat and complain about the snow!

A view of the collapsed tack tent after the "Snowpocalypse event."

The only thing we knew for sure was unless the weather improved dramatically, we weren't going to make it over Deer Creek Pass. It seems nearly every time it snows in the Thorofare there's talk of riding to Jackson Hole, some seventy miles west. It's been done before, and will be done in the future, I'm sure! But this was the first time I wondered if we actually would have to go that way?

And what a mess if we did! Heading to Jackson would be a two-day trip at a minimum. Then, once you're at the trailhead you don't have any feed for the livestock, trucks, trailers or even corrals that you can count on for that matter. With Yellowstone closed for the winter, whoever was coming with trucks and trailers was looking at a seven-hour drive, too! One way!

A few days after the "snowpocalypse" event it had warmed up slightly and the snow was slowly melting off. We were all getting antsy to get back to chasing elk. There was still enough snow on the ridges that I knew it would be slim pickins' up there, so I resigned myself to the river bottoms in the never-ending quest for some elk.

The big scary snowman!

Generally speaking, upriver is best in this camp. Mainly because there's five or ten times the available country to hunt. And that's usually the emphasis. However, this snow closed down the country way up river because the resident elk had migrated out for easier feeding conditions. The main migration trail goes up a side canyon about half way up river. So, we were pretty limited on where we could go. Never-the-less, we tried upcountry.

There had been a local camp at the upper end of the horse pasture, above camp for the first ten days of the season but they had pulled out just after it quit snowing. Certainly not because they were weak hearted, they had been coming in for years and were a salty bunch of hands.

One evening while heading back to camp we rode by where their camp had been. I was riding my grey gelding, Klondike that day, and we had passed the spot while it was still dark that morning. However, on the way down, in the daylight was a different story! Unbeknownst to us, the locals had built a huge snowman in the meadow about twenty yards off the trail.

Klondike noticed that immediately and decided that whatever that thing was, it was certainly going to kill us! I wasn't paying attention at the time, and one quick and loud fart later we were high tailing it toward camp! Klondike isn't a jug head though and as soon as I picked up the reins he listened and calmed right down. But he still didn't trust me enough to go have a sniff! He was having no part of that what-so-ever!

The following evening while we were down country, away from the scary snowman, I spotted a bull about three-hundred yards off. A unique 6x6 with real reddish antlers. He was tall and narrow beamed with ivory white points. It was just before dark when I got my first hunter lined up and ready to shoot.

The hunter shot but the bull didn't flinch. Before we had time to send a second round downrange the bull disappeared back into the green timber. Almost immediately more bugles came from the timber. After talking it over, we decided to retreat and head back to camp as it was already getting dark. I figured if the bull ran into the trees and began bugling again, we hadn't hit him. Moreover, should we go looking for sign right at dark we were certainly going to blow what few elk we had, out of the countryside.

We had a new guide working for us who got into camp late that night. He had been guiding the complainers I mentioned previously. He said they shot a bull down river, but they hadn't found him yet. They didn't know how big he was for sure or anything, which seemed a little odd? We didn't think much of it though. Not that I would have anyway, I wasn't much of a fan after seeing him pounding green timber and previously letting a hunter kill a spike earlier in the season.

As far as spike hunting in an area with an, "Any elk" tag, my opinion is as follows. Remember, it's just my opinion! When you can take either a bull or a cow, I think about it like this- A cow will give you one calf a year if you're lucky! Assuming that calf even escapes the predators. Anyway, a bull can breed more than 50 cows in a season. So, if you're talking about a sustainable population, in my opinion you shouldn't shoot those young bulls. Only old ones. And if you absolutely must have the meat, find a cow. Preferably, a dry cow. Moving on!

The following morning was the last day of the hunt and our plan was to return to the same spot, hunt those elk with the hunter who hadn't shot, then wade into the timber around 10:30am to track the bull from last night, just to be sure we hadn't wounded him. The kid had tagged out his one-on-one hunter and came along to see some new country. I knew the guide who wounded the bull was going to be in the area looking for his bull so I asked him to wait until about 10:00 before he left camp. That way he wouldn't ride through our hunt.

As luck would have it, we ended up calling a small six-point right out into the meadow that morning and the hunter waylaid him with one shot. Out in the middle of the meadow left us nowhere to tie up our horses so we left them near our shooting position and headed over to start the hard work. Before long we were pealing

Larry and I headed for camp with a snowy Yellow Mountain in the background.

quarters off the elk so I sent the kid back to the horses to grab Larry. By the time he got back we had four extra visitors too! A sow with three cubs.

We had seen her the night before and knew she was around but now we were caught in open ground with a dead bull on the ground. Soon she was circling us at a hundred yards and the kid was trying to hold Larry still. To no avail, however, Larry was watching those bears, and keeping his hind end toward the bears. I assume to kick them if they decided to charge in to run us off the kill?

Before long I told the kid to drop the led rope and let Larry do his thing. Larry stayed right there and kept moving with those bears while we proceeded to pack the entire bull, cape and antlers on him. Quickly, we were loaded and ready so we walked back to our horses, got our elderly hunters mounted and I walked Larry as they all followed back to camp.

Just as we pulled into camp the guide was leaving with his hunter. We unloaded Larry, hung the meat on the meat pole and just the kid and I went to assess the situation with the elk from the previous night.

I found out later that the other guide with the complainers rode out of camp, got down country a ways and ran into a bear on a carcass. So, he rode in and ran the bear off, then cut the bull up and packed him into camp. Once again, as the kid and I long trotted out of camp we ran into the guide a ways down country bringing his bull in.

We reined in as the guide approached to have a look and congratulate his hunter. Packed on a mule was a tall, narrow, red antlered 6x6. I looked him over and asked where he found it? Both the guide and the hunter kind of shrugged it off as they explained their theories on how the bull could have traveled more than a mile from where they shot from the night before. Then I asked if they tracked it from where they shot from? To which they answered no, because they saw the crows and the bear in the trees so they figured that was it. My blood pressure was going through the roof so I decided to go look for our bull without causing a fuss in front of his hunter.

The kid and I trotted off to our spot and began side hilling up to where the elk was standing the previous day, we found blood right there and began tracking it. The second I saw the blood regret washed over me as I knew I had made a horrible mistake by not tracking that bull the night before. As we side hilled horseback on the snow-covered hillside the bleeding elk tracks led to a thick shrub like bush at the base of a tree. From there, based on the tracks we could see where a bear had attacked the elk, and as they struggled in the ice and snow, they both slid down a ravine about two hundred yards. As we approached, shotguns slung across the saddle horn, we saw the carcass remains. And then human and horse tracks all over.

It was clear what happened. So, we followed the human tracks back to the trail and headed towards camp. When we pulled into the hitching rails and tied up, we relayed what happened to the boss and the other guide. The boss thoroughly cussed me for not looking the night before. Which I couldn't really disagree with, having the benefit of hindsight. However, at the time I thought I was making a wise decision. Regardless, I took the tongue lashing because he was more right than wrong and I deserved it.

See, the situation at the time was that I had two hunters to tag out, and what I thought was two bulls bugling. Given the bull's reaction to the shot, I really believed he wasn't hit. And we were going to look for him, but at the same time didn't want to blow the elk that were there. I can say that I deserved the cussing I received from the boss, but I can honestly say that I would have had trouble doing that differently if given another chance? I think of myself as more of a conservationist than a hunter. Leaving an elk lay makes me sick to think about. But I really didn't believe we had a wounded elk.

Anyway, my hunter took that bull, and cried he was so happy to hear that he didn't miss, or wound the elk! He told me this was his last elk hunt and for that, it was worth the uncomfortable situation. I'm happy it worked out the way it did, it was just unfortunate for everyone involved.

Deep down the other hunter must have known that wasn't his bull? Because he didn't protest at all. I even offered to take them all out to see the tracks. But he didn't want to. Neither did the guide and that told me they knew. I did however give the guide a few hundred bucks for cutting that bull up for me! What a nice guy he was for doing that!

The following day we rode out of camp which concluded the hunt and the season! Luckily, the storm had passed long enough for us to squeak over the pass without too much trouble! A little-known secret about Deer Creek Pass when it's snowy is that all the Thorofare camps are headed out the same day. Therefore, you can often times wake up an hour later than usual and those other camps will have it shoveled for you when you arrive! Of course, this technique can backfire if there's wind to drift the snow back in or if the storm hasn't completely quit yet. This was one of those mornings the plan came together!

Just weeks after we got out of camp, Larry was soon losing weight. We had the vet look him over really good but we couldn't find anything really wrong. He was just old! By the next spring he had lost nearly three-hundred pounds. It was clear that he was done, so rather than prolong his misery we had him put down.

I like to think Larry wanted to go into the Thorofare that one last time. And once we got out, he knew it was his time to go.

Larry was one of the horses you're lucky to have once in a lifetime. My wife used to ride him around in the mountains while she drank coffee and looked around with the reins hanging slack. The kids could sit on his back in the pasture and he was always happy to babysit. My oldest boy, Corbin was best buds with Larry and Larry was always waiting at the gate for him when we'd get home. There might be horses as good, but there were none better!

Larry, topping out on Bruin ridge on a cold and windy day.

| 12 |

Green Eyes in the Darkness

I had been on a guiding hiatus for a year or two trying to do what society says a person should do. And had managed to convince some people to let me fly their jets. They put me in a class and turned on the firehose of information! Six tests, many simulator sessions (where we do all the stuff that's too dangerous to do with paying customers in the back) and two months later, I was flying seventy seat jets out of Chicago's O'Hare International Airport. I still lived in Cody and would commute back and forth to work. At the airlines, you are usually given two-, three-, or four-day trips for your work schedule. With a few days off in between trips. So, it is common for pilots to commute to work several states away.

The catch is, it's all based on seniority. All those jobs are unionized now so if you're low man on the totem pole, often you'll get a "Reserve Schedule" which is a special kind of hell. Reserve is just a fancy word for "On call" so you might fly, you might not? Regardless, we had to be two hours from the airport at all times. So, you might commute to Chicago just to sit for five days, then have two days off and get to do it all over again the next week.

Or even worse yet, you could get another special kind of torture known as, "Ready Reserve." Which meant you were required to be at the airport, in your monkey suit and ready to go anywhere in the system on a half-hour notice. I never have been good at sitting so as you could imagine, I didn't do well tucked in the crew room in the "F" terminal basement of the airport. You can only smell so much mold and mildew down there before you have to get up and move around. As you might imagine, in no time I knew the Chicago airport better than Jim Bridger knew the mountains!

A skull I had to recover after a bear stole our elk.

Not to bore you too much with semantics but an eastbound commute is even worse because of the time change, but what really exacerbated the problem was the fact that Cody, Wyoming is a Podunk little airport with lackluster instrument approaches. So, when the weather even thought about being bad, what few flights they had were canceled. Adding to the problem was that the airport is serviced by small, commuter-type airplanes, exactly what I flew, except these weren't always piloted by some salty hand who knew his way around the challenges of mountain flying.

To make a long story short, I had employee parking passes for Billings, Bozeman and Cody. And most of the time I had to leave in the middle of the day, one day prior to when I was required to be in Chicago. When I figured it out, I was averaging twenty-eight hours a week at home. Flying is cool and everything, but it wasn't worth that. So once again, I bowed out of my flying job, bid a good riddance to Chicago, and was home just in time to get another job guiding.

This was the best and worst season I'd ever had all rolled into one. I had signed on with a brand-new outfitter for the year. We had been hunting hard and tagging guys out. Working our butts off and unwinding when we could. In fact, one particular evening the hunters got a little too deep in the booze which prompted our high-strung boss to outright ban any alcohol in camp!

I just kept quiet and kept smuggling whiskey in, in my duffle. Don't get me wrong, I wasn't out to get rip roaring drunk, but having a whiskey and water at the end of a hard day in the mountains is refreshing. And hey, even the mountain men from the 1800's had whiskey. It just wouldn't be right to be in the mountains without it? Almost sacrilegious! Anyway, a few hunts after prohibition had been declared the boss walked by as I lounged in my camp chair next to the fireplace. Relaxing after a meal of pork loin with all the fixin's. He gave me a funny look and asked for a drink from my water bottle. When I hesitated, he asked what it was.

"Oh, just some mountain water" as I handed him the bottle.

He took several long swigs and tossed it back to me. After that he'd always ask for some of that, "mountain water." And I was glad to share! And even more relieved that we had an unspoken understanding. I wasn't going to abuse it, and he wasn't going to make an issue out of it.

About the time the fourth rifle hunt rolled around several members of our crew were looking pretty shabby. The camp jack, a big, 240-pound teenager when we started, was now down to around 195 pounds! He had been on the mountain diet. Bacon, eggs, prime rib and potatoes every day! For the first time in his life, he was working his butt off though! It's a good hundred yard walk to the outhouse tent! And the camp jack had to be there several times a day on camp business. Let alone another trip on personal. Water was another hundred yards in the opposite direction, and he had to pack two, five-gallon jugs back and forth several times a day. Plus, helping saddle and unsaddle, and running errands for the cook which always involved climbing the ladder to the cache for food several times a day. The boy was getting skinny! And his mules appreciated it! His biggest issue was he only had pants that fit him before he lost the weight. So, he looked more like a hobo than a camp jack.

Our cook this year was top notch! A fifty-something-year-old slender gal who knew her way around the kitchen. We all gave her a fairly wide birth however because she wasn't much for conversation. I'm not saying anything good or bad, I'm just saying the lady didn't talk much. So, we steered clear as all of us understood the consequences of pissing a cook off. Well, almost everyone! We all loved her cooking, so we minded our manners. No cussing in the cook tent!

The wrangler was another young kid. Around eighteen years old. A decent horseman but he was brand new to the mountain. A quiet and soft-spoken kid from Montana. He had been acting weird the last few weeks and none of us really could put our finger on it. He wasn't his usual self though. He had become distant and slightly aloof. As I said, we just didn't know what to make of it? The only certainty was that after a sudden shift in attitude, the boss wasn't going to let the kid near town until we were done for fear of never seeing him again. Who wants to invite someone twisting off in the middle of the season?

We found out later that when no one was in camp, the cook was, um... how should we say it? Having her way with him. Teaching him things. Things that can't be taught with clothes on. You get the drift? That poor little eighteen-year-old was learning things few young men under forty are aware even exist. So, it was no wonder the fella was acting a little weird. That kind of education will make a guy question everything he's ever been taught in life. Of course, we didn't know any of that at the time.

I've already explained why the bosses don't like to let many people out of camp during the season. The cook is just too valuable. Plus, logistically it's a pain in the neck if they don't start the spaghetti dinner until they arrive with the hunters. It's just better customer service to have the meal ready when everyone rolls in from a twelve-hour ride into camp.

The camp jack and wrangler were both low risks as far as quitting goes. They both seemed to be enjoying their jobs. That said, they were also both extremely high risk for getting to town, and partying so hard they would miss the ride in. We all knew it and that's why they stayed in camp. The camp jack was allowed out one time on a previous hunt and had gotten drunk, fell down and chipped a tooth. His front tooth! We were all relieved that he opted to ride into camp rather than get his tooth fixed! That event however sealed their fate. They were officially sentenced to stay in camp until we broke camp and were done for the season. It was odd to us at the time that the wrangler was the only one who didn't complain about it!

The summer had been a hot one and thus far it had been a dry fall so the bears were really making us pay for it. The newly acquired camp had been around forever. Previously run by a Frenchman who thought he was an Indian. Anyhow, Frenchy didn't allow dogs in his camp nor were his guides allowed to carry side arms. That's mainly why he had to hire guides from out of the area, I guess? The camp had not been very well kept either. He fed his horses their cubes in round rubber buckets that result in a lot of spillage. And we had spent a lot of time getting a lot of stuff out of there during the summer just to tidy up. We had found a log with a dozen or so old elk skulls and other bones right by camp. An obvious cache of elk parts from the previous owner who had been too lazy to dispose of the parts properly. Which is not only illegal, it's also extremely stupid. Suffice it to say, by bear standards camp had been the Golden Corral the Thorofare for the twenty years prior to our arrival!

No one told the bears that the camp changed owners though. And bears had been coming to those hitching rails for twenty years or more looking for horse feed that had been carelessly dropped on the ground. Bears will go to horse cubes before they'll go to a pan full of bacon grease! I believe they compress the alfalfa cubes together with molasses as the binding agent but don't quote me on that? The bears were able to leisurely patrol camp from dark until light without being bothered by humans or their dogs. However, on the twenty-first year, all that changed.

All of the sudden a bunch of cowboys, dogs and whatnot, all came to camp. We immediately went to nose bags for feeding mules precisely because it's a lot harder to spill cubes on the ground with a nose bag. And the camp jack and wrangler were tasked with doing a cube patrol after every feeding. Which was twice a day.

We had bears all over us in this camp. Constantly! Every day and night, this particular year we had bears up the wazoo! We had an ongoing battle with a sow and cubs at the meat pole. First, she figured out how to reach over our new electric bear fence and slap the lash ropes with enough force to flip the elk quarters over the meat pole. So, we moved the tie offs out of reach. Then she figured out how to bulldoze her way over the electric fence. Then chew through the ropes that held the meat on the pole. When we found this out, we started tying the ropes from a ladder ten or so feet high in a nearby tree. Then she taught her cubs to climb the meat pole and chew through the ropes. It just went on and on. We were also battling several others at the same time. So, we were all pretty short on sleep! All of us were jumpy to say the least.

If you want to see a mule wreck, tie ten mules to a four-inch thick, twelve-foot-long hitching rail while it's still dark, put nose bags on every one of them and watch a bear appear out of the darkness and try to snatch a nose bag off an unsuspecting mule. That son, is a rodeo! We learned that mules don't particularly fancy the thought of a bear trying to slip a feed bag off their head. It gets really hairy when a guy is standing nearby when the mule panics and pulls back hard enough to break the hitching rail, wiping out the hand and spooking the rest of the mules. That's when you get a stampede of all the mules leaving camp, nose bags still attached, with their halters on and lead ropes dangling along underneath each and every one of them for them to trip on. That's a good wreck! And it had happened more than once this season already. It was a dangerous place that year. No one dared walk through camp unarmed!

In fact, it was so bad that when we followed the instructions of the Forest Service and the Game and Fish, they threatened to shut us down! All of their rules regarding camp cleanliness and what to do about certain issues are spelled out to the letter in the camp permits and general rules of the forest. We followed their rules and reported our issues. In turn, they threatened to not let us go back in to conduct any more hunts that year because it was so dangerous!

If that's not a wakeup call as to how things really work, there never was one! From that day on it was clear that if you operated by the letter of the law, the law would just shut you down. As such, it's not hard to understand how people started dealing with these types of issues in the wilderness! And the governing bodies turn a blind-eye provided that word never gets to town, no evidence is found, no one ever speaks of it and most importantly, no one makes their jobs hard. With a tremendous emphasis on the last part, do not make their jobs hard. That's the truth of how it works.

Don't misinterpret that either, it's a circle. If no one is complaining about having bears chase them every day except you, then naturally, the desk riders in their office far below believe you might be the problem. And who could blame them? They certainly have no clue of what's going on, save for a select few who traded in their outfitting jobs for that government pension! And they pretend they don't know anything and put on a Grammy level performance of acting shocked when something does occur.

Short of a summer trip or two, which isn't during hyperphasia, those folks are sitting at their desks. So why would they know unless the outfitters tell them? Perhaps the problem is the largely self-sufficient nature of the outfitters? They know that alerting the bureaucracy just starts a process that if you're lucky takes weeks to get an approval on. But usually, it takes months. It also forces people to get involved who aren't too keen on riding a horse over a 10,000-foot pass in the middle of hunting season. There might be snow? So, you can't really blame the guy who has a problem, for solving said problem as quickly and efficiently as possible. I mean, why would you intentionally make yourself a target? Why draw unnecessary attention to the outfit?

I'm not confirming or denying anything because each camp is different. However, I am confirming that the struggle between the bureaucracy and state agencies, and the outfitters exists. Casting blame on how it started is irrelevant. What's relevant is that it, in fact does exist. This outfitter tried to go about solving issues the way they're "supposed to" according to the Game and Fish and the

A US Forest Service horse I ran across one day. He was being ridden by a trail crewmember who was nearby. The odd angle of the picture was intentionally taken so you could see he was tied to a green tree. Which is against policy. I used it to poke fun at them!

Forest Service's own rules. For his efforts, he became a target. That lack of mutual respect and professionalism is unfortunate.

Truly the best part is when the fuzz says in a condescending tone, "Well bears don't do that unless you're giving them treats!"

"Us? Hell, we've been here a week but they've been getting that treat for the last twenty years. They're aggressive now because we took their treats away, you asshats!"

I don't need to explain how well that went over. Because apparently, no one had considered that a bear thirty miles from a road could have been habituated by the former owner. That, or considering such obvious things would make someone's job hard? It certainly would have opened a can of worms for the people in charge of the Forest! First, they would have to consider that their policies hadn't worked. And so-on and so-on.

When you follow that thought to its logical conclusion, regardless of politics you're left with one bad answer to solve the problem. We all know that the Endangered Species Act is nothing more than a political weapon in regards to predators in the Greater Yellowstone Ecosystem. And coming to grips with the fact that ten (or however many) bears needed removal isn't something anyone who works for the government and cares about their pension is willing to consider.

Just in case people are getting the wrong impression here, I personally know a few outfitters who would have nipped that problem in the bud, so-to-speak. I admit that. Likewise, I know an equal number who wouldn't allow that kind of stuff to happen in their camp. And I know a dozen others that hold a poker face when it comes to that stuff. I honestly don't know where they stand and I suspect that's the smartest way to play that hand? Sadly, this particular outfitter wasn't a vigilante. In my experience he was the one outfitter who had every right to, and should have killed all of those problem bears. But he wouldn't and wouldn't let anyone else maliciously hunt them either. So, we were stuck.

I had been hunting a couple of guys that week and the bear trouble both in the field and in camp had been horrendous. The boss had banned the kids from shooting in camp thinking that might be a sound the bears were coming to. One evening I was on a ridge above camp when I heard a shot come from that direction. Knowing those kids wouldn't do anything that the boss didn't like on purpose, I decided to head down a few minutes early. I didn't want to show up at the hitching rails after dark riding a green mule only to find a dead bear laying there.

As we approached camp you could see that it wasn't peaceful. You could just feel it in the air. As you approach camp, there's a gap of meadow about fifty feet wide that the trail went through with trees on either side. The meat pole is on the left while camp sits straight ahead. As we approached the turnoff to the meat pole, I spotted a bear wandering over that way. I smooched my mule up and we hit a gallop to close the distance. The plan was to run the bear off. By the time we got close, the bear was at the base of the meat pole and turned to face me. My mule thought better of it when the distance closed to around twenty feet so he darted off to the left before I stopped him. My yelling and the mule running didn't faze the bear. Quickly, I noticed my hunters were coming over so I turned and headed back towards camp, not wanting them to be in needless danger. As we rode into camp, I yelled for the camp jack and wrangler to come over.

Once to the hitching rails I could see the cook and several of the tagged-out hunters standing around the fire pit. All of them holding their rifles. The camp jack and wrangler were already at the hitching rails and told me the bear had been in camp all afternoon. They tried everything and they couldn't make it leave. They explained that they would run him out of the east side of camp and five minutes later he would come in the north side. They'd run him out of the north side and he would come in the west. And so on it had gone since the early afternoon. They had been dealing with this bear for several hours by the time I arrived. The results were a bunch of scared hunters and a cook refusing to go in the tent to cook until the bear was gone.

The boss and the number two man in charge of the camp were packing an elk off the mountain and I was the only guide in camp. So, I decided first things first, let's get the livestock taken care of then we'll figure something out about the bear.

While we were waiting on the mules to finish their evening ration of cubes the two kids filled me in some more about what had been going on. While we talked the bear came in again, just walking through the tents! Quickly, we ran over, me with my sawed-off shotgun, the camp jack with a worthless 22 pistol and the wrangler with another shotgun. We aligned ourselves shoulder to shoulder and yelled until the bear finally turned and walked away. We took some time to make sure he was gone because he walked into the thick green trees and out of site. Then we headed back to the mules. On the way we had to walk by the fire pit. Several of the hunters voiced their opinions, wondering why we didn't just kill the bear. While in the middle of that we spotted the bear under the cache where we had just got the feed bags from. We ran over and repeated the process until he left again. By now it was almost completely dark.

We quickly got the mules into the corrals and repeated the process of finding the bear in camp. Someone at the fire pit would yell, "He's at the guide tents!"

So, we'd go push him out and before we could even get situated someone else would yell, "There he is by the cook tent!"

And so on. Throughout the whole process we tried everything but we could never get the bear to actually run off. He would just reluctantly mosey off into the pitch black only to be seen a few moments later in another location.

Looking back on this encounter, I can say without hesitation that I should have just shot that bear and got it over with. Regardless of the outfitter specifically ordering us not to kill one unless it was attacking. I should not have put myself and my coworkers, not to mention the clients in that much danger for that long. I recall being absolutely livid. Not totally with the bear, mostly mad that the outfitter was putting us in this difficult of a situation. But back then, we were all very scared of the Game and Fish, Fish and Wildlife Service and the Forest Service. You see, back then, if you had a dead bear, you had better be bloody. That was their attitude as we interpreted it, whether that's actually true or false doesn't matter. That's what everyone in camp thought.

At one point, one of the hunters wanted to help so he joined us. He was a good guy, an Iranian from down south somewhere. It goes without saying that this guy isn't your typical elk hunter! When we picked him up from the airport, he basically had a gun and a suitcase. Wearing slacks and penny loafers! We had to take him to the store to get him adequately equipped for the hunt. I had found a newer Sitka vest on the trail the week prior that I let him borrow. And I haven't seen it since! He was a great guy though and a lot of fun to have in camp. We think he didn't know what he was signing up for?

Anyway, the bear made another approach from the hitching rails. Now the four of us, all armed started walking shoulder to shoulder, guns at the ready, pushing him off. Finally, he trotted about ten-yards then quickly whirled and lowered his head and started rocking back and forth. All we could see however was his green eyes, reflecting in our headlamps, swaying back and forth. He was standing his ground.

As soon as the bear turned, the hunter started to run! I grabbed him by the arm and stopped him.

"Hey, knock that shit off! Stand your ground or get back to the fire but don't you dare run!"

That's when we threw a bear deterrent at him. It's basically an M-80. You light it, throw it and hope it makes a big bang next to the bear and it scares him off. Yeah, and it didn't work. The bear simply didn't care. All we did was make noise.

After a short standoff, we pushed a little more and that's when the bear had enough. He squared off with us again and was rocking back and forth. Green eyes swaying in the pitch black.

"If he charges us, take him guys!" I said as we all drew down on him.

In a nanosecond, the bear popped his jaws several times and charged! I was taking the slack out of my trigger when a small, "PEW!" Sound erupted from the camp jack's gun!

Immediately the bear dropped like a sack of potatoes and remained motionless. He merely looked like a stump as he laid there in the darkness. Silver tipped grizzly hair shined in our headlamps as we looked on, not believing what we just witnessed.

Knees shaking, I glanced down the line at the three others. Everyone stood motionless, still ready to fire.

"Did you just shoot a grizzly bear with a 22 pistol?" I asked the camp jack.

"Yep." He replied.

"You're a stupid bastard aren't ya'?"

"Yep"

We stood for another five minutes, ready. Watching. During those five minutes the camp jack broke the silence by asking if he could bum a dip of Copenhagen. Sure!

Pretty soon everyone's radios cracked through, "I told you dip shits no shooting in camp!!!" Came the boss's very angry voice.

"Hey, don't come up the main trail, boss. Come in the alley trail" I said.

Our bear was laying five feet off the main trail that leads to camp. Right on the edge of a meadow that is surrounded by piss firs so thick you can't walk through them. I figured telling the boss to come into camp the back way would save a righteous mule wreck.

Just then we all heard a gargling sound from the bear. So, we cautiously approached to find him still breathing. I sent the hunter back to the fire and the camp jack to tell the cook it was safe for her to start dinner. While the wrangler and I waited for the boss to get into camp. Soon, the camp jack was back and we were deep in conversation about finishing the bear off. But none of us wanted to risk the boss's wrath if we fired another shot. So, we held off and kept our guns trained on the bear who was still just lying there.

Not long later the boss and the number two man came into camp and tied up their stock while we told him the story. The boss was hysterical and angry! Cussing all of us until the number two man got him calmed down. And who wouldn't be? With the law already making it clear they were going to shut us down if we had any more bear trouble. On one hand, I can't blame the guy. On the other, I eventually had enough of him cussing the camp jack. He was laying into the kid something fierce! Finally, I spoke up and told him we were all trying to shoot that bear. The camp jack just happened to be the quickest gun slinger that night. Soon we had the boss calmed down enough to form a logical thought. He was questioning all of us and while doing so, he was suddenly startled after realizing the bear was still breathing!

"Is that thing still alive?" he shrieked!

When we nodded to the affirmative, he ran to the tent and came back with the satellite phone. Soon he was on with the Game and Fish to ask them what to do next. They approved the dispatching of the bear and informed us they'd be in to conduct an investigation the following morning.

While dispatching the bear, point blank with a .44 magnum, we all learned some things about bears, and all animals for that matter. First of all, it took several shots. The .44, with 300 grain cast core bullets was blowing golf ball sized holes in the bear's skull. But the bear didn't die. In fact, he growled at us and started to roll over and get a paw up to swipe at us. All in ultra-slow motion of course. He died on the third shot that was perfectly centered. The previous two were off to the side just a touch and hadn't hit the brain.

The big take away was that a bear's brain is smaller than you would think it is. And the thought of having to be that accurate in a surprise encounter seems like a tall task? Which is why the fuzz advocates so hard over pepper spray. And that sounds logical to anyone who has never used pepper spray and seen it fail to be effective. So really, it's a pretty solid argument for a 12 gauge and buckshot!

Secondly, paralyzed animals that are still drawing breath should still be considered dangerous. An important mental note that had escaped me about ten years later when the kid "Arkansas Tooth picked" the bull in the, "Swayback Horses" Chapter. I've personally witnessed two different paralyzed animals move after being what we thought was paralyzed. That will make you respect the toughness and the desire to live that these animals have. Bottom line is, unless you have an x-ray showing a severed spinal cord, you better treat them like they can still get up!

In the meantime, we had another big problem. The first thing was to dispatch the bear, and we had accomplished that much. Second, was that we couldn't have a dead bear in camp all night. So, we got our best gelding saddled and rolled the bear into a rubber tarp. All while being careful that the horse wouldn't be able to actually see that it was dragging a bear. Then tied a rope to the tarp, dallied off on the saddle horn and drug the bear out of camp. We drug him into a meadow several hundred yards down river. That may sound easy, and thankfully it was but had the horse noticed that it was a bear in the tarp, and the bear was following the horse, you can imagine how big that wreck could have been. Luckily for us, we got the bear out of camp smoothly.

The following morning the Fish and Game arrived via a helicopter which scares a lot of elk and mules but I digress. After they flew up and down the valley, losing altitude, they eventually landed right in camp. They did their whole act where they split everybody up and question everyone individually to make sure the stories all jive. Next, they asked us to walk out to the meadow and point to where the bear was. They would be in their helicopter and they would chase all the other bears off of it, then we would help them roll the bear into a net and the pilot would fly him to the trailhead. From there the truck would take him to headquarters where they would perform an autopsy to ensure our stories matched the physical evidence. Make sure the bear hadn't been shot from behind, and all that good stuff.

Meanwhile, the helicopter would fly back in to pick up the remaining officers and we would all be set free until the completion of the investigation (which basically never happens).

Soon the helicopter was fired up with the Game and Fish guys on board while a few of us armed ourselves and headed to the meadow. As the chopper flew over us at tree top height we pointed across the meadow to where we had left the bear. As the helicopter hover taxied to the spot, bears erupted from the forest scattering in all directions. It reminded me of cockroaches when someone flips a light on. They were everywhere! The helicopter was pushing them all away when one particular bear emerged into the meadow at a lope. Quickly, he saw us and immediately commenced his charge even though we stood one hundred and fifty yards from him. We all aimed our weapons and prepared to fire when the helicopter swooped in between us and the bear. The bear broke off his charge as the helicopter chased him away. We looked on for a tense ten minutes as the helicopter swooped around chasing bears off, then returning to the carcass and chasing more off only to return and do it all again. There were more than a dozen bears on that one dead bear. I believe I am qualified to say that was an impressive piece of flying!

As the helicopter began to set down in the meadow, we ran over to help. We figured there wouldn't be anything left of the dead bear with all the other bears around, but when we got there and were dragging him to the net that was attached to the helicopter, we noticed that the only thing that the other bears had done was to get one piece of intestine out. The rest of the time they had been fighting over it. Filthy cannibals!

Soon we were back in camp no worse for the wear. While we waited with the wardens one finally spoke up,

"Okay guys, you know we are going to do an autopsy, right?"

Yeah, we understand that"

"Alright then, this is your last chance to tell us what actually happened. You all are telling us that the bear was shot with a 22?"

"Yes sir"

"And there won't be any other bullet holes in the bear? That's your story?"

"Well, you'll find three more .44 rounds in his hea…." They cut us off.

"We understand about the three in his head. We are asking you guys to come clean. You're all telling us there's going to be one 22 round in the bear's neck? That's it? You want us to believe the camp jack shot and spined' a bear with a 22 pistol?"

"Yes sir, that's what we're saying."

Eventually they shrugged us off and a few minutes later the helicopter showed up and whisked them off to the safety of their offices.

From atop, "Telephone Rock" with Yellowstone in the distance. Back in the analog cell phone days, you could get a signal from the cell tower at Yellowstone Lake from this rock. Hence the name, Telephone Rock.

At that point, I was basically out of the interworking of this particular investigation. And I'm not sure whatever happened with it? I believe they closed it? I mean, how can a bear who threatens people's lives and property for over six hours straight not be deemed a threat? The obvious conclusion isn't always what happens on those deals though, and you never get a letter from the fuzz that says, "Good job! We're glad you kept everyone safe in a difficult situation. We are closing the books on this one!"

The reason they don't is because there is no statute of limitations on wildlife issues to my understanding? Which is exactly why this story is a combination of tales from about twenty other bear encounters. Several things are true and several aren't. Sorry to let all my readers down but I'm not interested in accidentally kicking a hornet's nest ten or so years after the fact. You never know when some overzealous fish cop who's looking to stir up trouble will show up!

You should all know that there was a bear shot in the spine by a camp jack with a 22 pistol. And it was investigated thoroughly, and no wrongdoing was found. As it turned out, the word from the fuzz after the autopsy concluded that the bear was nearly toothless and was around ten percent body fat. This was in October! It doesn't take a rocket scientist to figure out two things from those two facts. The first being that the bear would have died that winter. Secondly, and perhaps not as obvious to the casual reader, the bear wouldn't have just denned up that skinny. He was desperate! And when a bear is desperate humans, and all of their belongings are absolutely on the menu! It's good we got rid of that bear when we did!

| 13 |

Redemption

As usual in a deep wilderness camp, the wakeup call came long before the sun peaked over the canyon walls. I was up and with the help of the two wranglers we had a string of mules saddled and ready to pack long before daylight. We gathered, caught and saddled using our headlamps under a high overcast, moonless and starless, frosty morning. Once complete, and all the other guides and hunters had left on their morning hunt, we gathered in the dining tent. Soaking in the warmth of the nearby woodstove, I sat watching the steam floating upward from my cup of piping hot cowboy coffee. We waited for daylight silently, listening to the hiss of the Coleman lanterns. There's no sense going to the meat pole before the grey light starts.

The previous night it had been decided by the outfitter that I would take the meat run out. I was the only guide who had tagged out both hunters so far, so it made good sense. At this time, I was a pretty experienced guide, but this season I had been having tremendously bad luck with bears. Truth be told, we all were! I had gone from never losing an ounce of meat to a bear, to losing two elk and half a ram in just the last three hunts.

Taking a quick sandwich break while field dressing a nice 6x6.

Meat runs are where someone takes a load of meat out of camp and drops it off at the processor during the hunt. There are several reasons to do it, the first could be for spoilage. If the weather is too warm to safely keep meat, you have to get it out before it's ruined. Secondly, is baggage space! One elk takes two mules to get out of camps this far in the wilderness. If you had a camp with ten-hunters, that's twenty-head right there just for meat! Assuming everyone tags out, of course! Sure, you don't have all the food items coming out but, in an effort to keep the outfitters from overgrazing the meadows and stock from eroding the trails, the "Circus" decided to limit most every camp to thirty-five head. That would leave an outfitter who has ten hunters and ten elk down five extra head to pack out the guides, and everyone's gear. It's physically impossible to do that with thirty-five head!

The Forest Service knows it's impossible as well. In my opinion, those rules were instituted as a back handed measure to limit how many people an outfit could have in camp. Since they are a separate entity than the Game and Fish, they have no control over the number of tags allotted. In some ways, I agree with the limits, but I'd prefer they limited those numbers by issuing outfitter permits to people who have an interest in being good stewards of the land. You know, be up front and transparent about it rather than slipping a regulation through without stating their intentions. But who am I, you know?

The livestock allotment of thirty-five head is a serious issue. The most common answer is meat runs. But that has obvious issues as well. What if no guide is tagged out? The wrangler's job is to wrangle in camp. The camp-jack can't do it for the same reasons. What most outfitters were forced to do was to hire an extra employee, a packer. Their job is typically to come out when the hunters are riding in. Layover a day, sometimes two to rest the stock, then head back in with horse feed and staple food for the upcoming hunt. Rest the stock a day, sometimes two, then take the meat out. Rest the stock another day and then head back in with groceries the last day of the hunt which is ride out day for everyone else. Then they sit on camp until the process repeats itself.

You see, outfitters can have more than thirty-five head for basically a day, so long as they receive the blessing of the Forest Service beforehand. What happens is a guy will be say, ten head over in camp for the layover day. Then he'll skinny out of there the following day.

If you didn't catch the drift, the total number of stock in camp isn't the main cause of trail erosion. The number of animals and the frequency at which they travel the trails are! On the surface, without giving it any thought, limiting outfitters to thirty-five head seems like a plausible plan. But in reality, it hurts the environment more than anything else. And that's before discussing the issues that arise when everyone has to ride wore out stock. That poses its own issues, as does the problems that come with having an animal come up lame in camp. Your two options are to go short on stock and let them heal in the mountains or to try to get them out. And a thirty-mile trip on a crippled mule or horse is a terrible thing to ask of an animal just so the outfitter stays in compliance. It just isn't safe!

Anyway, I had been nominated to perform the meat run chore. And I didn't mind! Thirty-two miles is a long ride out by yourself but it was worth it. And often, being alone has as many advantages as it does disadvantages! I was riding a really fast, gaited mule that they called Sara. I had ridden her a few times that season and got along with her well.

Once daylight broke, we dropped the quartered elk from the meat pole and got everything packed. By 7:30am I was headed for the road! A few hours out of camp is a small pass that we usually walk down. However, I arrived on the pass in time to see a sow with a cub headed down in front of me. Not having a reason to fear humans, and being that the trail negotiated a path through massive blowdowns left over from the Yellowstone fires of '88, bears aren't really motivated to give you the road. They did end up giving me the road after a little persuading however, and soon I was headed up the creek toward the main pass.

Several miles later, as we rode up the creek my mules kept queuing on something on the other side of the creek and slightly ahead. Soon I saw, and passed another sow with a cub. No problem, I thought! We'll get these bear sightings out of the way early and have a good rest of the day. Getting that early of a start, I could leisurely ride out and still be to town before dark. I had almost forgotten about the two sows as we continued ascending the river bottom toward the pass.

Not nearly as treacherous as Deer Creek, this pass is still over 10,000 feet. Once through the first twenty-seven switchbacks the trail drops off into a densely wooded canyon. Thirty-seven switchbacks later, is mostly flat and gently descending trail all the way to the road, twenty-some miles due north.

As we approached the first switchback, I was digging a dip of Copenhagen out of the can when my mules all suddenly stopped. When I looked up there was another bear, standing on the first switchback, just looking at me. I quickly put my chew in my lip, returned the can into my pocket and hollered at the bear. Reluctantly, he moseyed off the trail. I gave Sara a little kick and we began climbing through the steep switchbacks.

Roughly two-thirds of the way up the pass the trail narrows through a series of tight and quick switchbacks. There are several logs staked into the ground to prevent erosion and that makes a series of steps. Naturally, we called it the, "staircase." While in the staircase, one side is a steep drop off, not a cliff, but steep enough you'd roll all the way to the bottom of you fell off your mule! On the other side it's the same thing, just uphill.

When we were about half way through the staircase we ran into a big boar coming down the trail. And while there wasn't any blowdown for him to negotiate, he really didn't want to leave the trail! I yelled for a couple minutes as we had a standoff. He just stood there checking the wind. All of the sudden it occurred to me that the thermals had started and all that elk meat was wafting right up the mountain towards him! With a string of six mules, plus Sara turning around wasn't an option. And even if it was, we don't want to make it a habit of backing down from those dang bears. So, I smooched up Sara and we rode right at the bear. He held his ground though and at about ten-yards there was a small area where I could cut the switchback off. And that's what we did! The mules had to bear-down and really work to climb the steep mountain side, all the while having heavy packs of bloody, smelly elk meat, ten-yards from a bear! But alas, we got around him! Compromising our route not withstanding! The blatant disrespect and lack of fear of these bears nowadays is incredible.

Having seen that many bears all in a row I talked myself into believing that was all the bears we'd see for the day. So, once we summited the pass, I jumped down and began leading the string down the backside. Before long we made it off the switchbacks and later through the meadow. The bear sightings still had us all on edge, but we continued our march towards civilization.

I had been daydreaming for who knows how long when all of the sudden chaos erupted. We were starting across an open hillside we had dubbed, "the back nine" because it looked like a golf course. Suddenly, one mule passed me on the left, another on the right, and the lead rope connecting the two mules was pushing me forward in my saddle! It spooked Sara too and she took off like a rocket! Soon we outran the two mules that were trying to pass us and without the lead rope pushing me down in the saddle I snuck a glance behind us. I was very alarmed to see another big bear chasing the string!

Your natural reaction in a runaway is to pull the mule's head around so they'll run in a circle that eventually gets too small of a radius to continue to run. And out of reaction I had reached down and pulled Sara's head around. Without achieving the desired results, I reached further down and grabbed the metal bit where the reins attach pulling her head even further towards my lap. Seeing the bear, I immediately let her head go and she caught a gear and accelerated more! By now we had crossed the open hillside and were dropping off the back side. Dust and sod were flying as the trail weaves between several lines of short rim rocks. The rocks are only two to four feet high in that area, but as I gathered my wits enough to start processing the information, I saw that we weren't even on the trail.

As we started the descent I looked back and the bear was still there. Running full bore and we hadn't increased our distance on him by much. He was holding steady at what I'd estimate to be about ten-fifteen yards behind my whip mule! (Which is the last mule in the string.)

Admittedly, I'm no bear expert. But I've been bluff charged, chased and I've watched bears get after a lot of other people and animals. Seems to me that when it's a bluff, or they are just checking things out they kind of appear to be higher in the front when they run. They almost look like they are bouncing as they run with their head up. But when they are serious their front seems lower, their paws appear to be pulling the earth together, under their body? Almost pigeon toed. Anyway, this bear was pulling the ground, ears pinned, head low and coming hard and fast!

As I turned forward in the saddle Sara jumped off of a rim rock, never breaking stride and continuing on. We did that four or five more times before I suddenly noticed we were back on the trail. I snuck another quick look back and didn't see the bear anymore! But I saw something almost worse! A pack had slipped on my second to last mule and it was almost completely under her belly!

It took several hundred yards to get the mules slowed down to a trot and another few hundred to get them to a walk. After seeing the upside-down pack, I figured that we had lost some meat and that's probably why the bear stopped chasing us? Another hundred or so yards I found a good open place to tie up and fix the load. And when I did, the whole string was still so spooked I couldn't go to the mule with the slipped pack. They kept spooking with me on the ground and running in circles. I had to tie up the first mule, easily and cautiously sneak to the side to get the next lead rope off the back of the saddle, untie it, find another tree to tie to, then repeat. Eventually, I got to the slipped pack and got it fixed! To my surprise, we hadn't lost any meat!

I repacked as quickly as I could while nervously looking over my shoulder for a bear the whole time. Before long, I had my string tied back together and was ready to get moving. I untied Sara and went to get on. Just as my foot hit the stirrup she tried to bolt! Honestly, I was lucky to keep a hold of a rein and got her stopped after only sliding a few feet behind her. But I did lose the string! So, I re-caught the string, but this time decided to tie the string up. This way I could let Sara do whatever she wanted to do, be it bolt, buck or just stand there, without having the extra complications of hanging onto a lead rope. So, I tied the lead mule up in a nearby tree, then I swung into the saddle on Sara and she bolted again! This time I was ready and expecting it though, so we soon got her calmed down and rode the several hundred yards back to the tree where the string was tied. Staying in the saddle, I untied the string and soon we were back on the trail headed out.

As it turned out, being run by that bear loosened all those packs because I had to stop five more times to repack. And every time we would have a repeat of Sara running off as soon as I stepped into the saddle, then we'd ride back, get the string, and continue on. Finally, after what turned out to be the last runaway, I had the bright idea to tie Sara up too. That way she couldn't bolt when I got on. Once in the saddle I could untie her by leaning forward a bit. That was the one time she didn't run off. I suppose being a slow learner is better than not learning at all!

When I left camp that morning, I figured I'd be to town well before dark. Unsaddled, unpacked, fed and watered. As it turned out, runaways might help you make good time briefly, but the repacking that must be done ends up costing you a lot. We had turned a ten-hour ride into a thirteen-hour ride! Eventually, I made it out safe and sound!

Except there was a small group of buffalo hanging out at the trailhead when we arrived. No doubt, looking for some leftover hay to feed on. I tied the mules up on the opposite end of the corrals than the buffalo were on and snuck over to my pickup with the buffalo just feet away. I opened the passenger door because they were too close for comfort on the driver's side. Then jumped across the seats and drove over to my string. I didn't want to pack the quarters that far. Or deal with those dang buffalo!

When I finally arrived home, I was ready to quit! Quit the whole lifestyle! It was just getting too dangerous! I spoke with my girlfriend at the time, (who is my wife now) and we agreed. I would quit when the boss rode out after this hunt. I wouldn't go back in! I didn't want or need to go back in! This was getting ridiculous!

The following morning the phone rang bright and early. I could tell it was a satellite phone by the caller ID, so I answered reluctantly.

"Hello?"

"Hey, change of plans! I need you to go to my house and get a bunch of electric fence, then go to the tent store and get a bunch of canvas repair supplies and get back in here!" the boss said.

"Uh, no, why can't that wait?" I replied.

"A bear came through camp last night and tore a hole in the back of the cook tent and knocked half the son-of-a-bitch down!

The cook is too scared to cook unless someone is around! We're in a bind man! We need ya!"

The meadow on the way to camp. Just short of halfway to camp.

"Ah, shit! Alright, I'll see you guys tomorrow!" I said with a sigh. "Oh, one thing, I'm not riding that Sara mule again, that runnin' off piece of crap!"

"She ran off? Weird? She's usually great! Yeah, go grab the big blood bay out of the corral at the house! See you tomorrow!" He said.

And just like that, I had "un-quit!" my girlfriend smiled and rolled her eyes when we hung up. I just didn't want that feeling I had last time I quit and I figured this was God's way of making me pay it back! This was harder and a lot more stressful than an idiot outfitter running me over! Plus, those were my friends in there and they needed a hand!

The following morning, I headed back into camp with the requested supplies. It was only me, the blood bay we called Spooky and one pack animal. The electric bear fence, issued by the Forest Service is decent stuff but I had to sling in as it was too long to pack in a pannier or something like that. I hadn't had much experience slinging loads, but I got it on and was proud it made it all the way to camp!

I was on the trail early and back in camp by the mid-afternoon. We only had one incident on the trail that scared the bejesus out of an already bear scared guide, and that was running into three moose on the trail! And once I saw they were moose and got my heart rate back under control, it turned out to be quite the treat!

The following hunt I was paired off with a couple of Midwest friends. One a farmer, the other a rancher. We had also brought in two new mules we called Butch and Cassidy. Big blonde draft cross mules that were new to the outfitter and didn't know the other livestock or the country. Within a day they were lost! The wrangler couldn't find them anywhere. All of the guides were told to keep an eye out for two big blonde mules, but we figured they had quit the country and headed for the road? After all, that was the only trail they knew!

My rancher was a tough dude, but he was crippled up too bad to really get around well. But we were making do and had a close call up in some rocks that overlook the basin whose river flows into Yellowstone Lake. One evening while glassing I looked way up country. I found some elk up in a high basin that was difficult to gain access too. Not wanting to make a big pound unless we knew what we were getting into, I broke out the spotting scope to see if I could pick out any bulls. After watching elk for years and understanding a few of their habits you get to where you can pick a bull out of a group of cows based only on their confirmation, mannerisms and how they intermingle with other elk. Color isn't always true as an old cow will sometimes appear really yellow in color, while wet or even bad lighting can trick you into thinking that a real dark elk is a cow. Not to mention that these hunts are conducted during the rut and a lot of those bulls have been in the wallow and are covered in mud. At this range, if you could find antlers, they were going to be big!

Before long I found a bull that I thought was worth chasing the following morning. To my surprise, I also found Butch and Cassidy! They were living with that herd of elk! They were grazing alongside of them, and we even saw them touching noses with some of the cows! How they got all the way up in the rocks, that far from camp I'll never know? But there they were! And we had a plan to kill two birds with one stone so-to-speak!

When we got back to camp, over a full turkey dinner with all the fixings I told the boss what we found. I asked to bring the wrangler who would bring a pack mule, we would pack Butch and Cassidy's saddles, shoot the elk, catch the mules and bring everything back in one shot! The boss liked the idea and everything was set! Except the rancher, who wanted to rest up for a day. No problem, the farmer can shoot that bull!

I had gotten to the point that I wasn't a huge breakfast fan. Well, at least not at 4:00am. And make no mistake, we had a great cook, but I'm a bacon and egg snob. Medium rare, floppy, chewy bacon is one of the things that makes the world a wonderful place! And a runny egg? What could be better? But we kept getting hard as a rock, crispy bacon that's more akin to biting into a piece of fiber board that explodes into salty sawdust inside your mouth. It's not even food folks! We were also getting over hard eggs, so usually I just didn't eat. I know better than to piss off a cook so I didn't dare mention it! I would usually use breakfast time to saddle and drink some coffee. However, the following morning I was hungry so I suffered through a few boards of bacon and a couple over hard eggs.

Anyhow, a two-hour ride later we were tying up in some short trees in the sub alpine just below the upper basin. We could hear the elk and knew we had a good chance! The only issue I could see was there was going to be a lot of open ground between us and the elk if they were at the back of the basin.

The farmer assured me he was ready and we started up, to peak over the rim of the basin. We were immediately busted by the elk, and Butch and Cassidy, who were at the time in a perfect spot off to the side of the herd! But when the elk busted us, they took off deeper in the basin, luckily, the basin was cliffed out on the back side. It's the only time in my life that I've actually trapped elk! So, we ran to close the distance. I found a big rock, the size of a Volkswagen Bug up ahead that would serve as a perfect rest for the farmer and cut our distance to four-hundred yards.

Arriving at the rock, I could tell the farmer was out of sorts. But I assumed it was due to the two-hundred-yard sprint above 10,000 feet that we had just completed. The elk were on the hillside above us bunching up. I told him to use the rock as a rest and shoot that bull before he has time to make a break for it! I looked through my binoculars and waited for the shot. And shoot he did! Bang!... Bang!.. Bang! Bang! To my horror a calf was standing thirty yards to the right of the bull and I saw him get hit out of the corner of my eye! The farmer was hysterical! I've never seen anything like it!

"Did I hit him?" He screamed. Meaning the bull.

Taken totally off guard all I could get out was "Hey, stop it!"

Bang! Bang!

The son-of-a-bitch was flock shooting at the elk! And our two mules were in the same herd! I ran over and jerked the gun away from him as the elk made a break for it. Butch and Cassidy blew past us breaking away from the elk and nearly running over the wrangler who we had left with the stock!

To be honest I don't remember what I said to the farmer. And I remember the hunter being mad because I took his gun. Which I didn't give back until we were at the trailhead after the hunt.

As the elk filed off the calf walked into a small stand of white barks and laid down. I was so mad I sort of lost focus, so I got the hunter back to camp and told the boss what had transpired.

"What do you want to do?" The boss asked.

"He wounded that calf! I think I should ride him back up there and we should make the son-of-a-bitch tag him!"

The boss agreed and the following morning we headed back up to the basin. I rode right to the white bark stand I'd last seen the calf in and he was still laying there looking at us.

"There he is, use your pistol, walk down there and finish him off" I said while still sitting on my horse pointing.

"Oh, I don't think I can shoot that calf, Zach" He said.

I didn't bother explaining to him that he already did. I just walked down and did it myself. And let me tell you, we're all supposed to be big, bad, tough hunters, but the way that yearling bull calf looked at me sure made a guy feel pretty low. It just makes me sick to think about that. But it's a classic example of the chaos that is nature. No mercy, no rhyme or reason, it's just brutal on the mountain. But humans are supposed to be above that I thought? At least the good part, if there was one, was that we tagged the elk and although the farmer didn't want him, the rancher gladly took the meat and told me several years later how amazing he tasted. I believe we did the right thing after a bad situation. The farmer was damn lucky to have an "any elk" tag too! If he would have had an antler tag, we wouldn't have had a choice other than to turn him in.

Meanwhile, the wrangler still couldn't manage to catch Butch and Cassidy. They had continued their run down into the river bottom. Once he caught up to them there, he pushed them into the corrals in camp and we soon gave one of them lessons on how a picket worked. By forcing them to stay with the herd they quickly intermixed with the rest of the stock and the next hunt we didn't have to picket them. After living with the elk for about a week, and living through a hunter shooting in their direction, they decided they liked living with the other mules better than the elk I suppose?

A few years later the farmer came into a different camp I had been working in. I wasn't thrilled to see him and avoided him and the whole conversation. And he avoided me as well. But when the opportunity presented itself, before the hunt started, I asked the boss to not pair me with him and told him why. I warned him to tell whoever was guiding him to be careful. The boss decided he would hunt the guy just in case.

However, as the hunt progressed, the farmer and I spoke more and more. I don't know what happened in that basin, but he seemed to be remorseful, and apologetic now. But he clearly didn't want anyone else to know about that either.

He seemed to be a pretty good guy. And he made it a point to show me his new gun and to explain how his old gun had a bad barrel, which he found out when he got home. I was still apprehensive but I figured there's nothing that can be done about it now so I might as well try not to hold it against him.

The next year he was back, and I had taken a one-on-one hunter and tagged him out the first day. The farmer was once again hunting with the outfitter. I was bumming around camp, cutting some wood, helping the wranglers with the stock but mostly smoking cigars and drinking water that I liked to dilute with whiskey. Not getting drunk or anything. Just enjoying camp and everything that comes with being in the mountains including a cocktail.

One evening the farmer and the boss rode in from an unsuccessful hunt. I was at the hitching rails ready to help unsaddle while we all were waiting for dinner. The boss was talking about a place I had always wanted to go to, but hadn't had the hunters to make it. In fact, no one in the camp had made it in there for several years so whoever went was going to have to cross-cut saw their way in. They had been talking about it in general terms, but I offered to come and help because I wanted to see it too. The boss agreed and the plan was set for the following morning.

High on the mountain, 10,500 feet above sea level is a double canyon with open hillsides, parks and sparsely timbered draws. There are several waterfalls, and there's snow year around slightly above. It's one of the legendary honey holes that you hear the old timer guides talk about around the campfire. I was excited because access, even by Thorofare standards is so limited and difficult! Not only do you need a hunter who is in shape, but you need them to be tough and not scared of the steep trails. Secondly, you need really good mules with small feet and lots of experience to negotiate the rocks and rough trails. And lastly, you need the weather to co-operate. This hunt, all three of those elements finally aligned.

That morning we rode out of camp a full two hours before daylight. I had cut "Smoke" out of the herd that morning because he was my all-time favorite mule. A little grey mule who was tougher than nails and a little mean. And if he caught you jacking around too much, he'd buck you off. Which was why we didn't let hunters ride him anymore. They are usually in a perpetual state of jacking around and a few found out!

Once across a side creek we crossed a meadow, then picked up the hidden and thin outfitter trail before starting the 3,000-foot ascent to our spot. We cut logs while the mules rested and eventually topped out on the first bench at 10:30 am. It was like being in a time machine, the elk were bugling everywhere in the distance. We tied up and began glassing under a brilliant, clear blue sky. Being at a high elevation on bluebird day with no wind in the mountains is about as close to heaven as you can get in my opinion!

One of my all-time favorite mules, "Smoke" headed up the trail. You can see in the picture he is watching me.

Soon we found some elk, deemed it both safe and wise to return to the mules and reposition them closer. After all that was done, we made our way down to a meadow and just like that, all the bugling stopped at noon. Patiently, we ate lunch while listening to the slight breeze blow through the treetops while the song birds chirped nearby. Later, we moved a little farther up the canyon into the next meadow. Before long we found a herd of elk eight-hundred yards in front of us. To our left and ahead was another herd, and below us was yet another. I bugled and all the herd bulls, plus some satellite bulls erupted. The bugling continued for a solid hour while the boss kept chirping on his cow call.

Common wisdom says you're never going to call a herd bull off his cows. But on this day, the boss kept it up and eventually the dominant bull in the herd straight ahead of us picked his head up, checked the wind, and came running straight for us leaving his ten cows behind! At this point the farmer had shuffled out a ways to have a better view in case something came in below us. The boss was twenty-yards behind him so I snuck up and got shoulder to shoulder with him.

"That herd bull is coming, be ready, He's going to pop out between those two big trees at the end of the meadow."

"What's the range to those trees?" The farmer asked in a deliberate, steady tone.

I clicked the button on the range finder feature that is integrated into my 10x40 Swarovski's and placed the red dot on the trunk of the tree. "A hundred and sixty-five yards"

About twenty minutes and fifty bugles from the surrounding elk later, the bull stepped out in the clearing at a hundred and sixty-five yards. The farmer waited, holding his aim. Not excited, not breathing hard, just steady.

"That's a damn good bull" I whispered.

Instantly, his gun fired as I peered through my binoculars. The bull turned 45-degrees and was now nearly facing us. "You missed! Hit him again!" I said.

BOOM!

Looking down river in the Thorofare on a nice day.

And the bull dropped like a brick. We gathered our wits as we watched to ensure the bull was down before making the walk over to him. When we arrived at the bull the other elk were still bugling at each other. It was like the shots didn't even phase them! We arrived to find a 330-bull laying there dead. One shot perfectly through the vitals, and another through the forehead. The farmer had made two spectacular shots, off a knee, at a hundred and sixty-five yards. He didn't get excited and I never heard his breathing change when the elk stepped out. I'd say that's a pretty sweet redemption for all parties involved.

A few years later the farmer called and told me he and a buddy were coming back to hunt and wanted me to guide them. Which was fine by me, but he also decided to get a hip replaced and as it turned out, he wasn't healed up enough to come when the season rolled around. But his buddy came and I took him out. Right off the bat, the buddy had a splotchy red, pot marked face, was overweight and out of shape. The marks on his face told me he liked his booze but most concerning was his obvious hypoxia symptoms.

We eased around staying in the low country for the first couple of days and the guy had trouble walking at all. And with all that, he seemed to have no trouble complaining that I wasn't taking him where I had taken the farmer. Even if he could have made it up there, it had been snowing on and off for a week and the trail hadn't been cleared. So, we lacked the hunter ability and the weather. I tried to explain the weather factor and that I could see he had symptoms of hypoxia.

"I do not have hypoxia!" he said during one of the conversations.

"Dude, your nose has been bleeding since we got here four days ago and you told me you've had a headache this whole time. And you get winded walking to the shitter! You can't bullshit a bull shitter!" I replied, trying to lighten the mood.

Anyhow, I took him on one hunt with a short but steep descent to see how he would do. As we were riding down a ridge that we should have been walking down, I was just trying to do the guy a favor because he was so slow, we rode past a white bark pine with a really brushy base. It was about fifty yards to the right, off the trail. I looked up to see a bear sitting there looking at us. So, naturally I yelled, "Hey Bear! Git!"

And holy crap the bushes at the base of the tree erupted and a mad momma sow, twice the other one's size came boiling out of the tree, smashed into the cub, the cub went flying and she turned and bluff charged us up to twenty-five or so feet. By the grace of God, we were both riding super broke and gentle horses because they both just stopped and looked at the sow. The bear stopped her bluff charge, stood up on her hind legs and then turned and left. With anyone else we would have been walking right there and it could have turned out a lot differently! And with most of the horses we had, that would have caused a big wreck! We just got lucky!

Bubbles the mule packing "the farmer's" bull out of the high country, deep in the Thorofare.

On another down river hunt we got into a small herd of elk with a smaller 5x6 herd bull, a few spikes and seven or eight cows. We were right there at a hundred and fifty yards and the guy decided the bull wasn't big enough. Which is fine by me, we don't need to kill anything we aren't happy with. Especially, with the dwindling elk numbers! But you better be just as happy going home empty handed! Add in the handicaps this particular guy had and I was astonished that he said no.

Anyhow, eventually the hunt was over, and we were packing up mules for the ride out. The hunter was holding it together but I could tell he wasn't happy. And frankly, I couldn't have cared less! After helping this guy get on his horse, off his horse, tie his horse up, getting charged by a bear, him passing up a bull, me having to babysit for a week, saddle and unsaddle his horse every day, good riddance! Better luck next time! See ya around!

It's customary that the hunters tip while we are packing the morning of ride out day. Personally, I am not a big believer in tipping people just for the sake of tipping, and I'm usually respectful enough of a person to appreciate whatever I get. Even though I had worked my ass off all week for a guy who didn't hold up his end of the deal by being prepared, capable, and most importantly, having a good attitude, I was just happy to be done with him.

Anyhow, he came up, shook my hand, handed me some cash and walked away. As was normal. I said thanks, and put the money in my pocket without looking at it just like I always do. Soon the hunters get mounted up and we get them going toward the road.

The cook was headed to the road too, and she rode with the hunters. We keep packing while whoever is taking the dudes out gets everyone mounted. I was busy packing a mule when I heard some screaming coming from the hitching rail the dudes were at. As it turned out, as the cook went to step on her horse, she fell over backwards with one foot in the stirrup. It looked completely benign. She just tipped over and fell on her back.

All the work stopped and when I saw it, I told the other guides, "Let's keep working guys, that bitch is faking!"

About when we all resumed our work, I looked up in time to see the camp jack and the wrangler picking her up. They were facing each other and locked hands behind her back and under her knees so she was in a sitting position. She was still squawking away but when they picked her up, I saw her lower leg flopping around like a wet noodle in a stiff breeze! Both bones were obviously broke!

"Oops! I guess she isn't faking!" I thought to myself as they packed her off to her tent. Before long the outfitter, who is as old school as they come, and at this point the same guy we sweated out of the tent in another chapter came walking up.

Packing up to head to town. All panniers must be weighed to the pound.

Now, I'm a fan of technology! I have a wife and kids at home and I believe that the single most important thing I have on my person at all times in the mountains is my satellite messaging device. But let me tell you, the ration of crap I endure constantly from the old school guys is amazing! They are genuinely appalled when someone texts in the Thorofare! I bought that thing when they first came out and keep it on me at all times. Heck, you can be fifteen miles from camp and need a helicopter! Those guys would have to leave whoever is injured on the mountain and haul ass to camp to get help. Me? I can press a button and the Calvary will show up in thirty minutes!

Anyhow, the outfitter shuffles up to me when I'm packing a mule, "Hey, uh... she broke her leg pretty bad. The satellite phone is frozen and not working... I was wondering if you could call the helicopter on your little toy?"

"HA! I'd be happy too! I would love nothing more than to call the helicopter for you!" I said with a laugh! As I turned to walk away from the work area to call the helicopter I sarcastically said, "No one needs those damn texting devices back here!" Mocking previous conversations, we'd had.

Now the way those things work is the moment you press the "Oh Shit!" button, they call the emergency number you provided when you signed up, in order to verify the SOS wasn't a mistake. My emergency number is my wife. So, I shot her a quick message with the details. Fifty-ish year old woman, a hundred and forty pounds, broken leg. I'M FINE! I DID NOT BREAK MY LEG!!! Then I pressed the button.

At the time, my real job was as a pilot for the local medevac company. Although I flew fixed wings, I knew all the helicopter pilots. Knowing from previous experience that sometimes the minutia gets thick between the messaging service and local first responders, because the service has no local knowledge. So, I shot a message to one of the medics, who told me who the on-duty pilot was. So, I messaged the pilot the location using local terminology, patient weight information, and the weather in the area. It worked slick and in thirty minutes we had a helicopter landing in the meadow.

Meanwhile, we finished packing the mules, built the strings and got the dudes out of there before the helicopter arrived. After going through the confirmation messages, I walked over to the cook tent to let her know that the chopper was on the way. I opened the flap and a cloud of smoke rolled out. The smell of marijuana wafted in the air creating a scene more akin to hippies opening a VW bus door on their way to Woodstock than it did a tent in the wilderness.

"Hey put that shit away! The helicopter will be here in a few and with that leg dangling like that they're going to put some opiates in you." And I turned and walked away feeling slightly guilty that I was glad we would be getting a new cook. I wasn't a fan of this gal's cooking and expressed my displeasure with her in a previous chapter.

Before long we had the cook loaded on the "meat wagon" and out of there. We were lucky none of the pack mules panicked when the chopper landed but soon the "whop, whop, whop" of the rotor blades fell silent in the distance and the peaceful serenity of the mountain was restored.

We usually overtake the dudes before we get to the road. But the strings don't leave without counting their tips first! Once the dudes were gone, I reached into my pocket and pulled out one $100 bill. An average tip is $800. And I'm not offended by a $600 tip if we had an awful hunt with no elk. Well, to put that into perspective, the wrangler or camp jacks average $200 per hunter, per hunt. $100 is the equivalent of leaving a dollar tip to a waitress when your bill was over $300.

I strive for some semblance of grace and class although I often fall well short of that. I had managed to not say anything to the other employees. I just took the insult and tried to bottle it up and forget about it. I had good luck with the strategy until we were back in town. My wife and kids always like to meet us at the trailhead when we come out, so they were there and it was great to see them!

My boy was three years old at the time and wanted to ride home with me. So, after everything was unpacked, unsaddled, fed and watered and the stock that was going home was loaded we headed for town. My son and I had a great time talking about, "the big dangerous mountains" as he calls them. Then all of the sudden I was a block from the Irma so I pulled in. I saw the hunter's pickup so

Having family show up at the trailhead after a long hunt sure makes a guy feel good! My wife never missed!

I blocked it in with my horse trailer, smiled at my boy and said, "Dad will be right back bud, stay here and watch the trailer, okay?"

"You bet dad!" he said excitedly!

So, I jumped out of the pickup and the hunter rolled his window down as I approached. He started to say something when I handed him the $100 back and told him that was the greatest insult a hunter could give a guide. If he needed money that bad, he should just keep it. Then I said a few more things I'm not proud of and probably shouldn't have said.

I figured I'd get a call from the outfitter but never did. So, the next day I called him and told him what happened? He said to me, "Well I've known you for more than ten years and you've never cussed a client. So, my feelings are that I agree with you. He probably had it coming."

And he wasn't wrong! But once again, I added another something to the list of things I am not proud of doing. But you live and learn, I guess?

| 14 |

Sore Feet

I was about four beers deep, sitting at the Silver Dollar Saloon in Cody, Wyoming. Solving the world's problems with a good friend and the local bail agent for the area. It's always good to keep a bail agent as a friend, in my opinion! That's just smart business. We looked up as the door squeaked open to see one of the outfitters, I had worked several seasons for come in. He ordered a beer and pulled up a stool at our buddy bar. It was June in the Greater Yellowstone Ecosystem and the snow melt in the high country still made the water too high to do much in the mountains.

The conversation started out the same as it always does when talking to an outfitter before the fall.

"How'd ya' draw?" I asked referencing the lottery draw system that the Wyoming Game and Fish uses to allot tags to perspective applicants.

"Good! Real good! We have thirty-two elk hunters for the rifle, eight archery elk hunters and four sheep hunters! Who are you going in for?"

I was booked in the Upper Thorofare for everything except the first and last hunts. So, I had a few dates available, but I avoided the first hunt, which was archery, like a politician avoids accountability! It had officially become no fun to be in the mountains with another person who wasn't armed. Cow calling had been far more effective at bringing bears in than it was an elk. Not to mention that in order to hunt effectively most of the time you have to post your hunter a hundred or so yards in front of you. In my estimation, it had just become too much risk and not enough reward to deal with.

The first look at good sheep country in the spring is always exhilarating!

The bears had figured out that every fall we were leaving gut piles all over the mountain. And with the population explosion resulting in the habitat no longer being able to support the population density, those gut piles had become a primary food source. In fact, there is GPS collar tracking data showing Yellowstone bears migrating into the Thorofare every fall just for those gut piles! As such, the bears followed us constantly. They knew what we were doing. Some were more patient than others. Wolves on the other hand had completely changed the bugling habits in the rut. It used to be that you could hardly sleep at night due to the racket of bulls bugling all night around camp. You quite literally could ride up the trail until you heard a bugle you liked, then go chase him. Not anymore! They barely talk at all because the wolves and bears had both figured out how to locate them. Why give away your position to a would-be assassin?

Anyway, I hadn't hunted sheep in years and always wanted to do more! And I hadn't hunted for this outfitter for a couple of seasons now. Typically, we run sheep hunters during the archery. So, it was a great way to stay away from the arrow flickers! Sheep guiding and outfitting for that matter is a disgustingly political event. And I wasn't much into the politics of hunting. There's better things to waste time on I figured? Like picking on the Forest Circus or the Fish and Feathers! Recognizing the opportunity, I figured I'd offer up my services as four sheep hunters were as many as he'd ever had.

The boss agreed to have me take one of them and that was a wonderful thing! It got me out of archery hunting altogether! Plus, it meant I had a mission all summer! Find sheep! Pound country and get my ponies in shape! Another benefit was that it was an extra hunt worth of income that I hadn't planned on. It was shaping up to be a good year!

By this time in my career, I had guided for most of the outfitters in the Thorofare and preferred to do a few hunts in different camps. It kept a guy from getting bored and another benefit is that you're in and out. If someone is having drama, or is buried in wolves, or whatever else, you're not there long enough for it to effect morale. I had my own stock so I just kind of eased around. Drifting. Also, I had several hunters who were more loyal to me than they were to the outfitters. So, they would follow me to whatever camp I was working in. This was a great racket because I could charge the outfitters a "Booking fee" for my hunters. It was good for them too because all they had to do was buy a little extra food, cover a few dude rides for my hunters, and pay my guiding wages of course! I would guide my hunters, collect my fairly and just deserved wages and fees, then leave and go to the next camp and hunt there for a hunt or two. And so on.

By the fourth of July the high water had come down enough to cover some country and do some effective scouting. And I did just that! Often getting turned around due to unknown mud slides, blow down timber or washed-out trails. It was a lot of work just getting to the sheep woods err, rocks! I had my eye on one drainage in particular that butted into the main drainage the camp was in. It was a jungle going this route though as the canyon walls are steep and narrow, so it's always cold. Beetle kill had riddled the forest so it was always a complete wreck getting in there the first part of the season due to down logs and bad creek crossings. Over twenty-five creek crossings in less than twelve miles, actually!

This year was no different than previous and I ended up being turned around due to impassable trails from blow down twice. So, I came up with the bright idea to call the Forest Circus to ask when the trail would be clear. The lady with a raspy voice condescendingly assured me that next Friday the trail crew would have it done.

I've learned enough about the bureaucracies to be skeptical of anything they say, so I waited until Monday to try again. Which predictably ended up with me coming back to town early as my old tracks were the only thing that were on the trail. Yes, I went and looked anyway because the horses needed the exercise, only to run into the same snag and impassable blowdown again.

When I got out and got back to town, I called the Circus once again and the lady on the other end, who sounded like she smoked a pack of cigarettes every hour, assured me I was wrong, and that the trail was in fact clear. Even though I told this lady I had already been up there, and saw it with my own eyes not six hours prior to talking to her, she assured me that my eyes had lied to me and the trail had in fact been cleared the week prior. I couldn't help but wonder if the trail crew had been cooking the books so-to-speak? Why not just clear it, or tell us that it isn't being maintained? Who knows?

I let another week pass before loading my big geldings in the trailer and heading back up to the trailhead. When I pulled in, the Fish and Feather guys were raising all kinds of hell a little up country. Shooting up in the air and causing a commotion trying to haze some buffalo farther up river towards Yellowstone. I didn't think much of it and saddled and headed up the trail with my own one man saw tied on my saddle.

About ten hours later I was the first human to enter the meadow that sits below the pass that year. It separates the two drainages and is another spectacular sight! Waterfalls, cliffs, parks and lines of green timber giving way to the tall summer grasses and wildflowers as it ascends into the scrub trees and rocks of the subalpine.

As I rode into the meadow the aroma of the clover, in full bloom was intoxicating. I let the horses sneak some bites of thistle as we strode up the trail. Taking it all in. Obviously, it isn't a competition to be the first one anywhere in the mountains, but it sure feels good to know that no one is in front of you!

At the upper end of the meadow the main trail brings you right into an outfitter camp. As I rode in, I was disgusted to find the place in complete disrepair. Bailing twine was hanging from trees, the horizontal tent poles hadn't been taken down. Garbage and microtrash was strewn about. My mission had been to scout sheep, but this was appalling! I decided to stop and assess what I was seeing.

I tied up right next to their kumbaya fire pit, which had been ravaged by bears, but that's expected. As I walked around the camp it quickly became obvious that this wasn't something that could be cleaned up in a few minutes. And I didn't want to pack a bunch of these nit-wits trash out of the mountains.

Don't misunderstand, there are certain times, in certain camps where you might have to leave a mess. Be it a big snowstorm coming, or lame horses, whatever. We've all left a camp or two dirtier than we found it. But whenever that's happened to me, it's because we are twenty-five or more miles in the backcountry and facing some unforeseen circumstance.

And you can bet your bottom dollar that I'm the first one back in to clean up my mess the following spring! I assume most of us are of the same opinion because I've helped a few guys go into their camps to clean it up after something happened the previous fall. There's an old lesson my dad taught us as kids that I still practice whenever possible- Leave it better than you found it! Add to all that that this camp was less than six hours from the road, and there is no circumstance on the face of the earth that makes this excusable!

Mad at how disrespectful whoever was running this camp was, I unsaddled my horses and hobbled them. Setting them free to enjoy the fresh mountain clover and grasses. Larry and Cricket stayed nearby as the grazing was easy and sufficient.

Next, I pulled my knife and cut down all the horizontal poles they had left up, sawed them up and made a fire in the fire pit and began burning the trash, mule tape, bailing twine and anything else I could find. I knew they would be mad about their poles, and it was a ruthless thing to do, but so is leaving your camp trashed.

As I walked the camp, I saw the bears had drug the bear proof metal box down off the hillside toward the creek. I opened it to find food. A lot of food! Potato chips, granola bars, cans of several kinds of soups, plastic sandwich bags, and various other food related items. I had to go get one of my panniers off the ground and empty it to carry all the crap up to the fire. I burned all of it except the cans. Those I stuck back in my panniers, except one can of ravioli that I warmed over the trash fire.

Before I knew it, it was 4:00pm and the fire had burned all the trash sufficiently. I walked out to the meadow to glass and soon found a band of rams, high up in the pass. It was too late to get close enough to get a good read on their size, so I returned to the camp. I caught and re-saddled and packed and just before leaving I doused the fire with my water bottle. And soon rode out to the trailhead, getting there after dark.

I rode back in several times that summer. Eventually, I spotted a very large, chocolate colored ram that I estimated to be in the high 170's with nicely broomed off horns. His partner was an absolute thug of a ram as well. When I found them, I was confused for the first several hours because I knew I was looking at a big ram. But something was off. Finally, I figured out that when the ram would turn his head, I could see he was broken off on one side. His good side was broomed as big as a man's fist and it appeared to be at least a 190-inch ram, but the other side of this old warrior was broken off about a foot down. Obviously, he wouldn't score that well, but he was unique! He had character! A unicorn, so-to-speak!

As soon as the Forest Service allowed, I booked the spike camp permit in that drainage. At the time I was completely unaware that the camp was in the process of changing ownership. That whole summer I had let Cricket and Larry graze off as much grass as they could all around that camp, just to be a jerk. But as the summer progressed, the rams had taken up residence on the other side of the pass in the drainage that my outfitter's camp was in.

This development had an obvious conclusion. Even though I wanted to set a spike camp right on top of the littering, lazy outfitter, I decided the rams were more accessible from the main camp from the outfitter I was guiding for. Plus, who wants to sleep in a dome tent and eat freeze dried food for ten days when you can stay in a wall tent with a wood stove? A cook and wrangler on staff? You bet! Bacon and eggs? You bet!

About the time the Rams moved was when I found out that my buddy was in the process of buying that camp. Oops! Sorry about your poles! I paid him back the following year by helping him pack in his camp with my horses though. I had nothing to do and horses standing in the pasture, so I helped out! It only cost him a Mountain House freeze dried meal, too!

As summer continued, the days flew by and soon I was picking up my hunter from the airport. We did a few last-minute things in town before dropping him off at the nicest hotel in town, the same one that my hunter from the "Empty Pockets" chapter deemed befitting!

The following morning, I picked him up and we headed to the trailhead. The main crew of elk guides had already set camp, so we were all going back in together. They had supplies to top off camp, and I had my hunter and our gear. A second sheep hunter was also there with another guide who is a great friend of mine.

The other guide was also the second in command of the camp. And undoubtedly, the best mountain hand I've ever been around. Bar none. By far the best packer! Horseman, muleskinner and just an all-around good guy. A lot of guys will have their employees ride the bad horses or mules. Pack the rotten ones, and guide the most difficult hunters. Not this one! He artfully got around the worst stock you can imagine, and he did it gentle! He didn't need to beat a horse or mule into complying. He just has a natural way of get around them. And he took the hardest hunters too, and he tagged them out consistently.

Interestingly, he was part of a family of mountain hands who were all of the same quality. His brothers and cousins are also as good and just as great of people from a great family. He always seemed to show up whenever someone was in a bind. To the point where the ongoing joke was that you could be having a mule wreck in Siberia, and this guide would come loping over the hill on his stocking legged mule to lend you a hand. They don't make many guys of that quality, but he is definitely one of them!

A nice ram who predictably disappeared into the mountains as soon as the snow melted.

After getting packed up, we were headed into camp. Not ten minutes into the twelve-hour ride into camp I heard the distinctive loud, "POP" of a mule breaking a piggin' line. Just then, four of my eight pack mules came by at a dead run! I trotted up the trail to catch up and soon found them hung up in a tree. Typical of a knot headed mule, one tried to go on one side of a tree and another mule tried a different side. Luckily the breakaway held and they were stuck in the trees until someone showed up.

Soon we had them sorted out and back in line and the rest of the trip was uneventful. I had decided to leave Cricket and Larry at home for this hunt and just ride the outfitter's mules and horses because I knew we were destined to put on a ton of vertical feet and probably a bunch of miles too. The old geldings had a busy summer and deserved a week off before they would be tasked with going over Deer Creek Pass and into another camp.

Our first day in camp was a day before the season opener, so the other guide and I rode a low ridge below where I figured the rams would be. I hadn't been into camp in a few years and they had opened a couple of new trails. I needed a quick orientation on how to hit some of the outfitter trails they had cut. We soon had sheep spotted, but we weren't sure if they were the group we were after? Erroring on the side of caution, we chose not to get a closer look. I knew where some sheep were and that was a start! We turned our attention across the canyon to the drainages that the other guide wanted to hunt and soon found more sheep for them to chase.

As we sat with our faces glued to our binoculars, I could feel the sharp pains of my severely chapped lips. Soon I was digging through my pockets looking for my chap stick. Usually, I keep three or four sticks handy. One always goes in my pants pocket before I leave the house. Another in my toiletry bag, one in my backpack that I have on while hunting and usually a spare gets thrown in somewhere. Somehow, I had missed the chap stick on this trip!

"Hey man, you got any chap stick?" I asked.

"No! I forgot mine too and my lips have been bleeding they're so chapped!"

We sat for a while complaining of our hardships. One of us had the idea to raid the first aid kit when we got back to camp. Which jogged my memory that I had a first aid kit in my backpack! Soon I was rummaging through my kit and found four paper packets, about one inch by one inch, that was chap stick! I threw one to my partner and we both eagerly tore open the pouches and smeared a bunch on! Oh, the relief! Before long, we were headed back to camp to rest up with our hunters.

Opening morning we found ourselves at about 11,000 feet peering into the cliff faces, chasms and ledges that might hold sheep. We spent most of the day there and looked over a lot of sheep. Even a few shooters but we opted to hold out for the two rams I had been watching all summer.

Our shooting position on the rams.

The hunter didn't seem nearly as excited about the old, broken warrior ram as I was, but he certainly liked the idea of the chocolate ram. He just wanted to see for himself before committing which was totally understandable!

On the third day of the hunt, I found the rams in a deep canyon wall, over a mile away. We traversed a few ridges and made a stalk to within three-hundred and fifty yards. Perched from a shooting position high above we crept into view of the bedded rams.

We watched and waited, like snipers, for hours to get a good look at both sheep. The hunter liked the chocolate, so we ranged him, doped the scope and waited for a clear shot. About an hour into it the rams both stood up and started feeding along the hillside, quartering away from us. This made a clear, broadside shot really difficult as they consistently moved, stopped to feed, then turned and continued.

Finally, we had our chance and the hunter's .338 barked through the canyon. I watched in dismay as the vapor trail of the bullet sank low, and dust flew between the ram's front and back legs. There was no time for a second shot before they were out of range and we couldn't do anything but watch as they climbed the cliff face into an area basically inaccessible to humans. Humans who aren't rock climbers and have the gear anyway?

We watched until they were out of sight before descending the ridge and heading back to camp for the night. The following morning, we were back at square one. So, we headed into the pass that I had been watching all summer from the opposite side.

We spotted sheep and soon had to leave the mules behind as we climbed into an area too steep and dangerous for the stock. A few hours later we were perched on the summit of one of the tallest mountains in the range. 11,335-feet above sea level we watched and waited. And before long a band of rams appeared five-hundred yards below us. Feeding slowly across the mountain. Quickly, I decided to stalk first, before they pinned us down. We could judge them once we were in position and decide to shoot there.

Quickly and quietly, we descended the rocky slope on our butts. After a bit we came to the top of a set of rim rock that we could look over, from the prone position. Not long after arriving five rams milled into full view a hundred yards below.

At noon we were zeroing in on the ram we wanted to shoot. A respectable ram, not as big as the chocolate, but a good ram regardless. Determined to not let another opportunity slip away, the hunter shot true on this ram. We didn't see where the ram went because the topography limited how far below us we could see. But we did see four rams run out the other side, stop about three-hundred yards away and were waiting on their herd mate.

The waiting game.

Eventually, the rams left as we made our way down through the steep rocks towards where we thought our ram had to be. From our shooting position, the terrain was steep enough that I couldn't tell exactly what was below us. Soon we came to find out that we were on the top of a several hundred-foot cliff! The area where we were was steep and grassy in spots, with rocks in others. Creating a maze of crevices for sheep to hide in. Especially when they are dead!

After a brief search, we found the ram on the side of one of the many rows of rocks. Even the grassy areas were almost too steep to stand on. To get to the ram we had to cross one of the rows of rocks. We took pictures, shook hands and were all smiles as I began to cut the ram up. We were several miles from the mules and the realization of how much work it was going to be to get the sheep off the mountain was setting in.

Sheep Country.

As we discussed the predicament the hunter reassured me, he could take some of the meat so we could get it all in one shot. Before long I was whittling quarters off the ram and handing them to the hunter who was patiently waiting on the other side of the row of rocks. Before long the ram was caped and cut up and ready to pack.

In this camp we all carried radios to communicate with other guides, after we killed the ram, I had turned mine on and left it on my pack. I crawled over the rock row to find a head, cape, all four quarters, a backstrap and a tenderloin laying neatly on the grass. The hunter took the other backstrap, tenderloin and my coat. It was late enough in the day I didn't feel like complicating the matter by having to return up the mountain for a second trip, so I threw it all in my backpack, along with my spotting scope and tripod and various other equipment and called it good.

About the time I was getting ready to put my pack on we heard a mule brae far below. We looked to see the other guide and hunter coming our way! They rolled high around the basin and got much closer than my mules were. We found out later they were across the canyon and watched the whole hunt unfold. The guide instantly recognized what I hadn't! That we were in a serious pinch!

Pretty soon the radio came to life, "Zach can you hear me?"

"Yessir! It's good to see you boys down there!"

"Holy shit you are screwed bud! You're on top of a big cliff! Whatever you do, don't go down or to the left!" He said with concern in his voice.

"Well, what's the best way down then?"

And with that, the guide led me down by radio communication. He gave us directions to get to an avalanche chute which we basically slid down on our butts. After two hours of careful walking, sliding and at times, crawling we made it out of the dangerous area to the rockslide below. The guide was on the grass on the opposite side of the slide waiting. Obviously, they couldn't get their stock across a boulder field.

The pack was insanely heavy when I put it on, but now, after the descent I could only make it about fifty yards before I'd have to find a big boulder and just sort of make a controlled crash onto my back. Once rested, it was too heavy to stand up on my own so the hunter had to help. Every step I could feel the rubber in my boots rupturing and my legs twitched uncontrollably. We never weighed the pack but it was certainly well over 125-pounds.

Found him!

The guide's eyes bulged as he saw my pack! "Is the whole sheep in there?"

"Sure is" I said. "Unboned too!"

And with that, I received one of the best compliments a guy can hear on the mountain, "Tough Bastard" is all he said!

The guide expertly packed the ram while I tried to help. But was mostly just in his way. Eventually, I let the other guide do his work and I got my first aid kit out to start doctoring my feet. I never get blisters, but after that pack out I had several big ones! Soon I was all taped and mole skinned up and sliding my boots back on. The hunters sat nearby and ate a sandwich and retold the story to each other. Soon the guide and his hunter were loaded and riding back down the mountain. We had to side hill about four miles to get back to our mules. So, we started back across the slide.

Once across the slide we traversed our way through sparse sub alpine timber and boulder fields. As we came to one area, I noticed tracks I didn't recognize. In my exhaustion, I paid it no mind and continued by a hole that was dug out on the ground. Still not paying attention I reached a rim rock that was shoulder high. Using the rock as a handle to keep my balance, I started across the base of the rim rock.

Suddenly, there were rocks crashing down the hill toward me and an obvious commotion directly above me. With only my head above the rim rock I was certain I was being charged by a bear! Quickly, I jerked my pistol as the ball of brown fur barreled down the hill in my direction!

My body was close enough to the rocks that I had to struggle to un-holster my smoke wagon and as I struggled, still watching the heap of brown fur coming, it suddenly stopped! Then pushed itself up with its front legs to get a better look at me. When he rose up, he had a white patch on his chest that contrasted with the shiny brown fur. It took a second to process it, then it hit me like a ton of bricks! It was a wolverine!

Unable to contain my excitement I yelled back to my hunter, "Holy smokes! Wolverine!"

The wolverine instantly turned tail and disappeared into the rocks and cliffs above. We then rehashed the sighting several times and talked about the tracks around his den, or rendezvous sight, or whatever they call them these days! That kind of experience is exactly what I seek out when I go to the mountains. Something unique, that very few people ever get to experience.

Me packing all four unboned quarters, head, cape, tenderloin and backstrap along with most of my gear off an 11.000ft peak.

Eventually, we made it to our mules, exhausted and with weak legs, we sat down and finished our lunches before walking our mules the rest of the way down the steep face where we were tied up. After the rest we made our way down the mountain and hit the main trail. I was careful to look for horse or mule tracks headed to camp. That way we would know the other guide didn't have any problems and our ram was safe.

Soon I found a set of three different tracks, headed down river. That had to be them! I climbed into the saddle and relaxed while my mule, Salty, carried me toward camp with my hunter close behind. When we finally made camp, I was perplexed that the other guide hadn't made it back yet. I was worn out and all I wanted was to sit down and get my feet cooled down. Have a glass of whiskey and water and sit by the fire while waiting on dinner. But if he wasn't back yet, something was probably wrong?

As I described earlier, this guide is the best mountain hand I know, and I tried to talk myself out of going back up country to look for them. But my conscience got the better of me so after unsaddling my hunter's mule, I mounted up and long trotted out of camp to find my friend. Three miles up country I ran into the guide and his hunter. They were in the meadow above the horse pasture glassing some sheep high above. I was glad, and felt sort of ridiculous for being worried. I stayed there and glassed with them before we all rode back together just before dark.

Never before in my life had I ever had blisters on my feet. But ever since that descent I have had to fight them on long side hills and big walks. I've been through about every brand of boot imaginable and have resigned myself to having bad feet from now on. It's not a big deal, just another pain in the neck to deal with.

Back in camp, I hobbled into the dining tent on my blistered feet to find that the cook remembered it was my birthday! My birthday always comes during hunting season and I rarely even remember.

My wife always made fun of me for that. I always figured it was just another day, to come and go as quietly as possible so as not to remind me of how old I was! The cook had made a cardboard picture drawn in marker and had everyone in camp sign it. The story was from a few years back, and is described in the, "Bubba Mule" chapter. It had made its rounds early this year and it was her reiteration of the tale. I still have it to this day and is a simple gift I'll always remember!

We came to find out later, the fuzz had ridden into camp. And he went up river to count horses and mules because each camp is only allowed so many head. Usually, thirty-five. He obviously had ridden above the horse pasture to see if we had any extras stashed somewhere. How those guys get the idea that we would do something like that is lost on me! We always played by the rules! It turned out that the tracks I cut earlier were his.

The first year I became aware of this warden he had killed a horse on Deer Creek Pass. Which happens occasionally, I guess? I have several friends who have run that pass for twenty years without killing one. I haven't killed one. I've come close, but we got them out. But to be fair, it can happen. It's a dangerous trail. You severely decrease the likelihood of that just by paying attention. If a mule in the string is having trouble, and you don't notice, bad things can happen!

This guy killed a horse and left it lay about thirty yards off the trail right on the steep portion of the pass. We had wreck after wreck up there for weeks due to the bears who were eating the carcass. If I didn't make myself clear, this guy, the guy who rides around and writes people tickets for things like not moving your dead horse at least one-hundred yards off the trail, like the law requires, couldn't be bothered to move his own horse the required distance. And he certainly didn't write himself a ticket if you know what I mean?

Anyway, Lefty Two Guns got his nickname because he's always packing his guns and swinging his hips around as if to show them off. A lot of the time you can't see his guns because he wears a big stupid looking trench coat like he thinks he's a Pinkerton from the old west or something? An even worse looking cowboy hat. He's become the brunt of many jokes due to his rude behavior when he comes in to check camps.

Anyway, the wrangler and the cook relayed the day's events to me and the other guide as we unsaddled. Seems Lefty Two Guns rode right into camp while the wrangler was away and began yelling at the cook for not knowing how many horses and mules we had. Trying to strong arm and intimidate the cook. Of course, the cook had no idea how much stock we had; it wasn't her job. But he persisted until he thought he saw a chainsaw cut log. That happened to be grey from age. Anyone who's been around any kind of firewood knows logs aren't grey when they are fresh cut. The cook said he yelled and screamed at her for several minutes demanding that she produce the chainsaw, before riding through camp to count horses in the meadow up river.

He ran into the wrangler in the horse pasture and tried the same tactics with him. But our wrangler barely knew more than the cook! And we only had twenty-five total head in camp at that time because we only had the two sheep hunters.

We definitely didn't have a chain saw! And if we did, he ought to know that's not how you run a camp with a chainsaw in it. Everyone knows that the way you do that is to stash the chainsaw and never tell anyone you have it. Then, when everyone is out of camp you make all your cuts at one time, then get the saw out of camp. That way you can just suggest the camp jack look for firewood in one particular spot. And they can drag the rounds in as needed. The point is, we didn't have a saw and if we did the cook and the wrangler are about the last two people who would know where to find it!

The law hated this particular outfitter so we toed the line for him. No funny business or shady dealing were allowed because he knew this particular tree cop, as well as another fish fuzz guy, had it out for him.

Showing off a ram once safely back in camp.

Lefty was clearly picking on us for some things that happened the years prior. To be fair, the outfitter is an outspoken, high-strung guy. But that doesn't make him an outlaw. What we know now though is that if you speak too loudly about anything the Circus or the Fish and Feathers do, you get awarded with a big, bright target on your back. Some of the events that get a guy awarded with a target aren't against the law, however. And Lefty was just one of those blow-hards who got made fun of too much in high school I suppose?

The next few days we rested up while the other guide and his hunter were out. One day, the owner came in with a string of mules. As soon as he pulled in, we could see something was wrong. He retold the story of running into Lefty on the trail. Lefty told him that he knew we had too many horses in camp and wanted to know where our chainsaw was. The outfitter gave it right back to him though and they ended up in a screaming match alongside the trail. At the end of the argument Lefty told the outfitter he was going to take the camp from him no matter what the outfitter did.

Well, you can't run your mouth like that to cowboys. Especially when you're thirty miles from a road with no backup. The outfitter suggested he step off his horse and find out just how hard that was going to be. But Lefty, turned tail and headed out!

I suppose my mother would have something to say about not being nice and all that, but chalk it up as a character flaw if you will? I just have trouble getting around blatant injustices and repeated rude behavior. So why not meet them with the same courtesy they extend to you? I better digress on that point!

It felt good to have a ram down again and I didn't get too wrapped up in the Lefty Two Gun drama. Soon we headed out and I was supposed to be done with this camp for the year. I had hunts booked in a couple other camps and was excited to get back to my favorite elk hunting spots. Getting out of the crosshairs of the law was an added bonus!

I had a successful couple of hunts on the other side of the Thorofare and had just rode out of camp the night before. I was at home with my wife and our new son when the outfitter who I did the sheep hunt for called. I answered and he explained that one of his guide's had just had to leave due to a family member having tragic accident. The guide was the brother of the one who helped me get the ram out. I always felt like I owed those guys for everything they had taught me about packing and livestock and would have helped regardless of the situation. The boss needed a guide to come finish two hunters as they had to get the guide to town to tend to his business.

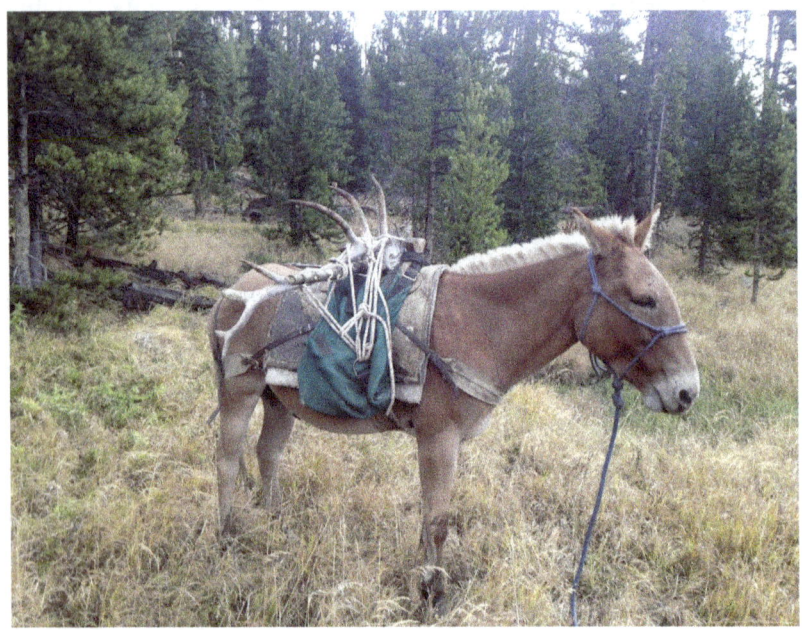

Tulip packing out an old skull I found near the Yellowstone line.

I quickly agreed and told the boss I had one condition. I would come in for $200 a day. And those wages were for the full eight days regardless of when I tagged out, which was very standard at the time. When he agreed to that I told him that he could just send that check to the guide. He was going to need it a heck of a lot more than I did, and I had already made all the money I needed to make that season. I would do the hunt for tip money because those guys are kind of like family. And any one of them would have done the same for me!

Once that was all agreed to and on six hours' notice I was making the thirty-mile ride into camp with my gear. Once there we began hunting right away. It was good to be back with so many old friends, in a camp I really enjoy.

The first morning we hunted we knocked down a good 6x6 near the Yellowstone line. Very near where I had the run-in talked about in the "John Wayne em!" chapter. As an added bonus, I found an old skull that we packed back to camp as well. But the real bonus was stumbling on an old cubby style bear trap! I'd been up and down and crisscrossed this area for several years and had never seen it.

The way the traps worked, as explained to me from someone else, was they built a three-sided cabin. Usually with a roof. The old trappers would set the bait in the back of the cabin and set their trap at the front. Which would force the bear to step in the trap to access the bait. Now, stop and consider this for a second. You're a trapper, back when trapping grizzlies was legal. Rescue helicopters hadn't been invented yet. InReach and satellite phones weren't even a gleam in some inventor's eye. You're walking through the woods, thirty-three miles from a road. You come upon an angry bear with his foot in the trap. Yikes! Better hope that chain holds!

The second morning I was riding what was reported to be the good mule of the guide I had relieved. A sorrel Molly mule named Bull. I didn't know the mule, and have already described my opinions about riding stock I don't know. But the guide who was on the sheep hunt with me assured me that she was a great mule.

Often, in the dark and cold of the mornings I will not hook up my crupper. Which is the leather strap that goes under the mule's tail and attaches to the back of your saddle. It is designed to keep your saddle from running forward because most mules don't have withers like a horse does. I admit that it's a bad habit but, number one, it's cold and I wouldn't like it if someone put a frozen piece of leather under my tail first thing in the morning. Number two, without exception, we are going up the mountain in the mornings so it's not needed. And lastly, Number three, if I learned anything from the Bubba Mule it's that I don't like getting kicked in the morning by a mule. So why not just hook that crupper up in the daylight, after it's warmed up?

That afternoon as we were headed back to camp, we arrived back at our tie up spot. I grabbed Bull, hooked up the crupper and we began walking down the mountain. About a quarter mile into the descent Bull broke in two and began bucking in the middle of the trail surrounded by '88 fire and blowdowns. All I could do was get out of the way, so I jumped onto a set of logs that were several feet off the ground. At the same time, knowing that if I let the lead rope go, I probably wouldn't see Bull, or my saddle until we were back in camp. If I was lucky!

As Bull bucked, and I could see she knew how, I gave a yank on the lead rope with all my might. The intended effect was to steer her into a triangle shaped stack of blowdown. Essentially, corralling her with her head at the peak of the triangle. Luckily, she gave up the buck as soon as she saw she was cornered and let me unhook the crupper while still standing on the logs.

I didn't think much of it and soon we made it to the bottom without further incident. However, I crawled back into the saddle and as we made our way to camp all the sudden my head snapped back and I was looking at the sky! Quickly, I got my chin tucked back and Bull jumped skyward again. It felt as though she was jumping as high as the treetops as I had plenty of time to think before we hit the ground. She bellered and sent us skyward once again for the third jump, but this time she turned a hard ninety-degree corner to the right and somehow, I lost my left stirrup. Eventually, we hit the ground again and with another grunt Bull blasted off again. This time getting more air. So much air in fact that I briefly considered giving up and bailing off. There wouldn't be any shame in that I figured since she already got my stirrup! But a quick glance to the side to see what lay below to cushion my fall, all I saw were sticks, branches and more down logs.

The old bear trap in the Thorofare. Usually, they had a roof, and the trapper would set a snare on the entry, chaining the other end to a tree.

With rekindled motivation to stay on, I bared down and got one rein shortened up and pulled her head nearly into my lap. We made several circles where I got my foot back in the stirrup before she gave up.

As soon as she calmed down, I got off and checked my saddle and cinches for anything that might be poking or pinching her. My concern was more about screwing up a buddy's mule than anything else. I'm not going to say that I wouldn't have been concerned if Bull belonged to the outfitter. Just less so. And the owner of the mule isn't renowned for having bucking mules so my first thought was that I had done something to cause her fit. After not finding anything, I remounted and rode back into camp. When we arrived, I told the boss to take her off my ride list. That mule knew how to buck way too well!

The next morning was the last day of the hunt and I was back on a trusted mule I had ridden many times over the years called Salty. That evening, on the last day of the hunt we shot another good 6x6. It was good to fill those two hunters out. It felt good to help out both my friends and the clients.

The guide who had the tragedy had been on everyone's mind a lot. I already had a good season. And earned as much money as I had planned. But I knew he was going to need more than what little bit I donated from this hunt. So, I hatched a plan.

I had done the math on how many employees were in camp. And I knew roughly what they made, generally speaking. So, I asked them one by one if they would donate two days of work a piece. That would be a pretty good chunk of change for our friend! Essentially, he would make what wages he would have made had he been able to complete the season. To their credit, and as a testament to how well everyone liked the guide, everyone agreed without hesitation. Soon I told the boss the plan and what everyone had agreed to do.

There were several hunters in camp that I knew from previous hunts and they were all stand up guys. One of them who I knew the best pulled me aside and asked if it was true that we were all donating days to the guide? When I told him it was, he just smiled and asked about how much of our income is based on tips? I told him roughly fifty percent. He nodded and left.

A while later he returned. He had talked to all the other hunters. Many had never even met this guide before. He smiled and set a wad of cash on the table in front of us. When it was all said and done, and we had combined the employee and the hunter's money we had raised well over five digits worth of cash. That's how a good team is supposed to work in my opinion!

Another nice 6x6.

CLOSING THOUGHTS

Closing thoughts- First, I truly am humbled and grateful that you spent your hard-earned money to purchase this book! I am honored! Even more so, I'm thrilled that you made it to the end without using it to start your own campfire! Thanks to everyone for that. This project is the culmination of several years of sporadic writing, and a lot of hard work at the end to finally push it across the finish line. I hope you enjoyed it and I hope I didn't ruffle too many feathers! Yes, I know I'm hard on the bureaucracies. They deserve it; however, it would be an injustice to not acknowledge some of the great people who work for them. Some, I even consider friends! I don't want people to think it's a personal vendetta against them. It's just too easy to not pick that low hanging fruit!

The root of the issue is the National Park Service's hands off approach to predators. They like to act like it was some giant success that they introduced wolves and decided not to touch bears and the population exploded. I'm not sure what they thought was going to happen? Regardless, as a result of doing nothing we have a trophic cascade of animals moving out of the ecosystem due to a lack of habitat.

I don't want to be misinterpreted here. I don't hate bears or wolves and I don't know many who do. What I do hate is introducing a predator that the land can't support. The downstream effects of such irresponsibility are far reaching. From a decline in ungulate populations in, to the impact on the flora and fauna in the area. Man is proven that they can't leave well enough alone and are terribly slow at correcting their mistakes.

As a result of predation, elk numbers have been in freefall in the Thorofare. The Game and Fish took note and reduced the number of tags for the area. The problem is not all the elk were killed. A lot of them just stopped migrating back into the wilderness. Opting for the relative safety of some farmer's field all year. The farmers and ranchers are seeing more elk than ever, and their livelihoods are being threatened having been forced into using their land to feed elk. As you might imagine, they aren't thrilled about that. Being the reactive problem solvers that they are, the Game and Fish increased the tags in the areas around the agricultural land. You can't blame the farmers and ranchers! But the elk are getting a double whammy.

If the goal is to have a healthy environment and sustainable wildlife populations, you have to manage the predators aggressively.

And even then, given the gestation periods of wolves I have my doubts that effective management can occur. Even the Yellowstone propaganda shows can't hide it. They'll have a narrator explaining that only the "Alfas" breed but in the same seen they show a rouge male trot over the hill and breed a female. All animals instinctually want to breed. Look no further than ugly humans if you question what I just wrote.

I pick on the guys I know more than I should because some things are more important than them keeping their government funded retirements. Like, having sustainable habitat. All I want is a place I can show my kids and they can show there's. A place that the reach of man hasn't ruined. An untouched wilderness.

Some of my best and worst memories are from the Thorofare. And that's what makes it such a special place. If you haven't been there, you should book a summer trip or a hunting trip through a local outfitter. If you have been there, then I hope you found this book entertaining!

Thanks again and watch your top knot!

Zach Bowman

ABOUT THE AUTHOR

About the Author- Zach Bowman is a former Mountain Guide with over fifteen years of experience in the Wyoming backcountry. A former professional bull rider and bareback rider. An Airline Transport Pilot and former Alaskan bush pilot. An owner of several businesses. A Nascar licensed race car driver, Realtor and embarrassingly, a former political candidate. Most importantly, a husband to a wonderful wife and a father to three amazing children, Corbin, Vali and Rylan.

www.ingramcontent.com/pod-product-compliance
Lightning Source LLC
LaVergne TN
LVHW021956060526
838201LV00048B/1590